CLASSICAL INDIVIDUALISM

Machan's book is one of the most thorough accounts of political and moral individualism available. . . . However classical its origins, classical individualism provides us with a new alternative perspective through which to make sense of the competing claims, interests and programs found in our world.

Douglas J. Den Uyl, Bellarmine College, Louisville, USA

In *Classical Individualism*, Tibor R. Machan argues that individualism is far from dead. Machan identifies, develops and defends what he calls classical individualism – an individualism humanized by classical philosophy, rooted in Aristotle rather than in Hobbes.

Classical Individualism does not reject the social nature of human beings, but finds that everyone is a self-directed agent who is responsible for what he or she does. Machan rejects all types of collectivism, including communitarianism, ethnic solidarity, racial unity and gender identity. The ideas expressed in *Classical Individualism* have important social and political implications, and will be of interest to anyone concerned with the notion of individuality and individual responsibility.

Anyone with an interest in social and political affairs, social ethics, political philosophy, economics, rights theory, the nature of the human being, libertarianism, capitalism, or environmentalism will want to read this book.

Tibor R. Machan is Professor at Auburn University, Alabama, but is currently Professor and Distinguished Fellow at the School of Business and Economics, Chapman University, California. He is also a research fellow at the Hoover Institution at Stanford University. His most recent books include *Generosity: Virtue in Civil Society*, *Private Rights and Public Illusions* and *Liberty and Culture: Essays on the Idea of a Free Society*.

ROUTLEDGE STUDIES
IN SOCIAL AND POLITICAL THOUGHT

CLASSICAL INDIVIDUALISM

The supreme importance of each human being

Tibor R. Machan

London and New York

First published 1998
by Routledge
11 New Fetter Lane, London EC4P 4EE

Simultaneously published in the USA and Canada
by Routledge
29 West 35th Street, New York, NY 10001

Typeset in Goudy by Routledge
Printed and bound in Great Britain by MPG Books Ltd, Bodmin

British Library Cataloguing in Publication Data
A catalogue record for this book is available from the British Library

Library of Congress Cataloging in Publication Data
Machan, Tibor R.
Classical indiviualism: the supreme importance of each human being / Tibor R.
Machan
(Routledge studies in social and political thought: 11)
1. Indiviualism. I. Title. II. Series.
HM136.M1553   1988   98–9404
302.5'4–dc21   CIP

ISBN 0–415–16572–5

FOR YONITA

The beauty of life is nothing but this, that each should act in conformity with his nature and his business.

Fray Luis de Leon

CONTENTS

PREFACE

Over the last three decades, I have been spelling out some of the details of a position in ethics and political philosophy that I have called classical individualism. It is the view, put briefly, that human beings are identifiable as a distinct species in the natural world and have as at least one of their central attributes the capacity to be rational individuals. Whatever else, then, is central about being a human being, it includes that each one, unless crucially debilitated, has the capacity to govern his or her life by means of the individually initiated process of thought, of conceptual consciousness. Furthermore, excelling as such an individual human being is the primary purpose in each person's life. A just political community, in turn, is one that renders it possible for this purpose to be pursued by all (or as many as is realistically possible).

As the novelist–philosopher Ayn Rand put the point – following similar observations by Aristotle and Thomas Aquinas – adult persons are "beings of volitional consciousness."[1] This involves, among other things, the crucial capacity to choose to embark upon – to *initiate* – a process of (thoughtful) action. The following work is animated by Rand's thought, although mostly not in the precise terms she made use of in the presentation of her ideas. Instead I will couch the case for classical individualism in the philosophically familiar – as well as ordinary – language of virtue ethics. The classical-individualist stance I develop in the ensuing pages is to be seen as fitting within the tradition of eudaimonistic ethics *and* Lockean politics.[2]

If we are the type of entity that can be a causal agent, the initiator of its behavior, this serves as a crucial basis for individuation: different human beings will be able to choose to exercise their conscious capacities and direct their ensuing actions differently. Putting it more simply, if we have free will, our diverse ways of exercising it can make us unique. So even if there were nothing else unique about different persons, their free will could introduce an essential individuality into their lives. (This is something that will have a major impact on the social sciences, on psychology and psychotherapy, and, of course, on ethics and morality.)

Yet different people are also uniquely configured, as it were, as human beings; thus they can face different yet equally vital tasks in their lives. Our fingerprints, voices, shapes, ages, locations, talents, and, most of all, choices are all individu-ating features, so we are all unique. This is the crux of the individualist thesis. Nonetheless, since we are *all* such individuals, we constitute one species with a definite nature possessed by each member. This may seem paradoxical, as existen-tialists have been known to point out, but ultimately it is not: one of the defining attributes of the human (kind of) being is the distinctive potential for individu-ality, based on both diversity and personal choice.

The position being advanced here has certain implications that are very close to what is usually thought to follow from a different version of individualism, namely, radical individualism. These implications are the classical–liberal polit-ical ideas and ideals of individual rights to life, liberty, and property. Yet, as I have argued in my book *Capitalism and Individualism: Reframing the Argument for the Free Society*,[3] classical individualism supports these more firmly and cogently than the radical individualism on which the case for classical liberalism had previously rested.

Such radical individualism, often dubbed atomistic, bourgeois, or rugged indi-vidualism, is distinct from classical individualism. It is usually linked to Thomas Hobbes and his nominalist and moral–subjectivist followers. Its most basic, onto-logical thesis is that human beings are numerically separate bare particulars, and it has serious weaknesses.

For one, according to this neo-Hobbesian tradition, political norms are ulti-mately subjective – usually taken to be mere preferences by its proponents. For Hobbes, to start with, "whatsoever is the object of any man's appetite or desire, that is it which he for his part calleth good: and the object of his hate and aver-sion, evil."[4] So the classical–liberal polity is itself, by the tenets of such individualism, no more than some people's preference, one that others may not share, quite legitimately. As some put the point, liberty is just one among many different values people desire. This political tradition has, thus, been vulnerable to the charge of arbitrariness, of resting simply on preferences that some people – for example, the bourgeoisie, capitalists, or white European males – happen to have.

What Hobbes and his followers have advanced, however, is just one possible version of individualism. Even in Hobbes's time there were other versions afoot, usually linked to Christianity. By the tenets of a Christian version, each person is a unique child of God, thus uniquely important and not to be sacrificed to some purpose of the tribe or state, for example. This, at least, is one path to the conclu-sion that a just political community must make room for the sovereignty of the individual human being – one's ultimate and decisive role in what one will do, be it right or wrong.

There is also a heretical school of Christian individualism called Manichaean individualism. "These people," said Saint Augustine, "want to be light, not in the Lord but in themselves, because they think that the nature of the soul is the same as God."[5] This radical doctrine of self-love, based on a view that human individ-uals are in fact godlike, even gods, has a mystical origin and thus can result in extreme libertinism since no rational, naturalistic limits to individuality are possible to it. As Paul Zweig points out, however, Augustine and others helped to demean, even destroy or at least drive underground, this version of individualism, by "castigating the 'pride' of self, and emphasizing the terrible abyss which separates God from man."[6] He notes that "Augustine strengthens a traditional bulwark of the Church that will continue to serve throughout its history, setting definite limits to the spiritual autonomy of the individual." Those limits, of course, as well as the diminution of self, make good sense in light of the implications of a mystical individualism.[7]

Yet another form of individualism is found within (and may be developed into) an elaborate social–political doctrine from an Aristotelian foundation. As Zeller notes:

> To [Aristotle] the Individual is the primary reality, and has the first claim to recognition. In his metaphysics individual things are regarded, not as the mere shadows of the idea, but as independent realities; universal conceptions not as independent substances but as the expression for the common peculiarity of a number of individuals. Similarly in his moral philosophy he transfers the ultimate end of human action and social institutions from the State to the individual, and looks for its attainment in his free self-development. The highest aim of the State consists in the happiness of its citizens.[8]

There were signs of the influence of this position in the natural-rights doctrines developed, albeit incompletely, prior to John Locke, in the tenth century and thereafter, for example, by William of Ockham in the fourteenth century. This was possible despite the claim by some, such as Shirley Robin Letwin, that "there is no more room for individuality in Aristotle's *philia* than in Plato's *eros* . . . because for Aristotle, as for Plato, rationality is the power to recognize a universal order. Aristotle cannot account for rational consciousness that is ultimately unique."[9] Furthermore, even though Aristotle is usually taken to have been something of a communitarian – due to his claim that human beings are by nature social animals and that the self-actualization of the individual must take place within the *polis* – some have argued convincingly that even Aristotle embraced a moderate individualism.[10] This counters those who have claimed that he was an out-and-out collectivist who saw greater value in the *polis* than in those individuals who comprise it.

Some of this is the stuff of intense scholarly disputation. What I identify as crucial in the Aristotelian philosophical tradition is that its basic metaphysical and epistemological teachings do not preclude understanding human beings fundamentally – though not solely – as individuals. Aristotle, for example, understood a person to have the capacity to make moral choices and thus to be personally responsible for becoming or failing to become virtuous, for flourishing or failing to do so. When he distinguished between the intellectual and the moral virtues, he argued that moral virtue involves choice. That, in turn, lays the foundation for an ethics and politics of classical individualism, a form of ethical individualism and libertarianism. Aristotle identified human beings as individually responsible for their moral character, even if in an early stage of their lives they could be helped toward this objective by proper habituation. The *polis*, then, will exhibit justice only if it is a suitable setting for such self-directed agents, who need to have room for development.

I make mention of the Aristotelian position that is relevant to understanding the human individual only to indicate that this is not some wild idea, entirely unheard of in the history of moral and political thought. It is in this sense – without, however, being completely tied to all of Aristotle's ideas – that I wish to elaborate some of the precepts of classical individualism. Needless to say, the issue is not so much what Aristotle said or what may be reconciled with his position, but what is the case. Since, however, we rarely manage to identify brand-new truths in well-traveled areas of reality, it would be impertinent to make claims to originality where in fact little of it exists. The only thing that may be original in philosophy is the way we forge an understanding from disparate philosophies. Classical individualism, as we will see, amounts to putting some good old ideas into novel and, of course, coherent and consistent combinations.

The crucial feature of this position stems from human individuals having the capacity to make and then to sustain commitments to original choices they are responsible for by reference to certain objective standards of human excellence. This is the essence of the individualism I wish to explore and elaborate in this work. *It does not deny the immense value of community, or that human beings are essentially social.* The thesis does, however, regard each human individual as being of supreme importance both for that person and for the polity in which human beings make their home. The thesis places the human individual in the role of ultimate decision maker, as the initiator regarding his or her most basic behavior, namely, rational thought. It does not deny that elaborate, complex conceptual thinking is amply assisted, indeed largely made possible, by one's social involvements – that is, one's community life. Still, classical individualism identifies individuals in the role of initiating, or igniting, as it were, the significant forces that guide society – art, science, commerce, philosophy, and so forth. Without the causal efficacy that individuals contribute, what follows would be impossible.

There is something of this understanding of human life in John Locke's work, not only in his development of the individualist natural-rights theory, but also when he suggests moral underpinnings for the rights everyone has by nature within human communities, as when he states:

> The state of nature has a law of nature to govern it, which obliges every one: and reason, which is that law, teaches all mankind, who will but consult it, that, being all equal and independent, no one ought to harm another in his life, health, liberty, or possessions.[11]

Contrary to much received opinion, this line of thinking shows that Locke believed that natural rights are not the ultimate moral principles. Instead, there is the law of nature, reason, which obliges each of us "who will but consult it." This is very close to Aristotle's idea that we are to employ right, or practical, reason, to be prudent in the conduct of our lives. Why? So that everyone can achieve the happy life – not eternal salvation, not the greatest satisfaction of the greatest number, not the welfare of humanity, society, the race, the gender, the tribe. No, one's proper, albeit possibly distinctive, individual end is one's own happiness in life, in accordance with one's human nature *and* individuality. Such an understanding, as I will be stressing throughout this work, accommodates both the universalist and individualist aspects of human morality and politics.

This is the gist of classical individualism, or, as it could also be called, ethical and political egoism.[12] The result of this understanding of ethics and politics is what the subtitle of this work notes: each human being is supremely important. The concept "importance" involves the proper ranking of concerns; to put the matter bluntly first, each person ought, first and foremost, to regard his or her own success in life as supremely important, with other objectives, including the well-being of others, deriving their importance in relation to one's life as the human being one is (something that can bring in very important matters besides oneself).

All of this is in drastic contrast to the broadest attack on the individualist tradition, Marxism. Marx's idea that the "human essence is the true collectivity of man"[13] has been picked up by non-Marxists: communitarians, socialists, and the rest of those who take human individuality to be negligible. Indeed, the official, articulated ethics and politics of the bulk of the world has been collectivist: tribes, clans, races, nations, teams, clubs, and other collections of human beings have been posited as superior entities to which individuals may often be sacrificed.

Now and then, of course, we hear some expression that reminds us that a different stance is possible, perhaps even merits respect. We often hear that we are all special! We are told, off and on, that we are individually precious, that each and every one of us has worth, and so forth.

The classical–individualist view, while eschewing the fictional atomism of human beings, affirms as a general philosophical and ethical stance what is said only in whispers and, perhaps, in the privacy of psychotherapeutic sessions: the individual human being is of supreme importance. He or she merits the utmost care, to be provided by that very same individual. The virtue of prudence is, after all, the first of the cardinal virtues, and Aristotle realized how vital it is to living the good human life.

Furthermore, this version of individualism also supports classical–liberal institutions, because of the vital element of sovereignty every person needs to have in a social context so as to aspire to excellence. It is this social–political stance, nowadays called libertarianism, that pays the utmost attention to individuals in society and their need for a sphere of personal authority, or private jurisdiction, one that respects their moral nature.

A word about how I understand the ongoing discussion of philosophical, ethical, political, and related ideas: These ideas are fundamental to human living and thus get reconsidered by some members of every new generation, with each adding some nuances, repairing or adding some errors, seeking to get a handle on what human living comes to in the most general terms, so as to guide each of us in our endeavors to have some measure of success in our lives. This suggests that there is less room for originality in philosophy than some might wish for.

Fundamental truths are not likely to change a whole lot over even a millennium. How they are best articulated, expressed in the language of the era, will, of course, amount to certain alterations of earlier versions. It is my view, though, that all good and most bad ideas in philosophy have gone around innumerable times as each generation of philosophers has fulfilled the basic human need of coming to terms with basic ideas on their own. Truths can be recovered, recast, forgotten, obscured, with the whole process itself constantly recurring. That alone would be expected from the fact that human beings are essentially creative beings, needing to affirm their capacity to create their own lives soundly, successfully, rather than as other animals are wont to do; they repeat pretty much what their ancestors did, with little or no variation, and without the need to make sure their approaches to living function well enough.

In this book I go over some perennial topics and contend that a somewhat unorthodox way of handling them makes the best sense, though others have surely advanced a thesis in the same tradition in the past. That is not a negligible point: In the sphere of normative concerns, the truth will have to be something that is neither radical nor wholly novel, lest it make no sense to ask of human beings throughout their history to heed it. If slavery's evil was not widely recognized until the nineteenth century, how could it make sense to protest and condemn it before? And if beating one's spouse or children was not widely understood as morally wrong until the twentieth century, that, too, would make it unjust to blame earlier perpetrators for such misdeeds.

But this is bizarre. It would make all criticism unjust because ignorance could be used an as excuse. That they didn't realize it was wrong, however, does not exculpate the guilty by any means. Still, some ideas of wrongful conduct are relative to certain possibilities that arose only at some point in history, so the matter needs to be handled with finesse.

Now, if the supreme importance of human individuals could not be appreciated before the time of, say, John Locke, it would be odd to make use of this idea in assessing the conduct of persons before Locke's era in terms of that norm. While a normative stance might not have attained prominence, let alone dominance, in various periods of human history, it is very problematic if it was entirely absent from human consciousness. And sure enough, the idea had been intimated from time immemorial.

Some of the essays in this book were published previously, in various scholarly journals and collections of papers. Most of them have been revised, more or less extensively. I thank the publishers for allowing me to bring together my works in this book. I also wish to thank several people for their help in my efforts to clarify the many ideas that appear in these essays: Jim Chesher, Doug Rasmussen, Douglas Den Uyl, Paul Christopher, Mark Turiano, Ernest van den Haag, Randall R. Dipert, Alexander Dunlop, J. Roger Lee, Eric Mack, Roger E. Bissell, Tom Palmer, Jack Wheeler, Ron Hamowy, Robert Campbell, Jane Shaw, Richard Stroup, Paul Varnell, Stephan Kinsella, Ronald Lipp, Tom Regan, Morton Schagrin, Fred D. Miller, Jr, Jeffrey Wallin, Cheri Adrian, Gregory Johnson , and the late David L. Norton. The editorial advice of Mark Ralph at Routledge and the copy-editing services of Kelly Russell Simpson and Susan Dunsmore are also very much appreciated.

I should also make note of my interpretation of the category of political philosophy. It is not what some – for example, students of Leo Strauss – take it to be, namely, a concern with the political maneuverings of philosophers in a world that doesn't understand and appreciate their work. Rather, it is philosophizing about political subjects. At least, that is how I use the term. This does not necessarily demean the Straussean focus; it is only different from it.

I wish to thank the editors of the following for permission to make use of materials I have had published in their journals or books: *The Journal of Applied Philosophy*, *The Journal of Social Philosophy*, *Res Publica*, *Philosophia*, *The Freeman*, *Public Affairs Quarterly*, *Poznan Studies in the Philosophy of the Sciences and the Humanities*, *Philosophy*, *Academic Questions*, and *The Philosophic Thought of Ayn Rand*.

1

INDIVIDUALISM AND
CLASSICAL LIBERALISM

IS INDIVIDUALISM A MONKEY ON THE BACK OF
CLASSICAL LIBERALISM?

Perhaps the most significant charge against the classical–liberal order has been that it is unjustifiably individualistic. This is one of the main claims Karl Marx made against the system, in his famous essay "On the Jewish Question,"[1] and it is a charge being repeated by the current champions of the most recent version of palatable collectivism, namely, communitarianism, by such thinkers as Charles Taylor, Alasdair MacIntyre, Michael J. Sandel, Robert Bellah, Amitai Etzioni, Thomas A. Spragens Jr and Richard Rorty.

This problem of being closely linked with individualism has plagued classical–liberal theory, whether advanced by John Locke, Adam Smith, or John Stuart Mill, and even those modern forms of liberalism favored more recently by John Maynard Keynes and John Rawls. The central charge is that the individualism that classical liberalism embodies is simply incapable of making room for morality. Even many supporters of the free market find fault with it on these grounds; for example, Irving Kristol made the point in his essay "When Virtue Loses All Her Loveliness" some years ago in an address to the Mt. Pelerin Society, the most distinguished international scholarly society devoted to exploring the philosophy of freedom, as well as in his pointedly titled book *Two Cheers for Capitalism*.[2]

Why is the individualist association deemed so problematic? What about it disturbs many people spread across the political spectrum? Leo Strauss from the right, Herbert Marcuse from the left, and many of their epigone have repeated the charge: Classical liberalism has been accused of fostering licentiousness, libertinism, hedonism, and moral subjectivism, as well as promoting atomism, alienation, and the loss of community and human fellowship. The list could go on to even more explosive matters, such as the fostering of crime, divorce, child abuse, and other contemporary social ills.

1

THE AMORALISM OF RADICAL INDIVIDUALISM

In short, in the difficult task of defending individual liberty, classical liberalism has not heeded ethics much, because it has relied on a type of individualism that precludes a coherent, intelligible concern with moral matters.

What is the central theme of classical liberalism in relation to this problem? Classical liberals have usually argued that a society organized wherein individuals have their right to pursue their chosen goals legally protected is for the best – it works to achieve the greatest public good. Put differently, via unimpeded self-interested behavior, the overall social good is supposed to be most efficiently promoted.[3] When they have addressed ethics, the sort at issue has been what we would better classify as mores or habits of behavior that various features of a society encourage or hinder, not so much what it is that human beings ought to do in their lives.[4]

The connection between unimpeded individual selfishness and the public good relies on a specific understanding of the human individual, forged initially by Thomas Hobbes and later developed by classical–political economists. It is an understanding that is repeatedly attacked by such writers as Robert Bellah and Thomas A. Spragens, Jr.[5] They note that such a view is false to the facts of human life, in which sociality is clearly and constantly manifest. They contend that the Hobbesian view of the individual is, at best, an analytical tool that can serve only limited purposes or, at worst, a grand illusion that has misguided Western political thought and institutions for several centuries.

Once they have finished with their criticism of individualism, these writers predictably go on to champion not only the fellow feeling they believe individualism fails to bring to prominence in human community life, but something of a coercive social system, one that issues in such public policy proposals as compulsory national service, compulsory health care, severe government regulation of the free exchange that is part and parcel of the classical–liberal political economy, and even more radical notions, such as the abolition of the system of individual rights.[6] Others may not be so harsh as to want to revamp classical liberalism completely, but even those from the right have suggested modifications that may have the identical result, namely, to undo the polity of individual liberty. Thus when Kristol calls for more attention to virtue, he is also championing censorship and a large dose of government regulation of the economy. Clearly, once the individualism underlying classical liberalism has come unhinged, a kind of deuces-wild situation develops with regard to the degree of statism that should reign in a community. Certainly, a principled adherence to individual freedom vanishes in the process.

THE ROOTS OF RADICAL INDIVIDUALISM

What is this individualism that has disturbed so many people with different orientations on politics?

Radical individualism, as spelled out prominently first by the seventeenth-century English philosopher Thomas Hobbes, is derived from a type of materialist metaphysics and nominalist epistemology. All of reality, by the tenets of this view, is matter in motion, and our ideas do not reflect some objective reality but are constructed classifications produced so as to suit our interests. In turn, human nature does not exist independently of social invention and cannot be known objectively. Hobbes advanced a kind of raw, barren, radical – or "atomistic" – individualism: only pure, particular, moving material things – no general classes – exist in reality.

The individualism of Hobbes was meant to be the application of the laws of motion to human life. Motion would occur most effectively, with the greatest efficiency, if something were left unimpeded, as per classical physics. Applied to human social life, Hobbes believed, the laws of motion – manifest in human affairs as the universal drive toward self-preservation and self-advancement – would at first (in the state of nature) lead to conflict, whereupon human intelligence would be driven to introduce social rules. This would be an improvement on the efficiency of self-preservation that is possible in an increasingly crowded state of nature. Individuals would thereafter behave in a more orderly, peaceful fashion, provided the rules were upheld – via the instrumentality of an absolute monarch.

Hobbes's endorsement of absolute monarchy is a tactical detail that his philosophical sympathizers later dropped. They accepted from Hobbes that societies are made up of these unique individuals striving to aggrandize themselves – striving to seek their own advantage in every way possible. They also believed that the social contract would only produce rules of social conduct that would guarantee the enhancement of the members' subjective self-interest. But the political economists who went along with Hobbes that far rejected his belief that absolute monarchy served the ends of peace and prosperity; in fact, they believed quite the contrary. This was most clearly laid out by Adam Smith, who held that the attempt to organize society through feudal, monarchical, or mercantilist economics was inefficient. Smith, while otherwise embracing Hobbes, suggested the idea – later developed in ever more refined fashion by subsequent political economists – that if we just adopt rules to which everyone will agree and protect natural liberty (the right of all individuals to pursue their self-interest), overall social prosperity and success will result.

RADICAL INDIVIDUALISM AND HOMO
ECONOMICUS

Classical and neoclassical economics, both of which embrace classical liberalism, tend to embrace the assumption that each person is "essentially a utility maximizer – in his home, in his office (be it public or private), in his church, in his scientific work – in short, everywhere." So argued the late George Stigler of the University of Chicago, a Nobel laureate and Smith scholar, in his famous Tanner Lectures.[7] Professor Gary Becker, the 1992 winner of the Nobel Prize in economics, is perhaps the most prominent and productive advocate and practitioner of this kind of economic imperialism, whereby all human affairs are to be studied as instances of primarily economic transactions, although Professor Gordon Tullock of the University of Arizona is a close second.

But classical liberalism suffers much because of its relationship to this Hobbesian view whereby each human being is entirely unique and taken to be in a sense complete, self-sufficient. Paradoxes arise immediately. First, the fact that human beings alone seem to name other groups of things suggests something distinctive about them by nature, not only by convention. Second, entirely unique, complete individuals have no natural need for society, nor any natural system of ethics or morality obligating them to act responsibly. Third, the Hobbesian individualism finds no easy place for political authority, for example, via the "social contract." What if some individuals desire to violate that contract? Nothing is wrong with this "by nature." Nothing well grounded can be said to morally object to it.

Furthermore, radical individualism leads to an untenable moral subjectivism – the view that what is right or wrong (for persons to choose to do) is a matter of what they prefer or like or feel or believe others will like, nothing else. This is where the position runs into serious trouble, because its subjectivism also applies to its own cherished political principles. According to radical individualism, one chooses to support the regime of liberty only to promote mutual self-interest understood in a purely subjective sense.[8] So such a regime really is not *necessary* to human life and cooperation; it is not a social–political framework that is required by human nature. The system has the status of the rules of a game that we have decided to play but need not have done so, not the way fighting an oil fire requires specific methods, as a matter of the nature – that is, the indispensable features – of the case. A game's rules can be changed by common consent even if in most cases they remain stable for quite some time. This conventionalist aspect of radical individualism, as far as ethical and political principles are concerned, lends to the classical–liberal regime an unavoidable element of instability. It is what so many critics of classical liberalism, from right and left, have made mention of throughout the history of this idea.

So, to recapitulate the problems of radical individualism: Its political values are what we have come, willy-nilly, to agree upon as useful for our subjective purposes. Any judgment of what is morally or politically good or bad, as well as right and wrong, comes to no more than a preference, a positive or negative feeling of the agent, lacking any objective, binding moral import. Thus the political principles of classical liberalism themselves become merely subjective or conventional, despite the fact that at first blush they seem to be well supported by this radical individualism. For example, the right to individual liberty or private property would seem to derive easily enough from this subjectivist individualism. In fact, by its own tenets, this right is only a matter of convention or convenience, something we have adopted but might just as easily not have; we might with equal justifiability have adopted something else, say, the right to equality or security or order.

Accordingly, if people prefer playing golf to defending liberty when the latter is in jeopardy, they do nothing objectively wrong thereby. If someone ignores the plight of the hapless or unjustly treated, there is nothing to be criticized about this choice. Embarking upon a creative artistic or scientific project, being active in one's community, or helping one's fellow human beings can in no way be superior to setting out on another visit to Las Vegas or lying about idly. Since there are no objective goods or objective values, neither the defense of liberty nor any other course of conduct is more important than any alternative.

Of course, subjectivists will argue that some stability can be found in our very likely common choice to embrace certain values and reject others, through a social contract or some such mutual decision. Yet there is no assurance that one who sees nothing wrong with breaking one's commitment to various rules will be convinced about sticking with the contract. By the tenets of radical individualism, no convincing argument can be given to someone who is unwilling to follow through on a promise, apart from reminding the person that this may not be what he or she prefers after all. That, of course, is something entirely up to the individual; nothing about the nature of the case, including the person's humanity and how it is fit for community life, can bear on the issue.

Now, if a social theory cannot even defend itself in terms dictated by its own tenets, it is seriously flawed to start with. And there are other problems. They are laid out in nearly every ethics textbook as the flaws of what most call egoism or individualism, whereby the social dimensions of human life are seen to be arrested and misrepresented. No advice as to what others ought to do can have persuasive force apart from appealing to the agent's preferences. No one's advice as to how people ought to act can be taken as anything apart from advancing a personal agenda. Egoists cannot have genuine friends or loved ones about whom they truly care, with no thought of one's own gain in the process. Community feeling, patriotism, loyalty to a just cause, and the like all turn out to be empty blather, without substance. The overall consequence is what Daniel Bell and others have called "the cultural contradictions of capitalism," a system that destroys itself from within because it can only stand up, logically, for pure, subjective hedonism.[9]

5

APPARENT ANTI-AUTHORITARIANISM IN
RADICAL INDIVIDUALISM

Of course, some philosophers and political economists welcome the radical individualism associated with classical liberalism. In what amounts to a suspiciously ideological form of reasoning, they welcome, in particular, that if values are subjective, then no one can justify coercing us to do anything. Never mind whether that position is actually true – what matters is that it gives support to the classical–liberal value of the right to freedom; to wit, if what a prospective moralist believes is merely subjective (an expression of one's personal taste or preference), no justification would exist for anyone's forcing us to conform to it. (A more sophisticated version of this thesis is value pluralism, whereby what is good and right, albeit objective or real, is, nonetheless, incompossible or mutually disharmonious, that is, incapable of mutual realization for those for whom it is good or right.) So some of those who prefer the classical–liberal order consider the radical–individualist stance on values to be a boost. It certainly appears to be a promising justification for fending off interventionism, authoritarianism, tyranny, intrusiveness, paternalism, and what have you. But it really is not at all.

Suppose an authoritarian moralist contends, "I don't need any justification to interfere with you. I just desire it; it is simply my strong preference to do it." Now, how is the subjectivist going to deflect this attack? Not by claiming, truly, that the aggressor *should not do* what he or she desires to do – after all, that claim is but a subjective preference. The criminal, tyrant, dictator, or government regulator wants to force you, and you want to be free. But neither the desire of the former nor that of the latter is an objective value or a moral political truth, so it comes down to a matter of power.

The alleged benefits of a subjective (radical-individualist) value theory are not benefits at all. *Indeed, from ignorance of what is right, nothing follows, not even the objection to acting on such ignorance.*

INDIVIDUALISM'S BAD PRESS

There is, also, a very serious public relations problem with classical liberalism's connection with radical individualism. Here what classical liberalism faces is having to explain its supposedly superior position *vis-à-vis* common sense, as well as alternative systems, some of which have lost their appeal except for their self-proclaimed moral high ground. (I have in mind Marxism–Leninism, Marxist national liberationism, fundamentalist theocracies, communitarianism, market socialism, and so forth.)

The first point to notice in this connection is that most people reject – at least in their common conduct and discourse – the subjectivity of values. Whether some institution is just or unjust is not for them a matter of personal

6

preference. They tend to think that if abortion is wrong, it is not just a matter of whether one prefers it. If laziness is a vice, that is because something is seriously wrong with it. And so forth with adultery, lying, recklessness, conceit, or cowardice. While there is, no doubt, much diversity in how these vices may obtain, or how one can, instead, stay the virtuous course, subjectivism is not what is implicit in how most folks live and even think about values.

And this is no mere prejudice on their part. Human beings are well enough aware of moral values, even while they may not be able to explain them clearly and convincingly. There is a kind of amateur frame of mind about ethics and politics, just as there is about physics, chemistry, and biology – one need not be technically well versed to know a thing or two about these subjects, provided the issue is not something highfalutin. The situation may be compared to how most folks would reject the claim by some physicists, for example, Erwin Schrödinger, that there are no solid objects since at the subatomic level, everything is composed of a great deal of empty space. The claim will go unheeded: a theory cannot argue away ordinary reality! Sound theories can only make clearer and deeper our amateur awareness of reality.

The same goes for ethics and politics. Skepticism can be intriguing, but it has no power to actually convince most folks about something as obviously true as that there are good and bad things, right and wrong ways of acting. At most it can prompt a measure of caution against arrogance; at worst it can produce confusion and hesitation, especially when it comes to standing up for one's values.

Accordingly, systems of ethics and politics that forthrightly propose certain ideas of what is good, or the right thing to do, have an advantage in reaching the minds of the public. They advance not an incredible theory but one that squares with what we ordinarily believe, at least to a certain extent. They back up the commonsense ideas that there are good things and bad, that this is something people can know well enough, and that some of this must guide our conduct and institutions.

In contrast, when it embraces value subjectivism, classical liberalism falls on deaf ears. Classical liberals themselves often enough betray this stance when they provide public policy advice based on instrumentalism or efficiency. Why, one can ask, should we care about efficiency, about economic cost? (That is just exactly what many environmentalists say in response to classical liberals who propose that laws protecting the environment be subjected to social cost–benefit analysis. Contrary to many classical liberals, not everyone prefers economic frugality to everything else. Perhaps they ought to, but from a subjective-value posture, such a claim cannot begin to be defended.)

INDIVIDUALISM: IS IT A LIABILITY?

Clearly, in light of these and related considerations, radical (subjectivist) individualism has become a target of not just criticism but even moral outrage. Some have rejected such individualism – especially as advanced within the field of economics – on simple moral grounds. They say the view engenders selfishness, social isolation, and alienation. Others, following Karl Marx, claim that while it may have had some uses as an ideology during the seventeenth, eighteenth, and nineteenth centuries, it has lost its value in our "postmodern" era. They say we should no longer be concerned with amassing great material wealth, which radical individualism encouraged; instead, we should be concerned with the quality of our lives, its spiritual dimensions, the ecosystem, community values, and so forth, and in these areas radical individualism is not just useless but a disvalue.

Need we, then, dismiss individualism and the liberalism with which it is so closely aligned? Should we embrace a new version of collectivism, for example, communitarianism, in order to recover from the consequences of subjectivism?

I do not believe that is necessary. Individualism has not had a full hearing. There are forms of it distinct from the version the classical–liberal tradition inherited. The type of individualism I have in mind focuses on individual *human* beings. This humanist individualism, which I call classical individualism, recognizes that there is in nature a class of human individuals. And their human nature has a lot to teach us about social life and personal ethics. It seems there are indeed good reasons to classify human beings as a distinct class of entities in nature. There is, however, also good reason to regard their individuality as one of their essential, central characteristics.

So, on one hand, we must abandon the radical individualism, but, on the other hand, we can firm up the foundation for individualism by noting that when we study human nature – when we carefully examine what it is to be a human being – we arrive at the conclusion that one of the crucial characteristics of human beings is that they are individuals. Instead of saying, with Hobbes, that there is no human essence, we can say, in opposition to both Marx and Hobbes, that the human essence is the true individuality of man. This may appear paradoxical, especially to an existentialist, but it is not if the Aristotelian idea of potentiality is sound, since something could have as one of its distinctive attributes a potential to be unique.

CLASSICAL INDIVIDUALISM: HUMANIZING THE RADICAL VERSION

A major criticism of the idea of an objective, or real, human nature has to do with the legacy of Platonism in both natural-law and natural-rights theories. There is a very serious problem with the Platonistic view of "the nature of something." In the Platonistic tradition, the nature of anything had to be a timeless, unchanging, perfect form. We may usefully think of the perfect circle this way, but that is because geometry is a purely formal field, concerned with measurement and precision, not with substance.

When we consider knowing the nature of human beings, justice, or governments, can we expect to know what is timeless, perfect, unchanging, eternal? Hardly. Human beings are actual, temporal. They are not unchanging, timeless. Nor are we in a position to demonstrate that a human or any other kind of being is timeless, perfect, and final. So Platonism in this area leads to skepticism. If we have to come up with a final truth to know the nature of man, we simply reach an impasse.

Such skepticism, of course, makes it impossible to rest any sort of stable social or political order or conception of a good society on human nature, natural law, or natural rights. This is what Hobbes concluded. We are now left with two extremes: radical skepticism, which issues in nominalism and radical individualism, à la Hobbes, and the Platonistic alternative of an unattainable, hopelessly utopian and ideal conception of human nature. Both favor skepticism in the end.

RECONCEIVING NATURALISM

Might we, however, reconceive naturalism instead of abandoning it? Yes, and quite promisingly. When we talk about the nature of something, we should have in mind what is reasonably justifiable given what we know to be so beyond a reasonable doubt. The evidence we can gather will be limited to the context of our present knowledge, but if we are consistent and reasonably historically complete, the evidence will yield a conception of what the nature of something is. And that is firm enough to guide us in our political and even our personal lives, as firm as we can expect the world to be from our knowledge of history and from common sense.

Actual aspects of the world – its substance – should not be thought of as we think of its formal features, for example, in mathematics and geometry. The subject matter of these latter fields is capable of yielding final definitions – although some dispute even that – because these definitions concern measurement devices, not actual objects. But human beings, for example, are not mere measurements – they actually exist and undergo changes, which our theory of understanding them must also accommodate. Now, when we study *Homo sapiens* over the estimated 92,000 years that they have been in roughly their current form on Earth, we are justified in concluding that they do have a stable nature as thinking animals – biological entities that are distinctively facilitated to think and depend upon exercising this faculty in order to live and do well at that task.

Furthermore, human beings seem to be always confronted with the possibility of mishaps through their own agency, which accounts for the pervasive fact of criticism among them! They can be wrong as well as right in what they do, and unlike other animals, it is often up to them. And the way they can be wrong is by their failure to act in accordance with their distinctive human nature – by not being in full focus, by failing to pay heed, by negligence, evasion, thoughtlessness, imprudence, dishonesty, and so forth.

These common features give rise to certain universal standards, but there is also an inescapable individuality to human nature. It is by their own particular initiative, circumscribed by their family backgrounds, traditions, habits, customs, environment, opportunities, climate, and so forth, that people must confront living their lives. So they must implement or establish their individuality every moment of their lives. This also points up the social nature of human life – being thinking animals implies that their flourishing is interwoven with their fellows. They will learn from them, find enjoyment and love from them, trade and play with them, and carry on all the most exciting aspects of their humanity with them.

How does all this help us out of some of the problems and paradoxes of individualism that I described earlier? For one thing, with a viable conception of human nature, we can identify some general principles that we could count on to guide our lives. These principles, alluded to above, are general enough to apply over time, to succeeding generations, even if they are not guaranteed to hold for eternity.

As Aristotle recognized, the application of the general principles that rest on our knowledge of human nature will not be identical in different situations, at different times. Being honest in the twentieth century probably requires applying the principles to telephones, fax machines, and computers. Earlier people did not have the responsibility to be honest just as we do because, for one thing, their tools of communication differed from ours. So honesty, although a general human virtue along with all the other virtues, such as prudence, generosity, and courage, will have individual, regional, temporal, and cultural manifestations.

CLASSICAL INDIVIDUALISM AND THE FREE MARKET

So how would classical individualism approach the points that neoclassical economists provide in support of the free market?

Take the claim that in free-market exchanges both parties necessarily benefit. Classical individualism rejects this understanding of market exchange. It is quite possible that a free exchange will not benefit both parties, or even either party. Both could be making a mistake. Sometimes people trade good money for bad goods or make exchanges that are harmful to one or both of the parties. Impulse buying and similarly thoughtless purchases also illustrate this clearly enough.

(Nor will it do to try to refute this by claiming that "it seemed to them to be to their benefit," since such a claim is not falsifiable. For more on this, see Chapter 3.)

Neoclassical economists tend to reject this because they think that if it is true, some central or collective planner might have second-guessed one or both of the trading parties and ordered them to behave differently "for their own best interest." If it were possible to know (objectively) what would benefit people in trade, even when they themselves deny this, it might be possible to admit to the legitimacy of paternalism and authoritarianism and to defeat free trade. In other words, the subjective theory of value stands for many of them as a bulwark against statism.

But does interventionism follow from classical individualism, simply because it rejects the theory of subjective value? No, not at all. A central feature of any objective ethical value judgment, as well as the ensuing conduct, is that a person must be able to choose. One must, that is, initiate one's ethically significant conduct. Bona fide moral theorists have all understood that one cannot force others to behave morally – ethical conduct must be of the agent's own choosing, meaning not that what is right is a matter of choice, but that doing it is morally right only if it has been chosen freely by the agent.

So a central feature of morally relevant conduct is that it is chosen; if imposed or regimented, its moral significance vanishes. Included in the range of choices every individual is confronted with is the entire array of issues concerned with the bulk of community life.

CLASSICAL INDIVIDUALISM AND MORALITY

Classical individualism, furthermore, places before us certain stable (enough) principles of community life that are necessary for us to even embark upon a morally independent, peaceful, and productive social existence. This aspect of the social moral nature of human life is a result of both one's humanity and one's inherent individuality as the author of one's moral character and conduct.

If one behaved as a good citizen or a charitable person simply because one was dreadfully scared of the state placing one in jail, one would not be a good citizen or person but barely more than a circus animal. So it is wrong to confuse conduct one should have engaged in of one's own free will with regimented behavior imposed by some planning authority, politburo, or regulatory agency. There is, in short, no such thing as coerced morally right conduct. Those aspects of the classical–liberal polity that concern individual rights, never mind whether they were founded on the right philosophical groundings, have validity here as well. Within the framework of individual rights, however, ample room for uncoerced communitarian values remains.

11

CLASSICAL INDIVIDUALISM AND PUBLIC AFFAIRS

This position also allows for moral criticism of commerce – including the behavior of commercial agents, from used-car sellers to corporate magnates – without sanctioning interference in it. Business ethics, for example, would be a branch of ethics. It would allow us to say, with full justice, that some individuals in the marketplace – some persons or entire firms – are behaving badly and should not do so. They might have chosen to do otherwise.

Of course, classical individualism and its resulting polity would not turn a blind eye toward corporate behavior with adverse impact in the form of violating individual rights. The entire sphere of corporate behavior *vis-à-vis* the environment, for example, as well as fraud, malpractice, and negligence in the production of goods and services, could still be seen, as it is by anti-individualists, as public wrongs that need to have legal sanctions applied. But these would be construed not, for example, in the murky fashion of the environmentalist ethics movement, as assaults upon nature or intrinsic values, but as dumping on and intruding upon individuals, as violations of their rights. The remedy would also shift from the more communitarian approach of social cost–benefit analysis to the individualist approach of giving full protection to those who might be dumped on or assaulted by means of toxic side effects of production or transportation processes. Furthermore, the conduct of merchants and corporations could be judged unethical, apart from any illegality, when such matters as tastelessness in advertising or mismanagement of employee relations are at issue.

CLASSICAL INDIVIDUALISM AND CLASSICAL LIBERALISM

Some of this is disturbing to various classical liberals because they realize that in terms of this form of individualism, sometimes what we do in the free market we *should not* do. Yet, as has been noted already, this does not at all imply that whatever I should not do may be prohibited or that what I should do may be commanded. Rather, it admits what common sense recognizes, namely, that free agents can do the wrong thing and that this may be pointed out to them in peaceful ways. Clearly, nothing about statist intervention follows.

What are the theoretical and political gains from classical individualism concerning how the classical liberal may analyze many aspects of contemporary society? For one thing, as noted before, this position allows for moral criticism of commerce without sanctioning the regulation of commerce. With perfect theoretical justification, we can write articles about unethical business practices and protest them by way of letters, boycotts, and ostracism. We might even attend a stockholders meeting and argue a company's management out of their current wrongheaded policy.

With radical – as distinct from classical – individualism, whatever people do

12

in the marketplace has to be accepted as what they ought to do. That is because the only clue as to what they ought to do is their doing it. I have already indicated what kind of difficulties that produces. Classical individualism recognizes that individual market agents might behave either in a morally praiseworthy fashion or in a morally blameworthy fashion; yet for them to earn praise or blame, *it has to be their choice whether they do one or the other*. That is the only way in which a socioeconomic system avoids becoming demoralized. Within certain "rules of market conduct" that identify the borders around us – which is where natural-rights theory comes into the picture – individuals must be left free to misbehave, because that is the only way that their human dignity is preserved in a commercial setting.

All this makes sense because it could now be said that, objectively speaking, some of what these people do in the market they should not be doing. But since morally relevant conduct must be chosen, it follows that market agents may not be regimented unless their morally wrong conduct infringes on the rights of others – that is, unless their conduct obstructs other people's liberty to make moral choices, the only avenue toward influencing them is to persuade them to do otherwise.

CLASSICAL INDIVIDUALISM AND NEOCLASSICAL ECONOMICS

Embracing classical individualism involves no loss at all to classical liberalism and neoclassical economics. Diversity of values still holds – not, however, because of ethical subjectivity, but because of enormous individual variations among people. The price system remains the best means by which to communicate human choices, although at times this means that wrong choices will also be communicated and responded to by market agents (for example, choices that may lead to the production of harmful drugs or trivial pursuits or pornography). Still, the point made by public-choice theorists still holds: any attempt to remedy market failures by means of political intervention involves the far greater risk of enshrining the errors of politicians in an aspect of a culture that is much less flexible than its market, namely, in its legal system. In addition, the point about trying to make people good by means of coercion must also be recalled. Both of these points count against any interventionist policies, so the free market remains intact, despite its somewhat altered philosophical foundations.

THE HOBBESIAN MONKEY OFF THE BACK OF
CLASSICAL LIBERALISM

This, then, is the crucial alteration that needs to be made in the standard classical–liberal doctrine of individualism. We must abandon the Hobbesian view, which states, in Hobbes's own words,

> But whatsoever is the object of any man's appetite or desire, that is it which he for his part calleth good: and the object of his hate and aversion, evil.... For these words of good and evil are ever used with relation to the person that useth them: there being nothing simply and absolutely so; nor any common rule of good and evil.[10]

Instead we must recognize that "good" and "bad" have objective meaning for individual human beings, based on their humanity and the individual persons they are. There are very general moral principles that apply to human life, based on human nature, as well as particular moral judgments based on the unique circumstances of the individual. While this preserves the full range of diversity that most classical liberals wish to call attention to in socioeconomic situations – ergo, the stress on the value of the price system, which communicates all these diverse value judgments – it does not embrace the flawed and self-defeating idea of subjective ethical value, whereby what is morally right or wrong is merely a matter of what a person happens to feel about some course of conduct.

There is another charge leveled at individualism, one that targets not its radical, neo-Hobbesian features but something akin to that, namely, its alleged denial of our fundamentally social nature. This view, championed by such writers as Richard Rorty, holds that human beings are inherently dependent creatures and can never, in any respect of their lives, exhibit individuality. They point to the elementary fact that human language is social, and they invoke certain esoteric arguments from philosophers such as Ludwig Wittgenstein, arguing that the very idea of privacy is incoherent because knowing anything is a social process.[11]

The public relations aspect of classical individualism amounts to the fact that no longer will there be an unbelievable, unpalatable doctrine of moral subjectivism attached to the defense of the free society. Individualism is true, but ethical subjectivism is false. Most people realize this as they conduct their lives. It is clear to them, for example, that persons have unique value, that they are not replaceable as friends or one's children. They also understand that male chauvinism is wrong, that slavery is evil, and that racism is vile. It is also clear to them that kindness, generosity, courage, and honesty are virtues. To claim, as radical individualism does, that all of that is a matter of personal preference simply makes the socioeconomic system derived from individualism quite confusing, if not outright incredible.

GIVE MATURE INDIVIDUALISM A CHANCE

All of this is especially important now, in light of the recent economic and cultural demise of the planned economic systems of Eastern Europe. The collapse of their system does not necessarily mean that a system that embraces freedom is going to be successfully sold to them. There is competition here – Western social democrats, or democratic socialists, are only too willing to rework their system, call it communitarianism, and sell it to the victims of Stalinist socialism. Unless individualism can be shown to be a sound position, it will not be successful in capturing the minds and hearts of those who have found its opposite, collectivism, practically impossible. One can always claim, after all, that collectivism has not failed but was merely misunderstood, misplayed, and will now have to be tried again, the right way.

In short, classical individualism addresses the concerns expressed by many anti-individualists with the amoralism of a social order based on radical individualism. At the same time, this view retains a principled adherence to the ultimate value of individual sovereignty, based on the moral nature of human individuals (that is, the requirement of self-governance in the bulk of their lives).

It is vital to note in conclusion that what the classical–liberal polity, including its private-enterprise system of economic life, faces from the anti-individualist critics is a fatal criticism – unless its individualism can be placed on a solid philosophical and, especially, moral footing. There is no question that freedom advances the lives of individual human beings. There is no question that those who find fault with the regime of liberty are not champions of such advancement but argue, mostly on the basis of their various moral and ethical theories, that service to the community is our primary and, indeed, enforceable moral and political obligation. It is not enough to respond to this with public policy studies showing that policies that force people to help others just do not work – the critics will reply that we must try harder, we must be more vigilant, we must use, indeed, greater force!

A far more germane response to such criticism of the free society is that the right to liberty, including the liberty to trade freely with willing others, rests on the supreme moral importance of individual human beings. This importance does not preclude community and fellow feeling. But it prohibits making it mandatory and enforced by the state or anyone else in society.

Unless this kind of response is available to the classical–liberal political economist, the system is doomed to public policies holding out some hope of serving the community by means of yet another scheme of coercion – be it more taxes, greater government involvement in the provision of goods and services, more regulation of commerce, or even regulation of such things as the arts and entertainment.

Piecemeal response to the assault on individual liberty simply will not suffice – it can always be met with a moral outcry to try yet another

15

restriction, prohibition, or regulation. A general moral–political theoretical case needs to be presented, showing that such restrictions, prohibitions, and regulations are immoral in light of human nature, a commonly recognizable fact of reality.

2

ETHICS AND FREE WILL

A neglected connection

Classical individualism, no less than other bona fide ethical or moral systems, presupposes that human beings can initiate some of their significant conduct – they can make choices of their own initiative. They are taken to be responsible for what they choose to do because of this, not only in that it was indeed they who did the deed – as a dog might have bit the mailman and thus be responsible for the mailman's injury – but in that they could have done otherwise and thus are accountable for the deed they did. Of course, this element of ethics, captured in the philosophical motto "ought implies can," is not uncontroversial and for any ethical system to be sound, it must be true, indeed, that human beings can make such choices or, in the familiar terms of this topic, possess free will.

It is the purpose of this chapter to explore the free will issue. It will be argued that people do, ordinarily, possess free will and that this is not some miracle or mysterious phenomenon but a part of their nature as beings of the natural world.

INCONSISTENCIES IN APPLIED ETHICS

Within much of applied ethics and public policy in our time, there appear to be certain inconsistencies or, at best, serious omissions concerning various actions that human beings should or should not take or institutions they should or should not establish. Many philosophers expound on ethics and public policy without questioning whether human beings have free will.[1] In the context of widespread acceptance of the deterministic view of human behavior, such silence amounts to acquiescence or at least tolerance of that view, in which individual moral responsibility is precluded from human affairs, private or public.

On one hand, there is no end of blaming and praising going on in both the academic and the non-academic world in our time. In applied ethics, in partic-ular, persons in the professions of medicine, law, business, science, and education are said to have certain responsibilities to conduct themselves in various ways, as well as to abstain from various kinds of conduct. These claims

17

are made in textbooks, treatises, and academic journals. Furthermore, during well-publicized congressional hearings, there is no end of blaming and praising, at first by the politicians associated with the various sides, but later by commentators and policy analysts. In the case of such issues as AIDS research, gun control, civil rights bills, entitlement programs, and so forth, we find that numerous academicians enter the fray, by means of radio and television appearances and op-ed commentaries, as well as articles in prestigious magazines. This is especially so during an election year.

On the other hand, we also find that many in our culture identify their own misbehavior in terms that do not fit the idea of moral responsibility, in other words, not in terms of blaming and praising. In academic social science, human behavior is treated primarily as if it were caused by factors over which individuals have no control – their upbringing, genetic makeup, economic class, cultural background, and so forth. In the fields of psychology, economics, sociology, anthropology, and political science, many of the prominent modes of analysis and explanation subscribe to some version of the nature/nurture deterministic framework, with no theoretical room left for individual self-determination that is not reducible to some outside or built-in forces. Furthermore, different types of addicts abound on talk shows, where some of the most lamentable conduct by people is deemed to be a result of an affliction or a disease. There are no drunks but merely victims of alcoholism; there are no philanderers or adulterers, only the sexually addicted; drug abusers are classified as suffering from addiction; those overweight or undernourished or abusive toward their children or their spouses, as well as many others, are identified as suffering from some condition that is supposed to explain this behavior in full. And, most notable of late, cigarette smoking is not a choice people make but an addiction that afflicts many of them, something they became hooked on even against their will. (President Bill Clinton even disputed the claim by his Republican opponent in 1996 that "cigarette smoking is not necessarily addictive," suggesting that it is.)

Among both groups – those who accept the moral viewpoint and ascribe to people the capacity to choose and to be responsible for their conduct, and those who deny this by invoking causal explanations for all human behavior – we often find philosophers as well as many others writing for popular as well as scholarly publications. Among those subjects addressed as if people did have the capacity for choice and personal responsibility are cases involving what are called ethical dilemmas that make front-page news – for example, assisted suicides, surrogate mothering, euthanasia, testing for the AIDS virus, accidents attributed to drug abuse, and racially motivated violence. Some other such cases in our time that have drawn evaluative comments include the Keating Five affair, the savings-and-loan fiasco, U.S. government dealings with the likes of Manuel Noriega or Saddam Hussein, the devastating factory fire in North Carolina, the Oklahoma City bombing, the People's Republic of China's human rights record, sexual harassment by military personnel, air and other types of pollution associated with the operation of businesses, recycling of renewable resources, alcohol consumption prior to using vehicles, safe-sex campaigns, and election campaigns by former KKK members. Among the subjects that tend often to be treated as if human beings lacked the capacity for choice and were practically hard wired to act as they do is child molestation, smoking, work deficiencies, gang violence, and a great many varieties of criminal conduct. The Americans with Disabilities Act – the USA's federal law designed to protect people with innumerable types of affliction against discrimination by employers – characterizes many forms of human conduct that might otherwise be deemed misbehavior as human maladies for which no one may be made to lose his or her job.[2]

CONFUSION AND INJUSTICE BASED ON INCONSISTENCY

The practical consequences of such a divided outlook, whereby much of the discussion in the culture both condemns and exonerates individuals when it comes to their lamentable conduct, may well be confusion as well as injustice. If in order to act effectively – including establishing institutions guiding long-range behavior and policies – people must have ideas by which to be guided, and if these ideas imply conflicting, even contradictory, courses of action, it seems reasonable to expect much confusion and even injustice to arise from the state of affairs described thus far.[3] We come to understand ourselves as (a) capable of being individually responsible for many problems in our lives, and as (b) unable to act by our own judgment, to formulate plans of action that counter influences upon us from our environment, our past, our genes, or whatnot. We cannot but see ourselves as divided in a rather fundamental way. And it seems that philosophers contribute amply to this problematic situation. Are they responsible? Should they – can they – alter their ways? Those questions are just the sort in need of greater attention.[4]

All this has, of course, been dismissed along lines heard from the late psychologist B. F. Skinner, namely, as so much "pre-scientific" talk based on no more than myth and by now eclipsed by the findings of modern science.[5] Nevertheless, we can easily move away from cases involving the remarks and conduct of lay people and draw our material from the forums where professional philosophers sound off and where we find that praising and blaming (and their cognates[6]) occur as frequently as they do anywhere else. In our time applied ethics is a flourishing field; philosophers make claims about how doctors, lawyers, politicians, soldiers, business managers, personnel directors, teachers, parents, and men and women fulfilling innumerable other roles in life should or should not act. Journals abound in business, medical, environmental, legal, and other varieties of applied ethics, as well as in the broader fields of social and political philosophy and of public policy, and many of the papers featured pertain to what those in these fields should or should not do or, alternatively, what laws or rules legislators or regulators should enact so as to force those in these fields to behave properly.[7]

THE PHILOSOPHERS' ROLE

Although I do not mean to denigrate any prescribing of courses of conduct, in the face of such moralizing from professional philosophers, it is curious, if not outright scandalous, that those doing work in applied ethics pay so little attention to whether human beings are equipped to direct or guide themselves so that they can be held responsible for how they act. In other words, given the widely admitted philosophical idea that "ought implies can," especially in circumstances not fraught with paradox,[8] it seems odd that philosophers are not eager to reconcile all their moralizing with their views of human nature and motivation. Let us explore here why it may be that no great effort is being made to draw together the normative and ontological aspects of substantive moral theorizing in our time.

I should note that there is not total silence on the relationship between ethics and human nature, specifically whether human individuals can be original initiators of their actions. But these discussions are not conducted in those forums where most of the substantive applied ethical analysis is carried out, or by those who focus most intensively on substantive ethics.

THE GENESIS OF DISJOINTEDNESS

To begin with, let us note that much of the late twentieth-century interest in moral public policy was started with the work of John Rawls, whose 1971 book *A Theory of Justice*[9] certainly launched a renewal of political philosophy, as well as a good deal of moral philosophy, in British and American philosophical circles. It was soon followed by Robert Nozick's *Anarchy, State, and Utopia*,[10] which also contributed to a resurgence of political argumentation. These two books, especially Rawls's, made more of an impact than earlier mid-twentieth-century books on politics, such as those by Brian Barry and Nicholas Rescher.[11]

Yet the resurrection occurred in combination with an expensive proviso, put explicitly by John Rawls in his 1974 presidential address to the American Philosophical Association. The address was called "The Independence of Moral Theory,"[12] and its thesis was basically that what we need to do is forget about the grand philosophical project and attend only to questions of morality. As Rawls put it:

[a] relation of methodological priority does not hold, I believe, between the theory of meaning, epistemology, and the philosophy of

20

mind on the one hand and moral philosophy on the other. To the contrary: a central part of moral philosophy is what I have called moral theory; it consists in the comparative study of moral conceptions, which is, in large part, independent.[13]

Ethics, morality, and public policy were to be approached without any of what used to be called "philosophical foundations."

In a way, Rawls's thesis echoed several decades of ordinary-language and analytic philosophy that had been antagonistic toward system building. It was, furthermore, just another turn away from the kind of moral theorizing that had been attacked by David Hume, in his *A Treatise of Human Nature*,[14] several centuries before. System building was once more declared to be useless and philosophically unjustified. Philosophy was supposed to scale down its scope and become more piecemeal. We were to look at various issues that had been the province of philosophy in isolation from philosophical thinking. Exactly how the recategorization of such traditional philosophical issues was to happen was a matter of the different methodologies and theories of the various competing schools, but these competing schools had tended to agree on one fundamental principle: that philosophy was pretty much impotent when it came to such questions as "What is the nature of knowledge and moral knowledge?" and "What is the nature of the good and the moral good?" Even such questions as "Do human beings possess freedom of will?" and "Is there a God?" were deemed by many to be out of bounds for philosophical investigations.

We may fairly associate these attitudes with subschools of empiricism, logical positivism, linguistic analysis, ordinary-language philosophy, pragmatism, existentialism, and so forth.[15] Rawls's thesis of independence of moral theory was another way of putting essentially the same point: ethics, philosophy of law, political philosophy, public policy issues, and the like were all to be handled on the basis of impressions, intuitions, what seems to make the best sense under ordinary circumstances and in ordinary terms, and so forth, placed, of course, in a "reflective equilibrium."[16] Following Rawls's work, as well as Nozick's partial endorsement of its methodology (Nozick, too, used ordinary intuitions to test the feasibility of his assumed natural rights), a great number of articles assuming the independence of moral theory began to appear in journals such as *Ethics*, *Philosophy and Public Affairs*, and *Social Theory and Practice*.[17]

STARTING WITH INTUITIONS

Evidence of this assumption may be gleaned from the fact that these articles usually began with an assertion concerning "our considered moral judgments" or "moral intuitions" and then proceeded to sketch out some kind of a derivation as it applied to some area of public policy, morality, law, or politics. It can be argued, however, that this tactic is misguided.[18] One consideration that had to

21

be neglected, in consequence of such "independence," is whether any of this moral and political exhortation had a realistic base in human nature, the nature of the beings that were the intended audience of such discussions. If we are moved by forces over which we have no control, how can it be possible that we ought to engage in redistribution of wealth and equal treatment of everyone in a society, or abstain from sexual discrimination and harassment, insider trading, tax evasion, exploitative or imperialistic foreign trade or policies, and greedy financial scheming?

Philosophers may not have outright endorsed the view B. F. Skinner placed on record – although John Rawls himself came extremely close to doing just that when he wrote that a person's "character depends in large part upon fortunate family and social circumstances for which he can claim no credit."[19] However, most of their colleagues within the social sciences, including economists, sociologists, psychologists, and anthropologists, have formulated or accepted theories that discount free human agency as regards our conduct, institutions, and laws.[20]

Assume it turns out that there is no way for us to do anything but what we must do, as determined by neural powers, the mechanics of our brain, the socioeconomic conditions that have surrounded us during our "formative" years, or some similar candidate. Assume, in other words, that the deterministic conception of human nature is correct.[21] Assume, furthermore, that no fundamental challenge of this essentially mechanistic model of the human mind and consciousness has been prominently advanced – and the model certainly has not been challenged much in nineteenth- and twentieth-century philosophy.[22] If all this is accepted, especially by those engaged in the promulgation of moral and political ideals, one can certainly wonder how anyone is to make any sense of the claims that people ought to do or abstain from doing the myriad of things that moral philosophers, public policy analysts, and political philosophers maintain.

THE IMPORTANCE OF HAVING FREE WILL

Let me briefly argue that there is indeed free will and that there is nothing odd about the supposition that we have it. I am going to defend the position that free will means that human beings can cause some of what they do, on their own. In other words, what they do is not explainable solely by references to factors that have influenced them, though, of course, their range of options is clearly circumscribed by the world in which they live and by their particular circumstances, capacities, options, talents, and so forth; human beings are able to cause their actions and are therefore responsible for some of what they do. In a basic sense, we are all original actors capable of making novel moves in the world. We are, in other words, initiators of some of our behavior. I will later indicate why this makes a difference in discussions of applied ethics and public affairs, contrary to the impression left by the numerous discussions in these fields that do not touch on the topic.

22

The first matter to be noted is that the suggestion that free will exists in no way contradicts science. Free will could well be a natural phenomenon, something that emerged in nature with the emergence of human beings, which have minds that can think and be aware of their own thinking. In other words, the idea that some animals might be facilitated to be original and creative, rather than largely reflexive, is not *ipso facto* a violation of the laws of nature.

Nature is complicated and multifaceted. It includes many different sorts of things, and one of these is human beings. Human beings exhibit unique, yet natural, attributes that other beings apparently do not exhibit, and free will appears to be one of these attributes.

I am going to offer several reasons why a belief in free will makes very good sense. The first few of these explain why there *can be* free will – that is, why nature does not preclude it. But these do not yet demonstrate that free will exists. That will be the job of the reasons I will advance next, which will establish that free will *actually exists*; it is not just a possibility but an actuality.

NATURE'S LAWS VERSUS FREE WILL

One of the major objections against free will is that nature is governed by a set of laws, mainly the laws of physics. Everything is controlled by these laws, and we human beings are basically more complicated versions of material substances, so whatever governs any other material substance in the universe must also govern human life. Basically, we are subject to the kind of causation that everything else is subjected to. Since nothing else exhibits free will but conforms to causal laws, so must we. Social science is merely looking into the particulars of those causes, but we all know that we are subject to them in any case. The only difference is that we are complicated things.

In response I want to point out that nature exhibits innumerable different domains, distinct not only in their complexity but also in the kinds of beings they include. So it is not possible to rule out ahead of time that there might be something in nature that exhibits agent causation – the phenomenon whereby a thing causes some of its own behavior. So there might be in nature a form of existence that exhibits free will. Whether there is or is not is something to be discovered, not ruled out by a narrow metaphysics that restricts everything to being just a variation on one kind of thing. Thus, taking account of what nature is composed of does not at all rule out free will.

CAN WE KNOW OF FREE WILL?

Another reason why some think that free will is not possible is that the dominant mode of learning about nature is what we call "empiricism." In other words, many believe that the only way we know about nature is by observing it with our various sensory organs. And since our sensory organs do not give us direct evidence of such a thing as free will, there really is not any such thing. Since no observable evidence for free will exists, free will does not or cannot be shown to exist.

But the doctrine that empiricism captures all forms of knowing is wrong. We know many things not simply through observation but through a combination of observation, inferences, and theory construction. (Consider that even the purported knowledge that empiricism is our form of knowledge is not "known" empirically!)

Many features of the universe, including criminal guilt, are detected not by eyewitnesses but by way of theories that serve the purpose of best explaining what we do have before us to observe. This is true, also, even in the natural sciences. Many of the phenomena in biology, physics, and chemistry – not to mention psychology – are explained not by what we detect through observation but by inferences based on theories. And the theory that explains things best – most completely and most consistently – is the best answer to the question of what is going on.

Free will may well turn out to be in this category. In other words, free will may be not something that we can see directly, but something that best explains what we do see in human life. It may explain, for example, the many mistakes that human beings make in contrast to the few mistakes that other animals make. We also notice that human beings do all kinds of odd things that cannot be accounted for in terms of mechanical causation, the type once associated with physics. We can examine people's backgrounds and find that some people with bad childhoods turn out to be decent, while others become crooks. And free will can be a very helpful explanation. For now all we need to consider is that this may well be so. If empiricism does not allow for it, so much the worse for empiricism. One could know something because it explains something else better than any alternative. And that is not strictly empirical knowledge.

IS FREE WILL WEIRD?

Another matter that very often counts against free will is that the rest of the beings in nature do not exhibit it. Dogs, cats, lizards, fish, frogs, and so forth have no free will, so it appears arbitrary to impute it to human beings. Why should we be free to do things when the rest of nature lacks any such capacity? It would be an impossible aberration.

The answer here is similar to what I gave earlier: There is variety in nature – some things swim, some fly, some just lie there, some breathe, some grow. Free will could be yet another addition to all the varieties of nature.

Let us now consider whether free will actually does exist.

ARE WE DETERMINED TO BE DETERMINISTS?

There is an argument that if we are fully determined in what we think, believe, and do, then of course the belief that determinism is true is also a result of this determinism. But the same holds for the belief that determinism is false: There is nothing you can do about whatever you believe – you had to believe it. There is no way to take an independent stance and consider the arguments without prejudice, because of all the various forces making us assimilate the evidence in the world just the way we do. One either turns out to be a determinist or does not, and in neither case can we appraise the issue objectively, because we are predetermined to have a view on the matter one way or the other.

But then, paradoxically, we'll never be able to resolve this debate, since there is no way of obtaining an objective assessment. Indeed, the very idea of scientific or judicial objectivity, as well as the idea of reaching philosophical truth, has to do with being free. Thus, if we are engaged in this enterprise of learning about truth and distinguishing it from falsehood, we are committed to the idea that human beings have some measure of mental freedom.

SHOULD WE BECOME DETERMINISTS?

There is another dilemma of determinism. Determinists want us to believe in determinism. In fact, they believe we ought to be determinists rather than believe in this myth called "free will." But as the saying goes in philosophy, "ought implies can." If we ought to believe in determinism, this implies that we are free to choose whether determinism or free will is a better doctrine.[23]

WE OFTEN KNOW WE ARE FREE

In many contexts of our lives, introspective knowledge is taken very seriously. When you go to a doctor and he asks you, "Are you in pain?" and you say, "Yes," and he says, "Where is the pain?" and you say, "It's in my knee," the doctor does not say, "Why, you can't know. This is not public evidence. I will now get verifiable, direct evidence of where you feel hurt." In fact, your evidence is very good evidence. Witnesses at trials give evidence as they report about what they have seen or heard, which is introspective evidence. Even in the various sciences, people report on what they have read in surveys or seen on gauges or other instruments. Thus they are giving us introspective evidence.

Introspection is one source of evidence that we take as reasonably reliable. What should we make of the fact that a lot of people say things like "Damn it! I didn't make the right choice" or "I neglected to do something"? They report to us that they have made various choices, that they intended this or that but not another thing. And they often blame themselves for not having done

25

something; thus they report that they are taking responsibility for what they have or have not done.

In short, there is a lot of evidence from people all around us of the existence of free choice.

MODERN SCIENCE DISCOVERS FREE WILL

There is also the evidence that we seem to have the capacity for self-monitoring. The human brain has a structure that allows us to govern ourselves, so to speak. We can inspect our lives, we can detect where we are going, and we can, therefore, change course. And the human brain itself makes it possible. The brain, because of its structure, can monitor itself, and as a result we can decide whether to continue in a certain pattern or to change that pattern and go in a different direction. That is the sort of free will that is demonstrable. At least some scientists, for example, Roger W. Sperry,[24] maintain that there is evidence of free will in this sense. This view depends on a number of points I have already mentioned. It assumes that there can be different causes in nature, so that the functioning of the brain would be a kind of *self*-causation. The organism with its brain would have to be able to cause some things about the organism's behavior, and that depends, of course, on the possibility of there being various kinds of causes apart from the efficient kind modeled on the way a bowling ball causes the fall of the pins or a cue ball causes the movement of the eight ball on the pool table. The sort of causation here is structural, from within the entity, not from without or even by means of some inner mechanism. It is the organism that produces its behavior or action.

Precisely the sort of thing Sperry thinks possible is evident in our lives. We make plans and revise them. We explore alternatives and decide to follow one of these. We change a course of conduct we have embarked upon, or we continue with it. In other words, there is a locus of individual self-responsibility that is evident in the way in which we look upon ourselves and in the way in which we in fact behave.

THE BEST THEORY IS TRUE

Finally, there is what I alluded to earlier, namely, that when we put all of this together, we get a more sensible understanding of the complexities of human life than otherwise – we get a better understanding, for example, of why social engineering and government regulation and regimentation do not work, why there are so many individual and cultural differences, why people can be wrong, why they can disagree with each other, and so forth. It is because people are free to be different, because they are not set in some pattern the way cats and dogs and orangutans and birds tend to be.

Most of the behavior of these creatures around us can be predicted. With human beings we can make some predictions because we often have our minds made up, and from that we can estimate what we are going to do. But our predictions are often wrong. Very often people change their minds and surprise or annoy us. And if we go to different cultures, they will surprise us even more. This complexity, diversity, and individuation about human beings are best explained if human beings have free will.

WE HAVE GOOD REASON TO TRUST FREE WILL

So these several reasons provide a kind of argumentative collage in support of the free-will position. Can anyone do better with this issue? I don't know. I think it is best to ask only for what is the best of the various competing theories. Are human beings behaving solely in response to forces impinging on them? Or do they have the capacity to take charge of their lives? Which supposition explains the human world and its complexities around us?

I think the latter makes much better sense. It explains, much better than do deterministic theories, how it is possible that human life involves such a wide range of possibilities – accomplishments as well as defeats, joys as well as sorrows, creation as well as destruction. It explains, also, why in human life there is so much change – in language, custom, style, art, science. Unlike other living beings, for which what is possible is pretty much fixed by instincts and reflexes, people initiate much of what they do, for better and for worse. From their most distinctive capacity of forming ideas and theories to their artistic and athletic inventiveness, human beings remake the world without, so to speak, having to do so! And this can make good sense if we understand them to have the distinctive capacity for initiating their own conduct, rather than relying on mere stimulation and reaction. It also poses for them certain very difficult tasks, not the least of which is accepting that no formula or system can predictably manage human societies. Social engineering is, thus, not a genuine prospect for solving human problems – only education and individual initiative can do that.

PROBLEMS WITH THE "AS IF" THESIS

There are those, of course, who hold that there is room for both causal determinism and praise/blame, because even if there were no free will, treating people *as if* they were free agents could be conducive to positive results (that is, results that all or most of us are causally destined to deem as positive). Yet this tact capitalizes on a conceptual difference between being convinced about something and being fooled into believing it, a distinction that itself assumes free will. Those who are fooled are deemed, generally, to have the capacity to watch out against that eventuality – unless, of course, they were destined to be fooled.

Furthermore, underlying this thesis we still find several questions that raise the issue of genuine free will. For example, should those who are aware of the illusion keep people in the dark about their belief in free will? Are we free to make that decision? Is it right to fool people about such matters? If not, is it up to us to desist?

Also, if the free-will matter is a case of "as if," what if most people discover it? Surely, if philosophers and psychologists can learn that it is merely a matter of treating us as if we had free will, so can others, in which case there is no point in continuing the subterfuge.

Finally, praising and blaming do not make sense if there is no factual base for them. When we praise or blame dogs or horses, it may be praise or blame to us, but for them it is nothing of the sort – at most it is a kind of reinforcement or encouragement, something that makes them feel good and induces repetition. In order to play the "as if" game, there must be some possibility of genuine praise or blame. Barring that, it cannot do its job, namely, of inducing bona fide pride or guilt. The language of ethics would be discovered to be no different from that of demonology or witchcraft, resting on nothing but error or myth.

PUBLIC POLICY AND FREE WILL

We can now return to the initial topic of this discussion. Why is the free-will subject matter a proper one to raise in connection with our understanding of applied ethics and public policies?

To start with, one might once again recall Kant's contribution to this issue with his discussion of "ought implies can" – that is, if we should or should not act in various ways, it must be possible for us to choose such acts or their alternatives. In other words, one cannot be said to have the responsibility to do or abstain from doing an action if the action is not something one can initiate. This initiation may be very well hidden when the action actually occurs, so that one may simply attribute its origin to character. But in such a case, one would have to be able to make sense of the idea that the character traits that prompted the action were somehow cultivated in large measure by the individual who has them.

Based on the insight expressed in Kant's motto – as well as in Aristotle's observation that "the virtues are modes of choice or involve choice" and "it is in our power to be virtuous or vicious"[25] – we can see that any effort to credit or discredit persons for good or bad behavior, including the support of good or bad public policies, institutions, and so forth, would amount to a meaningless gesture without free will. Indeed, in an intellectual climate in which free will is denied (as, for example, it seems clearly to be when most misconduct is attributed to addiction or other afflictions), the idea that people have the power to initiate their conduct – even the power to choose whether or how to think about the issues involved – would make no sense. This is just what we witness when someone is being urged to stop smoking and answers, "Well, I just can't stop." If all evaluations of human behavior could be met with "Well, I just cannot do otherwise," this surely would have something of an impact on how we view ourselves and whether there is a chance to make improvements in our lives and societies. Moral advice, exhortation, criticism, praise, reward, and the like would be robbed of their meaning, just as the idea that someone is a witch or inhabited by demons is largely looked upon as meaningless these days.

Accordingly, there seems to be a drastic gap between the idea of human nature that is circulating (and is tacitly pretty much accepted by most philosophers) and the persistent moralizing that goes on in philosophy journals. Perhaps this is of no concern to some people, but there is at least one moral reason to think of it as a serious issue. (One might even construe it as belonging in the framework of applied ethics, specifically, in the ethics of philosophical scholarship.) The reason has to do with integrity. Presumably, what integrity means is having the various facets of one's ideas, values, and policies in life, including one's professional pronouncements, placed in some sort of a consistent, coherent, integrated framework. If, in fact, one can live with both a deterministic conception of human action and extensive moralizing, maybe integrity is not a necessary part of human life (and certainly not of the life of a philosopher who dabbles in these issues). But then this could also have an impact on how we should view politicians and others whose lack of integrity is so often the topic of applied-ethics discussions.[26]

If, however, we affirm the reality of human free will – in some sensible form, never mind the details for now – we might also have to adjust some of our moral claims. In business ethics, for example, the doctrine of consumer sovereignty is commonly challenged on grounds advanced by John Kenneth Galbraith, namely, that consumers are easily manipulated by advertisements to purchase goods and services they do not actually need or want (except for being made to want them by the ads).[27] If, however, some version of free will is construed as necessarily presupposed by business ethics as such, it may well require construing consumer sovereignty as something more justified than it is within the Galbraith thesis.

Other issues that may be influenced by a thorough discussion of the free-will issue include "caveat emptor" ("let the buyer beware"), "unconscionable contract," surrogate mothering, sexual exploitation, and sexual domination. In the area of sexual harassment, molestation, and assault problems, the idea is often advanced that some people are incapable of resisting their urges to make advances toward, even at times to rape, people who appear very attractive or provocative to them. Here, too, the free-will stance would, if sound, pretty much discredit this way of understanding and open the way to assign responsibility to individuals who sexually harass, molest, or rape. There are also those who attribute racist, sexist, and other kinds of unjust sentiments entirely to their upbringing, claiming that given how or where they were brought up, it is impossible for them to feel and act differently from how they do. They say they should not be made to pay for something they cannot help, that it is, after all, a mere accident that they are the way they are.

It seems to me that these ways of looking at misconduct by human beings are undermined by the free-will thesis, provided it is sound. But if it is not sound, these ways of thinking seem to be quite feasible and possibly sound. In any case, without a direct examination of the connection between ethics and the free-will issue, we should be candid that the field of ethics is fundamentally disintegrated and that questions of morality, politics, and public policy are going to be left in disarray.

3

HUMAN ACTION AND THE NATURE OF MORAL EVIL

INTRODUCTION

In a very interesting and challenging paper, Laurie Calhoun advances a view denying the connection between rationality and morality. Via the example of Rhoda Penmark in the film *The Bad Seed*, Calhoun attempts to show that evil persons can be rational – by which she means, as she put it, that "Rhoda has no cognitive deficiencies whatsoever. She is meticulously perfectionistic about everything she does and always performs exceptionally. She is fully capable of understanding the facts about her murders, but they have absolutely no emotional effect upon her."[1]

My purpose here is to sketch a position on the nature of human evil that will serve to put on record a modified rationalistic view within an individualist framework. I will argue that when some*one* is morally evil – and only some*one*, an *individual*, can be such, via both commission and omission – that person is being irrational. "Irrational" will be used in a sense somewhat different from Calhoun's, but not in a sense that violates cogent employments of the concept. As such, moral evil will be shown to be less a species of cognitive "deficiency" than one of cognitive "malpractice." In line with the view I will advance, Rhoda Penmark's evildoing would be a species of irrationality (unless it turned out that she had the relevant sort of involuntary cognitive impediment, in which case her behavior would not be evil any more than the behavior of a mad dog is evil).

It should, however, also be noted that because Rhoda is a fictional child, she may be exemplifying traits of personality, even behavior, that will not be replicable in the case of bona fide evil (adult) persons who are morally responsible for their conduct. Yes, Rhoda behaves in ways that actual evil persons – for example, a hit man with a wife, children, a nice home, and pets around the house – could behave, namely, "rationally" *vis-à-vis* much of one's life. Yet there is something dubious in this contention about hit men and perhaps even Rhoda. Another film, *The Mechanic*, follows the activities of two hit men and depicts those in this line of work as having seriously warped personalities. Accordingly, once a person is blind in the way Calhoun believes Rhoda to be,

31

he or she will be emotionally numb to various experiences and will exhibit slippage from callousness about other people's lives to related areas.

But these matters cannot be explored here, so let me turn to the limited task of sketching a neo-rationalistic position of the nature of moral evil in human life. I want to outline a conception of human action that opens the way to provide (a) the prospect of good explanations of what people do, (b) the possibility of moral evaluations of their conduct, and (c) a conception of evil that involves voluntary subversion of one's cognitive functions.

HUMAN ACTION:
INTENTION, YES; DELIBERATION, MAYBE

What is the nature of human action? What distinguishes actions from, for example, behaviors, movements, or events? What is the difference between intending and deliberating? When we *think up* some behavior, do we always ponder it, weigh it against other possible ways of behaving? If so, then intentional action would be the same as deliberate action. It does seem that the following can be said, truly, about action:

> Actions – cutting, burning, weaving – have an independent nature of their own. If we wish to succeed, they cannot be performed in just any way the whims and desires of particular actors may dictate. The objective character of the world (the hardness of things to be cut, for example, the inflammability of things, the characteristics of yarns) determines the operations that must be performed, though only if the goals that are to be accomplished are also posited (shearing off one portion of a thing from the rest, consuming things by means of fire, separating the warp from the woof). The goal – what is to be accomplished, in general or in detail – also serves as the measure of adequacy of the operation. Moreover, all these and many other actions are performed "with a proper instrument" (Cratylus, 387d5), one that is suitable for the proper performance of the operation in question (387d–388b).[2]

Some social philosophers, for example, F. A. Hayek – who himself draws on such others as Adam Ferguson and Bernard Mandeville – are noted for having concluded that since the bulk of our behavior is not deliberate, it is, instead, unintended, spontaneous. They reach this assessment by observing that many of the consequences of human action have not been thought of and anticipated when the action was taken. Thus, they think, the action must not have been intentional. Hayek, for example, invokes this point to stress that since we reach most of our ends – especially those that amount to various institutional arrangements, such as language, a system of money, and the marketplace – without deliberation, these ends must not have been *intended* in any sense at all. That is why he is famous for having focused upon the *unintended* consequences of human action. He cites Adam Ferguson approvingly for coining the phrase about the "results of human action but not of human design."[3] This suggests that Hayek saw human action more as human behavior, as *driven* rather than *intended* ("intended" meaning produced, at least in part, by means of rational thought). But consider how J. L. Austin saw this, judging from the following passage:

> We walk along the cliff, and I feel a sudden impulse to push you over, which I promptly do: I acted on impulse, yet I certainly intended to push you over, and may even have devised a little ruse to achieve it: yet even then I did not act deliberately, for I did not (stop to) ask myself whether to do it or not.[4]

Austin shows here – by way of a quite ordinary example that we can all appreciate – that intentional action is not the same as deliberate action. Hayek conflates the two and is left, thus, with the conclusion that since most ordinary action is not deliberate, it must be "unintended."

The conflation of deliberation and intention leads to the claim that much of what we do is in some sense not up to us, not a result of human initiative. It just happens. To put it another way, such an understanding of human action suggests that what we do without deliberation comes about spontaneously, with no one being responsible for it. It may, indeed, amount to something totally arational, even instinctual. The order that Hayek sees in much of human social life appears to him to have come about spontaneously, without anyone having planned it. But, of course, there is planning and there is planning. Intentional action is planned, even if the planning is not elaborate, involved, self-conscious. In Austin's illustration, for example, even though the person acts on impulse, this may mean simply that he gave *little thought* to what he set out to do, not that he did not set out to do it, did not plan to push him and for him to fall. Premeditated planning isn't the only kind.

Hayek's conflation also suggests that deliberative action, involving self-conscious planning and monitoring of what we set out to do (in contrast to action that is "not intended"), is somehow unnatural; that it is not really part of the normal proceedings people embark upon in life or that the deliberative behavior of human beings may be artificial.[5]

Hayek uses his distinction to mark off actions that are benign from those that are likely to be harmful – market transactions versus government planning – and has convinced many in the field of political economy that one can do this without recourse to normative political theory (for example, a theory of justice such as that of Rawls or Nozick). He is not the only one who has tried this route. There is considerable talk among environmentalists, too, about how what human beings do may well be alien to the natural world – trampling on nature, controlling their environment, building, developing, and so forth. This, too, is an approach that helps to avoid ethical or moral theorizing in favor of what is deemed to be a scientific approach.

It seems to me that this attempt to deal with different types of human action without recourse to the normative sphere is misguided. (There is something inherently normative about it anyway, for what is spontaneous or natural – in line with human nature – in the human sphere is infused with choice.) It leaves us at sea when we face evil, when we consider such matters as the Holocaust, rape, serial murder and child molestation, leading many to turn to social and natural science, such as evolutionary psychology and biology, and avoid the waxing problems of morality. Yet those problems nevertheless reappear if only because even to say that one *ought to* look at human affairs in one light rather than another carries with it a moral tinge. Such a claim is usually followed by charges of stubbornness or intransigence, both of which are clearly morally pregnant.

It is, thus, crucial that we address here one of the most troublesome areas of moral philosophy, the problem of human evil. But this will take a bit of preparation.

ACTION IS BEHAVING INTENTIONALLY, PURPOSEFULLY, AND NORMATIVELY

Let me suggest, first, that action (or perhaps conduct, so as to distinguish human action from the actions ascribed to other animals) is behavior (of a living organism) willed and guided by means of a judgment formed, either intentionally or deliberately. When one acts, or engages in some conduct, one wills – initiates or embarks upon – some behavior. One thinks, often unselfconsciously, of some objective or end and produces the behavior one believes is needed to achieve it. The thinking need not have been deliberate – reflected upon, as when one *thinks about the thinking* that guides the behavior. (Self-conscious conduct is characteristic, for example, of intoxicated people *vis-à-vis* ordinarily unmonitored conduct and engineers or surgeons *vis-à-vis* complex tasks. Editing a text, too, exemplifies clearly such deliberative action.)

What seems to be needed for behavior to amount to conduct, or human action, is only that *some level* of thinking guides it or shaped the behavior to begin with, when one developed it – for example, as when a person learned how to play the concert piano but by now does it "nearly automatically." In other words, the behavior has to have been intended, willed by means of thinking, even while the thinking itself need not have been reflected or deliberated upon – one "did not (stop to) ask" oneself "whether to do it or not."

The topic of exactly how a thought that would guide or shape behavior is formed would lead us too far astray here. Suffice it for my purposes to suggest that we think by engaging in the mental – driven by the higher brain (cerebral cortex) – process of integrating and differentiating the content or substance of our direct (perceptual) and indirect (simple or more complex levels of conceptual) awareness. This integrating and differentiating is a mental action. In contrast to actions undertaken intentionally and deliberately, such as tying one's shoes or building bridges, it involves not overt, public behavior, but primary initiative or origination (creative thought) at the level of brain processes.

Thus mental "action" is *primary*, the direct willing of the agent. However, actions of the sort we observe persons undertaking are guided or governed by the mental "actions" of thinking. (Willing itself is but the beginning point of mental action, something we initiate on our own. There is no entity such as the will; rather, the will is the outset of action by a free agent, one facilitated to cause what he or she is going to do.[6])

Some believe, following David Hume, that in order for behavior to commence, there must be an emotion or passion that produces it, reasoning being passive and impotent to produce motion. The will is, thus, motivated by emotions such as fears, hopes, and anxieties. This approach to understanding human action seems to fit with the modern propensity to seek an antecedent *cause or variable*, the behavior of which produces the overt behavior of the human agent. It also seems to satisfy one commonsense notion, namely, that much of what we do comes about because of how or what we feel.

I will not address the broad issue of seeking antecedent causes, since if that framework is sound, the very idea of evil must be given up or so drastically reformulated that no place for individual culpable wrongdoing would be left. Evil would then turn out, at most, to be another bad thing that happens, in this case involving human behavior. Some philosophers, following Socrates or others, do see evil as a kind of force that impedes good – thus David L. Norton states, "The pitfalls through which evil appears are ignorance and obstruction." And although he also states, "In eudaimonistic theory no one is born with an evil will, though everyone is born with the possibility of acquiring an evil will," he adds, "The evil will is a reactive phenomenon, arising from the thwarting or frustration of the innate incentive to live a worthy life."[7] This view seems to require some kind of efficient cause for evil to occur – a thwarting or frustration. Yet moral evil proper requires that the evil be done by the person, on his or her own initiative – for example, a failure to carry out some task or an effort to cover up such failure, at the agent's initiative or because he or she chose or did not choose to do something.

There may still be a way to accommodate the commonsense impression that emotions have a powerful role in human behavior. Suppose we take emotions to be certain facts about us – we feel fear, anger, delight, hope, and so forth, and as we think about what we will do or refrain from doing, emotions line up among the facts that could be relevant in our decision, in what we are "determined" to do (in the sense of "Judy was determined to become a good architect"). Our emotions are important responses, often clueing us into what goes on in the world – when we fear something, it is pretty likely that the thing we fear will be dangerous, although this is not decisive. When we consider what to do, we could take our fear as *one* fact to consider, but if we also realized that running away would endanger, say, our child, we would refuse to let our fear be decisive concerning what we should and will do.

And this seems to fit another of our commonsense ideas, namely, that we do not always allow emotions to be exculpating facts – the mere fact that Harry felt very angry at John does not suffice to account for Harry's having decked John. Harry's feeling angry at John could, we take it, be outweighed by Harry's realization or understanding that John's having insulted him does not objectively merit the drastic behavior of decking him, or that the probable result of permanently alienating John is not worth indulging one's feeling of anger.

Of course, the determinations involving such decisions – weighing of the various facts that bear on what we will do – are not always done self-consciously; that is, they do not have to involve some self-monitoring (stopping to consider) process. This is so even if that process is an option (outside of emergency and reflex cases, as when one swerves to avoid a child but then hits someone else).

What I propose (following some others, such as Immanuel Kant and Ayn Rand) is that the ultimate *free action*, one that underlies or sets on their way the myriad behaviors we undertake, is *thinking*. Indeed, this may explain why being thoughtful is widely deemed to be so vital in how human beings come to do what they do. It is clearly important in deliberate behavior, such as making arguments, conceiving theories, forging foreign policy, or embarking upon a complex business venture.

What is not realized sufficiently is that the process of thinking – started by the agent, in the capacity of a kind of first-cause agency – is also vital in ordinary conduct that is "spontaneous," or not self-monitored. It is natural to expect human adults to keep their wits about them and attempt to forestall mishaps even in the course of doing ordinary things (intentionally but not deliberately). This is why negligence may be deemed legally actionable, for example, in auto accidents or medical malpractice.

When one acts, the behavior that is evident occurs in light of some judgment or conceptualization of what was to be done. Even small actions, such as the movements of one's hand during gesticulation or the stirring of a cup of coffee, involve the prior (but nondeliberative) judgments that direct or guide the behavior that ensues. When the judgment prior to the behavior would have to have been made is quite possibly a particular question, pertaining to given actions and not answerable in general terms. As already suggested, some tasks are performed in light of judgments made long before. If I turn on the lights by nearly automatically flipping the switch as I enter the bedroom where my spouse is trying to go to sleep, I am not doing such a thing deliberately; quite the contrary. Yet it does not suffice for me to invoke that fact as exculpation when she, upon having been (rudely) awakened, whispers, annoyed, "Haven't I asked you to please keep the lights off when you come to bed while I'm trying to go to sleep!"

Indeed, even in the course of verbal arguments, whereby one advances a line of reasoning that is supposed to be sound, or at least valid, one does not always check back over what was just said; yet if one were to be found to have made an error in reasoning, it is deemed to be a fault – as anyone involved in philosophical or other intellectual discourse knows well enough. The recognition of the plausibility of the position being laid out here is, thus, pretty universal, even if it is not widely articulated.

One way to consider the merits of this understanding of human action is by checking how it may help us with some other concerns we have about actions. Thus, if we construe actions along lines sketched above, it seems we can make sense of assessing some of what we do as wrong, ill conceived, messy, lazy, inconsiderate, or misguided by virtue of being badly thought out to begin with. The actions and their impact on the world often reflect this fact about them. Thoughtless, sloppy judgments result in behavior that is ill formed, misguided, and so forth, thus destructive, injurious, harmful, even fatal – to which the law courts of various societies testify when they entertain charges of malpractice, negligence, oversight, and omission as responses to such misconduct.

This picture would appear to make sense of how we address the way people act: A continuum seems to exist, from actions that have but the most minimal (sloppy, vague, inconsistent, shallow) thought guiding them to those guided by the most clearly conceived judgments. This gradual differentiation between minimally thoughtful and fully focused action appears possible even with behavior that is intended but not deliberated about. This would follow from understanding action as involving a significant and initial measure of thoughtfulness, of conceptual focus – better or worse, careful or reckless. The issue then comes down to whether nondeliberative thinking can be so characterized.

BELIEF, RATIONALITY, AND ACTION

Some hold that when an action occurs, the agent *must* have the belief that this action is the best course warranted, or, to put it differently, "The action seemed to the agent to be the best thing to do." This is the thinking exhibited by some economists who appear to have a rather powerful influence on at least economic public policy matters in our time. As Nobel-Laureate economist Gary Becker puts it:

> My research has convinced me that people generally engage in rational behavior. They tend to make rational choices, whether it is the marriage partner they choose, the number of children they have, or when they get a divorce. These decisions have costs and benefits.[8]

For an action to be rational, it must involve an accurate calculation of its costs and benefits to the person who takes it. Becker explains, for example, that

> couples divorce when they no longer believe they are better off by staying married. In particular, divorce rates grow when women's earnings are higher compared with those of men; the gain to such women of remaining married is thus diminished.[9]

That is to say, what explains the action is that the agent thought it was not only something to do but also *the most worthwhile* alternative, based on a cost–benefit calculation by standards chosen by the agent. This seems to be the view not only of neoclassical economists, such as Gary Becker, but also of those who follow the lead of the late Ludwig von Mises, the founder of the Austrian school of economics. As von Mises put it:

> Human action is necessarily always rational. . . . When applied to the ultimate ends of action, the terms rational and irrational are inappropriate and meaningless. The ultimate end of action is always the satisfaction of some desires of the acting man. . . . No man is qualified to declare what would make another man happier or less discontented.[10]

What this appears to mean is that we always have some idea as to the effectiveness, satisfactoriness, and propriety of an action *vis-à-vis* our goals. In short, whenever we act, what we do "seems to us to be the (best) thing to do," given objectives that are not themselves subject to objective evaluation.

ACTION LEFT UNEXPLAINED

But it appears that what we get from the economists here is not so much a framework of cogent explanations but rather a system of empty tautologies. First, we are supposed to conceive of rational action as stemming from a calculation of costs and benefits. But whether something is to be costly or beneficial is, in turn, subjective. Strictly speaking, a worker may be rational by choosing to work more hours and receiving less pay, because there is no objective basis for construing work as a cost and pay as a benefit. Pain and pleasure, too, may be either avoided or desired, and there is nothing to say which is better. As far as rationality is concerned, there is no reason to construe anything as a cost or a benefit, a harm or an advantage.

Second, the evidence for the claim that something we did "seems to us to be the (best) thing to do" is nothing more than that we did what we did – that is, the *revealed* preference or actual behavior. Presumably, *all* actions are necessarily characterized by their seeming to the agent to be the (best) thing to do. If one does something without another forcing one to do it, that is judged to be the best course for the agent. But saying the agent did what he or she did because it seemed to be the best course does not actually explain the action. It merely redescribes it. Why does this approach seem so attractive in economics, one of the most reputable social sciences wherein human action is constantly being analyzed?[11]

There is one main reason for the appeal of so looking at the matter. It is the widespread embrace of scientism. If, as most social scientists and many economists hold, all actions require some kind of *efficient cause* to be adequately explained, then something must occur prior to the action that *forces* its emergence. That this something is the belief-state or belief-event that *the behavior is the (best) thing to do* clearly suggests itself as attractive for purposes of filling in the causal role required by the mechanistic, scientistic conception of what counts as an explanation. The belief that some behavior is the best serves, then, as the (efficient) cause for the doing of what is done. The idea of such an efficient cause is required by the conception of what is a *scientific* account of human behavior. (One can see this both in von Mises' *Human Action* and in Becker's *The Economic Approach to Human Behavior*,[12] although von Mises is less inclined to physical-empirical reductionism than is Becker.)

WHAT SCIENCE REQUIRES

Yet this may be a serious fault based not on research, as Becker claims, but on a prescientific, philosophical view of what science *must* find. If the hallmark of science is the discovery of what things are and how they happen, such a prescientific, philosophical view turns out to be prejudicial and quite possibly unscientific.

The approach some economists take to understanding human action may be called into question on various grounds, including that actions are more successfully explained by reference not to efficient causes but to final causes, that is, purposes – more or less clear conceptions of what one will be doing guided by more or less clearly thought-out objectives. The (practical) thinking whereby the agent produces his or her actions is itself directed toward the fulfillment of some more or less clearly formulated objective – an idea as to what will be the result of the behavior one will engage in. This objective need not be deliberately formed; it may be merely intended, thought of as that result.

THE MORAL ASPECTS OF ACTIONS

An efficient causal explanation by reference to a belief (as to what actions seemed best to the agent) does not enable us to give a full enough account of a most important aspect of action, namely, its moral quality, that is, its success or failure in achieving what agents *ought to* achieve. We are not informed about this essential feature of the action, the feature we are often most interested in, when we are told that "it seemed the best thing to do for the agent," because by that account every action is of equal quality – every action is, as it were, always *meant* well!

Furthermore, the efficient causal explanation precludes even making clear sense of the idea that human agents ought to do one thing rather than another, since it denies self-determinism in favor of the determinism that requires events causing subsequent events in a never-ending causal chain. If we are compelled by forces over which we have no control – for example, by some belief-event or belief-state that we *happened to be in*, one that is itself explained by some prior facts – then we are not the sort of beings to which "ought" claims apply. This is the import of the philosophical motto "ought implies can."[13]

EXPLANATIONS MUST BE INFORMATIVE

But even apart from being unhelpful for purposes of moral assessment, to attempt to explain what one does by reference to the fact that one believed the act to be of benefit to oneself fails to be informative. In a sense, of course, by setting out to do something, one may be said to (implicitly) testify to its having seemed to oneself to be the best thing to do. But this is misleading if there are no actions taken voluntarily of which it could be false that it seems to be the best thing to do for the agent. If there are not, then it is doubtful that saying "it seemed to the agent the best thing to do" actually tells us anything about the action other than that it was taken. It is, to use one of Karl Popper's expressions, not a falsifiable causal proposition, one that we could ascertain to be either true or false. Yet it is offered as such by linking behavior to some prior belief as its distinct and (in principle) separate (efficient) cause. The point about something seeming to be the (best) thing for someone to do amounts, then, to no more than a contentless definition of action, rather than what it purports to be, namely, a causal explanation for which evidence could exist.

FOCUSED THINKING AND ACTION

There is an alternative way of explaining – or, if you will, giving an account of – conduct that both is informative and addresses its (moral) success or failure, namely, by reference to the degree of mental focus or attention, and the results thereof, that was paid when it was conceptualized. Sloppily thought-out conduct turns out to explain what we do and helps us identify it as either proper or improper, thus adjusting our theory to our persistent common need for evaluating (blaming and praising) human actions and our awareness that we might have done what we did differently, better or worse. And this sloppiness is the agent's own doing, not something he or she was forced to engage in. Such a framework, to be sure, requires its own controversial philosophical paraphernalia – causal capacity from the agent, free will, self-determinism, final causation, and other ontological conditions that would need to be established for the framework to be shown to be sound.

In summary, then, one aspect of an action is a preceding or concurrent (albeit not deliberated upon) judgment of a certain quality. A person who carries out an action and does not merely engage in some behavior (which may have been produced by forces outside himself) would have to have conceived of what he or she is to do, more or less accurately, carefully, thoughtfully, prudently, and so forth. The action is thus always intentional, involving as it must some degree of attention to what will result from the agent's making a move. But the degree may be minimal, so that some actions are nearly thoughtless, without rhyme or reason, not even the minimal consideration of aiming to please oneself or wishing to do well enough. So when it is claimed by some that all actions are at least minimally rational because they aim for something that seems best to the agent, this claim is unfounded. Some actions aim for nothing so specific at all – they merely fulfill some vague conception, sometimes without any distinct end other than to do something or other, to get on with things, to comply with vague expectations, to react to some desire, never mind the consequences.

Ordinarily, we are aware enough of this when we give voice to such laments as "Hell, I acted without thinking!" or "Damn it, I didn't think!" We also notice about one another the (unfortunate?) propensity to act on impulse, to do things thoughtlessly, to be, as it were, "out to lunch" now and then as we carry on with our various tasks. As one drives around one's city or the country's highways, one often takes notice of drivers who appear to be off someplace else, not paying attention, perhaps only half conscious of what they are doing. When some mishap stemming from such conduct occurs, the reason is not that the driver was doing what "seemed to be the best thing to do under the circumstances," as the rational-action theorists suppose. Rather, the explanation is that the person was not in focus, had lapsed in the task of attending to the world carefully enough. It is this that makes sense, also, of the legal concept of criminal negligence.

To call all such behavior "rational" is to deprive the term of any useful meaning and to produce what Becker and von Mises produced, a characterization of human action that is rational regardless of its quality – be it criminal, adulterous, or irresponsible toward children or spouses. Indeed, it is for this reason that one of Becker's teachers, the late George Stigler, claimed that all social and political states or situations are rational – that we live in the "best of all possible worlds," after all.[14] If people always act rationally, that is surely the result, whatever we may lament about the environment, child abuse, rape, or the federal deficit. The laments will then be akin to those all animals express as

41

part of their dissatisfaction – whining, wailing, sobbing, crying, screaming, and so forth.

Some economists have argued that we always engage in a cost–benefit assessment and that since at times paying heed to what we ought to do is "too expensive," we avoid it. Exactly how "ought" functions in this claim is uncertain. In any case, to know the expense of something (well enough) itself requires mental focus, so this generates an infinite regress. Indeed, if the first move we make is mentally focusing, there is no way to assess its expense at all, since prior to it we would have no way to weigh costs versus benefits. Not all actions appear to be subject to such a calculus.

As we have noted, if it were the case that whenever careless thinking occurs, the explanation is that people are doing what seems to them to be the best thing under the circumstances, no blame or praise could actually be assigned. After all, "they did the best they could." (Notably, of course, this is a familiar way of giving the social scientific way of thinking about human action ordinary expression.) But if the explanation is that they failed to focus on something that *they had the power to change* and *should have changed*, then blame can be reasonably assigned.

Alternatively, with those who focused firmly and discovered what is what and how one ought to cope with it, their actions would be laudable, praiseworthy. One might ask – and Calhoun would probably ask *vis-à-vis* her example of Rhoda Penmark's alleged rationality – "But what if they focused on evil ends?" Yet this question makes no sense prior to an analysis of the nature of human evil. If human evil *is* the willful neglect of full mental focus, and if the results of full mental focus are always as good as they could possibly be as far as the quality of human actions is concerned, then full mental focus cannot have as its target evil ends. Evil ends would be just those that would result from lack of such full focus!

Indeed, when one is tempted to link rationality to evil ends, one usually omits from consideration that rationality requires full, not partial or selective, focus on the facts that are available for consideration. When a criminal gang focuses very sharply and intently on how the bank vault is to be opened, they only appear rational if one forgets that the wealth in the vault belongs to others and they failed to take that into account to its full measure of importance. Rhoda Penmark, too, failed to consider that her victims had lives of their own that were for them, not someone else, to govern. Full focus would have availed her of that understanding and provided her with the suitable guidance for her ensuing actions. Moreover, by evading the relevant facts, Rhoda clearly jeopardizes success at the main task of her life, namely, to live it as an excellent or at least reasonably good human individual. Given that human nature involves being a rationally conscious biological entity, it is the volitional focus of one's attention on the circumstances of one's life that makes one good at the kind of being one is. And it is this central task that Rhoda is failing at dramatically by means of her narrow, selective, purely instrumental rationality.

ECONOMIC RESPONSE AND REBUTTAL

The first point, about the uninformativeness of the explanation offered by the economists, is often rejected on grounds that the view still possesses predictive value – that it can be used to test particular economic forecasts. This is doubtful, however, since nearly any prediction can be made to conform to the view.

Suppose we predict that Judy will divorce Michael and this happens. Then it must have been the case that Judy saw value in divorcing Michael. Suppose we predict that Judy will not divorce Michael and she does not. Then Judy saw value in not divorcing Michael. Since Judy's values are subjective – they come to light as they are revealed in Judy's behavior – whatever she does is, of course, rational if it is done by her (that is, if she was not made to do it). This is part of the reason why the economists at issue tend to favor the free market, since only under such a condition can (subjective) values come to light.

The second point, about not being able to assign praise or blame, is challenged by the economists on grounds that wishing to morally evaluate conduct is a nonscientific prejudice that should be abandoned. (They might draw here on B. F. Skinner's explicit declaration to this effect in his *Beyond Freedom and Dignity*[15] and *Science and Human Behavior*.[16]) As Milton Friedman argues, "of course, 'bad' and 'good' people may be the same people, depending on who is judging them."[17]

Yet the very proclamation that moral evaluation should be abandoned involves a kind of professional moral criticism of those whose view differs from those of the economist or social scientist. It reminds me of a discussion I once had with Milton Friedman, about whether moral judgments can be rationally made by human beings. Friedman, after much debate, turned to me and noted, "The value that seems to me most important and most neglected in the kind of approach [you take] here . . . is the value of humility."[18] Yet in saying this he failed to notice that he had just made a moral assessment, evidently thinking he could do something he found to be unjustified and, as it happens, also untoward when someone else did it. The charge of lacking humility is a moral criticism. The paradox is glaring.

As they criticize one another or their skeptical critics, economists are making (professional) moral judgments themselves, criticizing others for a kind of malpractice, for not thinking better about the topic they have taken up to discuss. And when they critically review submissions to their journals or books, not to mention books submitted to publishers for whom they referee works, they certainly make claims that are a kind of moral assessment – even akin to legal judgments involved in product liability or tort cases. They often claim that others culpably engage in unscientific thinking. Furthermore, they advise that this ought to matter to potential readers and policy shapers. Their discourse, in short, is fraught with moral import even as they deny that such import is intellectually possible.

HUMAN ACTION AND HUMAN EVIL

Does what has been said above help us with one of the crucial concerns human beings have had since time immemorial? Does it help us address the issue of what is the source of human good and evil? Let us consider evil as at least a test case.

When someone is said to be morally evil or when some act is said to be morally wrong, just what is being said about the person or the act, respectively? What is it that constitutes evil? Without a clear enough idea of what evil is, we are left perplexed about numerous problems in society. Let us just consider some random cases where human evil is said to be found: a jury in a trial subverts justice, so its members are blamed for something they should not have done; gang members are blamed for their violent deeds; politicians are accused of abusing their power or not doing their duty. In each case, we are blaming people, holding them morally responsible, for evildoing or negligence. Whenever we charge parents with child abuse, men with sexism, women with self-deprecation, teachers with indoctrination, drug traffickers with poisoning children, industry with polluting, or terrorists with senseless violence, we are claiming that something morally wrong was done and that someone may have been morally evil in doing it.

SKEPTICISM AND MORAL JUDGMENTS

Nevertheless, throughout history, as in our own time, there has been much skepticism about morality. Many people, erudite or plain, claim that evil is in the eye of the beholder and either that we cannot know what is right and wrong conduct or that no one is morally responsible for anything because no one can help doing what he or she does.

Indeed, much of social science rests on such skepticism. Many social scientists wish to engineer us to behave well because they do not believe that we are responsible for what we do. They take it that the way we behave is produced by factors outside our control and that if these factors could only be manipulated intelligently, our behavior would also change for the better, but not on our own account.

SKEPTICISM BELIED

Still, even social scientists blame people – for example, those in Congress who will not vote enough money for them to do their important work, those who find their outlook mistaken, and those who would subvert the work they believe is the only salvation of society. Paradoxically, also, social scientists often chide their own children or friends for wrongdoing, all the while doubting, officially, that such wrongdoing is anyone's fault or could be known as such.

Despite the complexity of this issue of whether human evil exists and what it amounts to, it is worthwhile at times to take a stab at the subject outside academic circles. The matter is not so difficult to comprehend as some may believe. And an understanding of moral goodness and evil cannot require a very special way of thinking, since it would then be unavailable to the people whom we praise or blame. In short, we ask that everyone understand morality enough to practice it. So how could it be so complex that only philosophers could comprehend it?

HUMAN NATURE, ACTION, AND MORAL RESPONSIBILITY

Ultimately, the explanation of all blameworthy human actions, even attitudes, is most sensibly understood in view of human nature. This is because whatever is good or bad about anything is assessed in terms of the nature of that thing. Whether we are judging a tomato or an orange, a tennis match or a football game, a home or an office, a movie or a play – whatever it is that we are evaluating, we begin the process by first grasping what kind of thing is involved.

Once we grasp what something is – not necessarily in some timeless fashion, but usually (except, perhaps, at the subatomic level) in a transhistorically stable fashion – we can begin to consider what would make it good or bad. A good apple is something that fulfills the requirements of being an apple, while a perfect apple is this to the utmost, exceptionally. Accordingly, what makes adults good is to be as fully, or maturely, human as they can be. The analogy is, of course, incomplete, since apples do not take part in making themselves good. But as living entities, what makes them good as apples is akin to what makes other living things good as the species of living things they are, namely, completeness and consistency in their nature. In the case of children, adjustments are made to account for their necessarily incomplete potential for full human development at the time when they are acting and being judged as doing well or badly at what they do.

To put it differently, while adult human beings (that is, human beings that are psychobiologically fully developed[19]) have the capacity to be fully, or maturely, human on their own initiative, a person may choose not to be such and thus will have chosen to amount to a less than good human being, one who does not choose to actualize his or her full potential for being a whole, complete, fully developed individual human being.

What, then, is it to be a human being? Our nature is just *what we must be to be human*, and that is to be thinking animals.[20] This means that we are the kind of biological organism that depends on thinking for its survival and flourishing. It is by virtue of our thinking faculty that we are different from other animals.

But it is by virtue of our biological attributes that we also are part of the animal world. Both of these are vital to our humanity.

Thinking is an (admittedly complicated, elusive because unique) activity of forming ideas, theories – a way of grasping or understanding what the world is conceptually, by means of abstractions based on primitive awareness, as it were, achieved by our sensory and perceptual faculties and organs. To have a biological nature is to be a living organism that survives by means of nutrition and self-development. This self-development, however, can occur at reflexive, instinctual, and conceptual levels. A thinking being must flourish by means of conceptual self-development.

CHOICE, THOUGHT, AND HUMAN ACTION

But perhaps the most unusual aspect of being a thinking animal is that we live largely by choice, not by reflex and instinct, since forming ideas is not automatic. Thinking is a mental process that one must initiate – it does not just happen. The idea that human beings have free will means that their thinking and, thus, their actions are self-produced. It is also the foundation of their moral nature – their individual responsibility to do the right thing and avoid doing the wrong thing, to be good.

To be good at being human, we must excel at being thinking animals. It is when they choose to get by with only half their minds tuned into reality that we see human beings doing badly at living their lives. Aristotle called the basic goodness of human beings the exercise of right reason. Plato believed that the choice to be guided by reason made the difference. Many other philosophers suggested something similar, prior to the time when they became enamored with "science," which they thought eliminated free will.

As I noted before, the idea that humans have free will means that their thinking is self-produced; they have the capacity to ignite the process of thinking, to start up the formation of ideas. Now, instead of putting our thinking into motion or, in other words, initiating thinking, we often just coast, without "engaging our gears," without even firing up the engines of our human lives, namely, our minds. That, more than anything else, would explain human malpractice, including thinking silly or half-baked stuff and acting on it.

The main difference between people and the rest of the living world is that *we must initiate the thinking* that is essential to our lives. We lack instincts to steer us on the right course. Other animals live largely automatically, instinctually, with their genetic makeup equipping them to *react* to circumstances successfully enough; they use ideas only minimally, and they do not reflect on this fact – they are not aware that they need to focus their minds, think carefully, attend to problems. We learn of this need very early in life. We can make mistakes because we fail, by our own volition, to pay heed to the world around us. Other animals tend to be victimized by new circumstances – especially by ones human beings introduce in the world, such as highways, dams, forest fires, and onrushing trucks, but also by natural disasters such as floods and tornadoes – whereas our task is to constantly reassess the world we face so as not to be found unawares. This requires the effort to think, to be aware, to be and to keep in focus.

THINKING AND MORALITY

It seems reasonable that most evil is not malicious – deliberately aimed at doing something wrong – but negligent. Only after a good deal of such negligence do some people move on to lie, cheat, destroy, assault, murder, and so forth. (These are the evils usually dramatized in simplistic novels or plays; more complicated depictions show that it begins with banal neglect – as in the case of Adolf Eichmann, who was supposedly "just doing his job.")

There is, first, evasion – mental laziness or refusal to take action. Then, once the evasion has occurred but we want to recoup, there is either acknowledgment of our failure (maybe contrition or an apology, when others are affected) or the selective focus culminating in the cover-up needed to keep pretending that the evasion has not occurred.

HUMAN GOOD AND EVIL ARE A GIVEN

The fact of human evil is too evident to be argued away by any theorist, so the only alternative is to try to understand what it comes to. (Even the moral skeptic *blames* others for not accepting his skepticism!) So, then, what is the nature of evil, given our commonsense awareness of its existence?

Since thinking is the activity that is most directly under our own volition – we must activate it; no one can make us think (which, to a teacher, is all too evident) – what we must ultimately be blamed for has to be our failure to think. (Recall, again, the frequent exclamation "Damn it, I didn't think!" upon one's having realized that one did the wrong thing.) This is also the best way to understand the fact that morality is neither something wired into us nor something arbitrary.

The debate, as old as the one about free will, concerning whether morality is objective or merely subjective may well be managed best along these lines, because although there is no morality without human beings electing to come under some set of principles, they do make this choice when they embark upon their own living experiences. They, as human beings, cannot avoid choosing either to be or not to be living a fully human life. "To be or not to be," as Shakespeare's Hamlet so poignantly put it, is the fundamental choice, and for humans it comes to the same as "To think or not to think."[21] Once we make the choice in favor of being, it immediately ushers in a set of principles, namely, whatever reason requires – most directly, the requirement of being in mental focus. The principles, or virtues, that are the heart of Aristotelian practical reason, or prudence, are what we all ought to put into effect.

"IS" IMPLIES "OUGHT"

Those moral skeptics who think that no "moral ought," such as what each of us *ought* to do, may be derived from a "factual is," such as what each of us *is*, have it partly right. But they also have it partly wrong. They seem to imagine that there can be judgments concerning the basic features of human living that do not embody "ought" propositions.

The fact, however, that one wills (if ever so implicitly, subtly) to live – given what living is, namely, a self-sustaining process – is not a neutral fact but one pregnant with value. Humans who have chosen to succeed at living have committed to doing what will enable them to succeed at that task, so they ought to think. This way of looking at morality may be appreciated a bit better from an analogy with choosing to embark upon any serious profession. The will to embark upon it commits a person to follow certain professional requirements, or ethics, which if not adequately fulfilled would expose the person to the charge of malpractice. In human living, the failure to think is the most fundamental malpractice.

NO ROOM FOR SUBSTITUTION

Many who reject any kind of naturalistic approach to morality – natural law and natural rights, for example – admit, however, that some kind of morality may be extracted from the fact that people commit themselves to various courses of conduct. They invoke some version of social compact or contract theory. Among them we find legal positivists who claim that although there exists no natural obligation or right, once the people have expressed their choice of laws in a constitution, for example, they have thereby committed themselves and may be held responsible for failing to abide.

Notice, however, that this assumes something not at all granted by those who think morality is invented or conventional. It assumes that when someone makes a commitment, this is something the person *ought* to keep. Now, unless something about the nature of human beings indicates that consistency with one's will is a good thing, it is not possible to reach this conclusion. A promise might well be made and yet not kept, and no blame could be assigned. There may be disappointment, yet even that is difficult to explain. Why would anyone count on people keeping their word? What would be wrong with not doing so?

By what standard, if not by the fact that for any rational agent a breach of a consciously made commitment would be inconsistent with one's true nature, would such a practice (and the rest of what can be done badly by human beings) be wrong?

LAST OBSERVATIONS ON HUMAN EVIL

It seems, then, that the problem of evil is not insoluble. Indeed, ordinary mortals do not seem to think so, insofar as they engage in blaming and praising – as well as in outright character assassination – throughout the globe and all of human history. Given what human action amounts to, namely, behavior guided by purposive ideas (that is, intentions), we may have a handle on action as both explainable and open to moral evaluation.

But this comes at something of a price, at least to those who harbor utopian hopes of a world engineered to be morally good. It is that each of us cannot do much to improve other people if those others do not make that choice entirely on their own. All the social engineering in the world, starting with the most gentle type evident in welfare states, all the way to massive regimentation, will not *create* morally good persons.

What, then, can we do? We can encourage the development of a community where the "evil that men do will come back to haunt them." That way, at least, people's failure to think will result in untoward consequences for themselves and those directly associated with them. Protecting people from their own evil will perpetuate the evil, because their failures will not come back to teach them lessons.

The best device for achieving such a feedback mechanism within communities is the institution of the principle of the right to private property. People's actions can, at least legally, be tied to them reasonably firmly, and any attempt to dump on others can have some penalties attached to it.

Without this approach, we will – indeed, we often do – suffer from a phenomenon I have dubbed "the moral tragedy of the commons," in which we have no way to differentiate between the good and evil deeds of different individuals; they all get mixed up with one another and thus lead to the perpetuation of the process of wrongdoing. Neither blame nor credit can be taken in the case of such dumping. The good that people do will not be a source of self-esteem, nor the evil a source of guilt.

Beyond the rather minimal help of instituting a system of private property, nothing much more can be done politically to produce good in the world. Making people good is not possible by anyone outside the individual people, and trying to make them good usually has the opposite effect.

Let me just summarize the thesis on evil advanced in this discussion. All forms of immorality are varieties of irrationality in the sense that they involve perverse understanding of the way things are (for example, refusing to see people as having rights and deserving care). This perversity, however, is self-induced, not "irrational" in the mentally incapacitated sense of that term. Both morally evil people and criminals[22] – those who actually violate just laws, not those who rebel against unjust or silly laws – are irrational in the sense of subverting their own reason as they view the world.

Since our sphere of freedom in our lives is in our thinking (we can, as it were, turn on the process and do it or be neglectful and omit doing it), this is where our fundamental moral responsibility lies in life: to think clearly (not necessarily in an intellectual or calculating way, but as attentive, conscientious men and women do). "Ought" implies "can," so where else would morality fit in with human existence if not in the sphere where we are genuinely free, where it is we who initiate conduct? The mind is free – it initiates thought and awareness, particularly conceptually. So what follows (conduct, action) is free derivatively, because it is guided by thought.

So the moral philosophy sketched here is very close to a view of epistemology that sees thinking as a form of action that one can embark upon or not. The reason we can criticize others' ways of thinking is that we are free to do it well or badly. And it is in this sphere that action that goes wrong originates and thus gets its quality, ultimately. Because this is free action, it is also the source of moral success or failure.

To return to Rhoda, now, the result of the above account is that either (a) she is a damaged child and is incapable of being aware of the value of human life, or (b) she is an adult (a person with fully developed capacities) who has evaded – that is, blinded herself, voluntarily – to this value. From the moral viewpoint, she is evil only if (b) is true, although we would probably be justified in removing her from society in either case. Rhoda's evil, furthermore, is a form of irrationality, of self-subversion of the essential human function of guiding oneself by the knowledge that is afforded by one's clear, attentive – rational – thinking.

4

WHY OBJECTIVE ETHICAL CLAIMS APPEAR SUBJECTIVE

SUBJECTIVIST INCLINATIONS

A perennial question about principles of conduct – statements as to what we should or should not do – is whether and how one might be able to establish that they are true (or false).[1] The disappointment with efforts at answering this question has produced skepticism about whether statements of norms – for example, "George ought to feed his child" or "Tyrannies are evil" – can be true at all. In some circles the preferred approach to ethics has become subjectivism, the view, essentially, that claims as to what someone should do or not do are statements of preferences or of feelings of approval or disapproval regarding how one might behave. In the social sciences, especially economics, this alternative is nearly the accepted orthodoxy. In any case, many believe that there is no justification for thinking that normative claims can be known to be true or false.

Most of us often make ethical, political, and aesthetic claims,[2] yet many doubt that such claims can be true. Instead, such claims are said – by some of the most prominent figures in the social sciences and philosophy – to be "subjective" or "relative" or even beyond the pale of reason. As we have already seen, political economist Milton Friedman, for example, states that "of course, 'bad' and 'good' people may be the same people, depending on who is judging them,"[3] and philosopher Richard Rorty tells us that concerning political principles, "we cannot say that democratic institutions reflect a moral reality and that tyrannical regimes do not reflect one, that tyrannies get something wrong that democratic societies get right."[4]

This view of subjective truth is widespread,[5] even as nearly universal agreement can be found regarding some norms. People in different cultures and at different periods of history clearly treat some of them as "objective"; that is, they think that the truth of such claims could be known.[6] For example, it is nearly universally agreed that parents ought to rear their children so as to ready them for adulthood; that life-preserving actions are superior to life-destroying ones, at least in nonextraordinary circumstances; and even that one ought to stay out of the way of angry beasts and powerful, angry persons.[7] I say "nearly" only to make room for cases where someone refuses to assent to the truth of such claims because, for example, he or she wishes to disguise a failing or is airing a wholly contrarian philosophical position.[8] In the main, however, such claims, as well as many others, are treated as if they were true, at least for specific circumstances involving particular persons and their choices.[9]

Yet there are many who deny all this. Among these we find many neoclassical, Austrian, and classical–liberal political economists. They claim that all value judgments are subjective, meaning that they are values because some agent (or subject) prefers them. For example, Don Bellante states, with no hesitation, that "the values and motives of individuals [are] entirely subjective [so] it is impossible for an analyst to pass judgment on the optimality of the individual's chosen actions."[10] Others, including Isaiah Berlin, have given voice to a type of value pluralism that comes close to metaethical subjectivism. Berlin states, "To assume that all values can be graded on one scale . . . seems to me to falsify our knowledge that all men are free agents, to represent moral decisions as an operation which a slide-rule could, in principle, perform."[11] It is especially notable that metaethical subjectivism is closely linked with classical–liberal politics in the hope that it would serve as a tool for repelling authoritarianism. If no one can know that something is the right thing for one to do, no one would have any justification for coercing another to do something apart from the idiosyncratic "reason" that the goal the action aims for is something the agent wants to achieve.

Yet this is not a very promising argument. As Richard Tuck notes:

> It is common nowadays for people to say that moral relativism should lead to a kind of liberal pluralism: that (say) the waning of religious dogmatism paved the way for modern religious toleration. But Hobbes's work illustrates that there is no reason why this should be so. Moral relativism, thought through properly, might lead instead to the Leviathan; and the Leviathan, while it will destroy older intolerances, may replace them by newer ones.[12]

Objective ethical claims appear to be subjective because, briefly, ethical claims pertain to how individual human beings ought to act, and that, in turn, depends to a considerable extent on who these individuals and their particular circumstances are. Only at the most fundamental level – vis-à-vis some very rare universal considerations – can we expect what is objective to be also universally applicable. In some respects this is close to the way health-related claims appear subjective – although some basic claims concerning human health are universally applicable, more often we face claims made in the discipline that apply to people in terms of their special or even unique situations.[13]

Before I turn to a detailed analysis of what it is about ethical claims that might make them only *appear* subjective, let me make doubly sure we understand our crucial terms. Let us, therefore, take another brief look at what "objective" and "subjective" mean when it comes to norms or ethics.[14]

"OBJECTIVITY" AND "SUBJECTIVITY"

For an ethical claim to be objective, it would have to be capable of being established independently of the feelings or preferences of the person making such a claim. For instance, Thomas Nagel suggests, "In [objective] deliberation [on what we ought to do] we are trying to arrive at conclusions that are correct in virtue of something *independent* of our arriving at them."[15]

By "subjective," as applied to claims about what is right or wrong, what is good or bad, or what someone should or should not do, many people mean that the claim arises from a person's "unique point of view" or "set of personal preferences." Or, putting it differently, a subjective claim is held to be "true" – or, perhaps, taken by one to apply to one as action-guiding – only for the person who advances it. There is no requirement of the claim being established independently of such unique feelings or preferences.

It seems, then, that when we use the term "objective," we mean that what we claim or think can be established as true or false in ways that can be followed by anyone who does not have serious brain damage, is familiar with the case at hand, and takes the time to investigate. The way to establish the truth or falsity of the claim can involve reference to facts about the person making the claim or something apart from that person, or even some relationship between the person and other features of the world.

It is crucial to note that there need be nothing universal about a judgment that is objective, in the sense that the judgment must apply throughout the class of human beings. The claim that a particular hat fits Harry, for example, is objective, but is not true that the hat fits everyone. And the claim that George ought to write to his mother for her birthday may be objective, but it need not be true that everyone ought to do the same. Of course, in the case of the hat that fits Harry but not necessarily anyone else, the means by which we show this – for example, sizing Harry's head and then sizing the hat – would have to be generalizable, so that when we say that another hat fits Joe, the means by which we show this to be true are none other than those we used to show the claim about Harry's hat.

Yet the same approach is not granted when it comes to making claims as to what Harry should or should not do. With claims of that sort, it is often suggested that they are subjective and "true for" Harry but not "true for" others, not only in the sense that the claim's truth pertains to what Harry ought to do, but also in the sense that whether Harry ought to do such and such is "true" only if Harry takes it to be such. Such claims are thus not objectively but only subjectively true – true from someone's point of view, in terms of someone's preferences, not open to be established as true. This way of viewing the matter also suggests that the objectivity available in other areas – for example, in science – does not concern these sorts of claims. Yet it is not evident that claims about what one should or should not do are not in fact much more akin to the claim about a hat fitting Harry. There is at least one respect in which they are, namely, regarding the relativity of the agent (or hat wearer). The fittingness of the hat is related to the hat wearer's particular head size.

The hat always fits some potential hat wearer. And whether it does is either true or false. What is universal is only that if it is true, then all those who are concerned with whether it is true or false and possess normal faculties for this purpose could identify the claim as such. This can be obscured by saying, "The claim that the hat fits is true only for Harry," as if the truth of the claim rather than the fittingness of the hat were something particular to Harry. But the claim that the hat fits Harry is true for anyone. And it may be that only one person, none other, ought to do something, but if it is true that the person ought to do it, then the claim that the person ought to do it is true for everyone.

Objectivity lies in the means of proving or grounding some claim, not in the range of its applicability. Such a proof, if we can obtain it, will connect the judgments we make with the world that the judgments aim to identify correctly. That is the point of stressing objectivity, to note the connection between what we think is reality and what is reality. Indeed, we note this when we admonish scientists or jurors or judges at the Olympic Games to be objective – to stick to evidence and sound reasoning, to avoid letting their feelings or wishes influence what they judge. The issue of universality comes into play only in that the claim that is supposedly objective could be established to the satisfaction of anyone who can understand the standard. So far, so good.

As an example of a reason why moral claims could both be objective and seem subjective, consider that ethical claims do not seem to identify some fact that is independent of some person(s). "George ought to write to his mother" is pertinent when the individual who is George exists and could do just that; it is not pertinent under any other conditions. This suggests the subjectivity – that is, the subject-dependence – of such claims, yet it is objective and agent-relative, given the case at hand.[16]

OBJECTIVITY AND ETHICAL DISAGREEMENT

Then, too, people often disagree on ethical or political subjects, more than on others, and these disagreements appear to be intractable. Consider that the wisdom of entering into international trade agreements, for example, is widely disputed. But these disagreements can be explained by other than what some claim, namely, that when people provide reasons for such beliefs, they are "not convincing, they are not rigorous, they are not logical, they are not coherent, they are semantic, they are arbitrary, and so forth."[17] Such an explanation would stress that people are free to make judgments and often these serve to further some objective that arises from their own past complicity in evasions, misconduct, fear of exposure, rationalization, etc. (This is most publicly evident in cases when convicted criminals cook up elaborate rationales for why their guilt is really no guilt at all.) Diversity of ethics can itself been seen as a symptom of ethical malpractice – covering up one's own misdeeds with obfuscation, for example. Furthermore, much ethical skepticism is produced mainly by intellectuals who are in the business of testing ideas with hard cases and preventing complacency.

An additional difficulty is that when it comes to ethical matters, what is true can be so intimately tied to an individual's unique circumstances that we cannot expect to get the answer from someone else. As Raimond Gaita observes:

> If I am deliberating about which is the best route off the mountain and I fail to arrive at an answer, I can pass the problem over to my partner; it is only accidentally *my* problem. If I am deliberating about what, morally, to do, then I cannot pass my problem over to anyone else: it is non-accidentally and inescapably mine.[18]

(This is indeed a very clear statement of the gist of classical individualism: each person is the volitional author of his or her significant conduct.) Should I receive advice from a wise person, I still must be the one to decide whether to take it. So it will ultimately fall on my shoulders how I act, including that I took or rejected the wise person's advice.

Does this disturb the objectivity of the issue at hand? If I conclude that I ought to abandon my friend and seek my own route when we are both lost on a treacherous mountain, is there no objective way to tell whether this is right, whether the claim that I should so proceed is true? The objectivity is not necessarily disturbed in the slightest by the inescapable personal element of the judgment, namely, that what I ought to do is intimately linked to the *I*, to who and what I am, something that is ultimately irreducibly individual.

Of course, it could turn out that I address the problem on a substantially subjective level – based on my unexamined fears, my prejudices, my preferences. This would contrast with addressing it, instead, on the basis of what is actually important to me, using as criteria what kind of being I am and what it takes for such a being to flourish, as well as my individual identity and circumstances. This is what would establish, objectively, what is right for me to do, how I ought to live my life. Subjectivity would enter from my disregard for or inattention to the important facts and from my letting less important matters guide my thinking. As in the case of a jury's refusal to pay attention to the evidence linking the defendant to a crime rather than to the defendant's looks, tastes in music, and preferences for certain sports – that is, immaterial, irrelevant matters

– the decision to do something would be subjective if immaterial, irrelevant factors were to influence it.

THE ROLE OF PERSONAL IDENTITY

Of course, when one admits that a person's identity is of vital importance to the determination of what that person ought to do, this suggests that in such cases subjective factors are inescapable. But that is because the question about one's identity is left unaddressed – and because even if we do consider it, it seems to be in constant flux, from infancy through old age. So let us consider whether what and who someone is turns out to be entirely a matter of the person's preferences. And let us also briefly touch on whether there is some constancy in one's identity.

If one's identity is in constant flux, then the personal, or individual, element in moral decisions would make them subjective. Moral decisions would arise from considering unstable elements within ourselves. But if we have identities with some stability and the personal element can be identified by one who is concerned about it (ourselves, a parent, a friend, a lover, a therapist, or, in circumstances that are dependent on the role we have taken on in life, a colleague or a consultant), then the objectivity available in other realms of decision making would be attainable. And we could even be held responsible, again akin to a juror, for failing to be objective about reaching our moral decisions. Such stability would consist in the fact that the kind of being one is, as well as one's particular identity, must be something that can change only in ways that its nature makes possible. And the possible changes are determinable – coal can burn, but water cannot; human beings can learn and alter their convictions, but flowers cannot.

The reason many do not believe that a standard of decision making is available is that they see the personal element providing us with quicksand, not stable, clear-cut data drawn from reality itself. But many ethical matters of greatest concern to us relate intimately to facts about us that range from utterly individual to, gradually, more widely shared and, finally, completely universal. The personal element, after all, includes not only aspects of ourselves that are wholly unique, such as our particular configuration of talents, our biological composition, our family–national–ethnic–cultural–regional setting, and the decisions we have made based in large measure on the combination of all these. The personal element also includes facts we share with many others – for example, being a parent, American or French, tall or short, diabetic or allergic to peanuts, a doctor or a teacher. And in the last analysis, we are all members of the human species (distinguished, presumably, by our capacity for rational thought).

The unique facts seem to many to be more decisive than those we share with others, and for some cases of making the right choices in life, they are. But unlike the way persons are regarded in a kind of Hobbesian framework – used often by economists and social theorists – our uniqueness is circumscribed by our objectively determinable human nature and more specialized general attributes (such as our role in a family, profession, polity, or athletic team).

No doubt, of the facts we share with others, many appear to be accidental, insignificant, unimportant, or contingent. So basing ethical claims on arguments that include such facts as premises seems still to be arbitrary or subjective. These facts about us seem like they could easily be otherwise or could be changed at will, so whatever follows from (practical) arguments in which they play a role appears to depend on something that could, but for our decision or some accident, be different.

But such facts are firm enough. First, consider facts *about the individual human being* one is – for example, when and where one is born, how tall one is, one's genetic make-up, parentage, early education, talents, aptitudes, and incapacitates, and one's particular history to the point of one's life where the decision is to be made. Second, consider some other facts that could be firm enough, such as one's profession, family status, and residence. If these alterable facts came about through an objective, rational judgment one has made – that is, if they were based on other facts about oneself and one's proper ranking of options in the world – they would be morally well established facts on the basis of which further objectively determined decisions ought to be made. The choice to become a film maker could have come from, among other things, the facts that the person is talented in some areas and had the opportunity to learn about film making, as well as the fact that being a productive person is better for anyone than simply lying around. This is where the more general facts of one's humanity enter into consideration, facts that help us develop a general policy of how to live our lives, a set of principles that overarches all of our decisions.

SUBJECTIVITY WITHIN OBJECTIVITY

So what appears to be subjective – in other words, a matter of what one feels or prefers or otherwise chooses for "reasons" of this type – could upon closer inspection turn out to be objective. Nor is the matter a mere contingent one, dependent on some features of the world that could be otherwise, not necessarily what they are.[19] That is to say, it could be grounded in such a way that anyone who is not crucially (cognitively) incapacitated *and* is willing to examine the (stable) facts of the case, including what kind of being one is as well as who one is, could conclude what he or she ought to do.

Yet it needs to be noted that a purely optional subjective element can enter basically objective moral decisions. We may have an admittedly fleeting, even trivial, taste for something. But if it is rational for us to indulge such tastes – say, since a human life is better lived when a person experiences some pleasures – then such an element does not deprive the conclusion as to what we ought to do of its objectivity. All it does is open up several options as to what, objec-tively, one ought to do. Objectivity does not imply singularity – it could be the case that one ought to choose any one of a number of courses of conduct, with any of them being objectively right if they do not differ from one another so far as morality is concerned. Thus it could be objectively true that "I ought to perform either a Mozart, a Liszt, or a Brahms piece during my concert," while it is entirely optional – and, perhaps, in this limited respect, subjective – which of these I perform. Many mean by "subjective" those factors that determine which of these pieces I will perform. Yet to characterize what one ought, basically, to do as determined subjectively would be a mistake, for it could be true that one ought, objectively, to perform at least one of them. Or, to put it differently, one may objectively have the moral responsibility to honor a promise to give a piano recital, but it will be a matter of one's subjective preference what music one will perform.

So it would probably be best to say that although there are objective deter-minants of what we ought to do, there are many optional – subjective – matters that will serve to determine our actual morally justified conduct. One should, objectively, dress formally for the wedding, but exactly which one of one's formal attire one will wear could be a matter of preference.

OBJECTIVITY IN ETHICS

But how might this objectivity of what one ought to do be ascertained? When we judge as to the goodness of something, in the last analysis we come down to ascertaining how it accords with its nature, with what it must be to be the kind of thing it is. A good apple, then, is an apple that is consistently, coherently, and fully satisfactory as an apple. So it is with a tennis game or a philosophy paper. A game or paper done by a novice is a genuine article but not a good specimen. In the case of good conduct, this judgment, too, would be made, at the most fundamental level, by reference to our human nature.

This nature, it seems to me, includes the fact that we share some characteris-tics with other human beings, although progressively fewer as we identify ourselves in particular. So we may be able to identify objectively good courses of conduct based on the fact that we are living beings for whom there can exist benefits and harms bearing on our success as such.

For example, given that we human beings are animals whose lives are uniquely guided by the thinking they do or do not do, it may be objectively true that we all ought to think well and always when we are awake and not engaging in rationally required recreation or enthrallment (although this is not to say that we all ought to be intellectuals). This may well be objectively true about human beings as such within the bounds of their capacity – for example, they cannot be overly tired when it applies, lest "ought implies can" is violated.

The idea that this is a mere Western prejudice can perhaps be entertained here, but only if one takes it that an unprejudiced understanding of human nature can yield something different. The "rational animal" characterization of human beings – provided "rational" is taken to mean a capacity for an attentive, focused approach to living, not a relentless articulation of ideas – would appear to be the most inclusive one in light of the evidence of the enormous creativity throughout human history around the globe, a creativity involving the implementation of conceptual thought and imagination. In short, this seems to be the definition of what human beings are that has the greatest and most consistent explanatory power for understanding even the debate about what human nature is.

Now, given one's specific identity and having done one's needed quotient of thinking that drew on various facts about oneself, one could objectively decide that one ought to aspire to a career in philosophy, electrical engineering, the performing arts, hunting, weaving, forming, or whatnot, and thus that one ought to move to a suitable accessible region of the world and embark upon a suitable training or education to reach that goal. These decisions would involve a series of judgments (potentially rendered into claims) as to what one ought to do. These judgments or claims would then be objectively supported by humanly (in many cases *publicly*) accessible facts about oneself (although few besides oneself and some intimates would wish to access them).

The idea that one might make wicked yet consistent and rational choices is foreclosed by the fact that one would be using the criteria of one's humanity as a very broad, but firm, restriction on what one may do. One could not rationally select as a career to be a junior executive in Murder, Inc., since being human by itself imposes certain broad restraints on what one is justified in doing – taking another's life is a violation of natural rights, principles that serve to circum-scribe interpersonal conduct among human beings as such. Other virtues that derive from one's humanity – or one's role as a parent, friend, citizen, or profes-sional in medicine, business, or law – would also circumscribe what one is justified in doing, what is optional based on one's talents and opportunities and what is off limits.

IS–OUGHT AND THE NATURALIST FALLACY

Of course, we now run up against an ancient obstacle. This thesis appears to conflict with the still widely embraced "is–ought gap" position.[20] Without entering the controversy in full (for more on this, see Chapter 8), let me just note here that the belief that one cannot derive true claims as to what one ought to do from true claims about what is the case rests on certain mistakes. It mistakenly assumes that a derivation must be a deductive argument at every step of the reasoning process. It is supplemented by G. E. Moore's naturalistic fallacy, namely, the view that a sound definition cannot be sensibly questioned. This, in turn, takes definitions to be far more Platonistic, fixed, and impossible to conceive as false.

If the assumption underlying the is–ought gap were true, we could never derive anything from anything, since concepts and definitions are not established deductively but are the products of scientific and ordinary theorizing or formation of general principles. (This was seen by Hume with reference to scientific knowledge and is now recognized by radical skeptics such as Rorty and Feyerabend.) A concept is not formed by means of some intellectual intuition – a sudden, unexplainable "seeing" – of a state of affairs (casting in a proposition) from which further states of affairs (or propositions stating them) may be formally deduced. It is more sensible to understand concepts as formed by abstraction – by what Aristotle refers to as integration and differentiation, by thinking of what one is aware of and arranging this material in a coherent, complete, and practical order.

We combine this concept formation process with the development of language – which is, in large measure, an economizing process, since words are easier to keep in mind and recall than lengthy strings of ideas. And when we ask about the meaning of a concept, we do indeed ask on what sorts of occasions, with what conditions surrounding us, we will make use of it. The nature of meaning is to carry out this process of conception formation objectively, and the nature of meaningful moral concepts – and, in the last analysis, a meaningful moral life – rests on such objectivity. It not only guides us to living rightly and well, but also enables us to know that we do so, should it become necessary to explain ourselves either to ourselves or to, for example, significant others.

As to Moore's objection that any definition of what "good" means can be earnestly questioned, let us note that such a question can be raised about definitions and theories in every branch of knowledge. When a new astrophysical entity, say, dark matter or a black hole, is identified and defined, questions about it abound, and only after a while do they subside, once the definition has caught on. In ethics, politics, and aesthetics, however, such questioning of definitions rarely subsides, since there are many motives for questioning them – including attempts at obfuscation, professional devil's advocacy, and the need (expressed by members of every new generation) to be sure about things so personally significant.

CONCEPT FORMATION IS UNIQUELY HUMAN

One reason much of this is so mystifying (so much so that many philosophers have abandoned the effort to render it generally, systematically intelligible) is that the central feature of the process of forming concepts in general and moral concepts specifically is *sui generis*. One will not be able to account for it by means of some neat analogy, since the capacity for concept formation is something uniquely human and quite extraordinary, probably dependent on biological attributes unreplicated elsewhere in nature.[21]

Still, I wish to propose how we embark on the formation of an idea – or decide how to organize what we are aware of and develop our conceptual economy. It involves a kind of mental (but not final or finished or eternal) *grasping* of the materials that normal sensory-perceptual activity supplies and which, by means of our faculty of reasoning, we can develop into an understanding of the world. And part of that understanding includes the relationship we ought to have to the world, how we ought to act. Arriving at an objective understanding is to have done this development consistently, guided by what is evident to awareness, within the framework of certain reasonable principles (for example, the laws of valid inference, parsimony, and experience).

As an example of a familiar concept that may well have been formed objectively – not necessarily in (Cartesian) isolation from the input gained from other people who have a concern for learning about the world – let us take the idea of causation. It means, roughly, that a being acts according to its attributes, not in defiance of them, and will continue to do this unless crucial facts about it change. Mere elapse of time is not such a change, so we can infer that the sun will (be caused to) appear on the eastern horizon tomorrow as in the past, given that there is no new cause for it not to. It is not the case, however, that the sun must, logically or with deductive certainty, rise tomorrow. Having so formed the concept, it is objective, not a construct based on attitudes or desires. Accordingly, a theory of the causal behavior of various beings can be developed and utilized to predict our own behavior and guide it so as to change things. Engineering is possible because of this, yet when we conclude that a bridge will be built best – that is, most reliably – in this or that way, the proposition is not deduced. This, roughly, indicates the sort of objective basis for complex concepts relating to the world and our involvement with it.

FORMING ETHICAL CONCEPTS

The same general objective approach may well apply to normative areas such as ethics. (I am not here concerned with the distinction between normative and deontic concepts, for I take it that deontic ones, such as "right" and "wrong," are parasitic on normative ones, such as "good" and "evil.") However, the variables will be greatly increased. Thus, because human beings have the capacity to cause some of their own behavior, in ethics we make claims that include "should" and "should not," "responsibility," "obligation," "duty," and so forth, and the only predictions we make are hypothetical, not categorical.

Yet the situation is not all that different from engineering; one might say that in ethics we conclude that life will be lived best in this or that way – that is, that most probably if we adhere to certain guidelines, our lives will come off most successfully as human lives. Thus, in an ethical argument, some theory of what concepts like "good" and "ethical" mean will be essential, yet such a theory is built up from experience and generalization and the application of the principles of concept formation in general. It will involve reference to certain unique aspects of life, such as its teleological character and its perishability, as well as the nature of human life, including its dependence upon self-determination and the initiation of conduct.

Accordingly, if it is true, for example, that "good" means "life-enhancing for the agent," so that, say, it is good for plants to gain sunlight because sunlight enhances plant life, and if "ethical" means "chosen by the agent because it is good," then it can be argued objectively (not necessarily deductively) that one should choose to do what enhances one's life as the kind of being one is, that is, given one's nature. Given human nature, then, one should, first and foremost, choose to think and then act on the results of that thinking, because that will, most likely, produce a successful life. (The thinking need not be deliberative, but it must be based on unprejudiced awareness.)[22]

VALUES AND ETHICS

It may help here to consider that we have an area of value judgment, or application of norms, outside of human life that is relatively uncontroversial and does afford us evidence for the objectivity of norms. I have in mind such life sciences as botany, ecology, biology, zoology, and medicine. In these areas we confidently refer to good and bad states, conditions, attributes, prospects, organs, and so forth, with no suggestion that these are good "to us" alone. When a botanist or physician judges the condition of some plants or living organs and proposes that these are doing badly or well, there is no suggestion here at all that the norms this judgment refers to are subjective, manufactured by human beings based on their preferences. A redwood tree can be faltering or a kidney can be malfunctioning quite apart from any human preference. Even if a patient were to prefer to die, this would not change the diagnosis of the kidney. Gardeners can report on whether the populations of their gardens are doing well or badly, even if the owner may wish for the garden to perish. It is not a subjective matter how a living thing is doing; rather, it is something determinable by reference to a sound theory of the nature of its life and what is needed to have it flourish and to avoid its demise.

The main difference regarding norms about human life is only that human beings live largely because they choose to do so, and who they are, their individuality, is vital to what they are, their nature. So the norms used to judge whether they are doing well or badly, whether they are good or evil, are much more complicated, much more dependent on details about them than the norms used to judge nonhuman life. Furthermore, when one establishes what they ought to do and avoid doing, this will mean something unusual in the scheme of norms in general. It will mean something bearing on how they ought to *choose* to act, not just on how they would behave under certain conditions, as would be the case with the well-being of, say, an oak tree, a whale, or a butterfly. These entities do well or badly not of their own accord, just as human beings do well or badly in some respects not of their own accord – for example, their genetic make-up or the climate in which they live can bear on their well-being. But in many other respects, human beings govern their own well-being; they are, in short, responsible for it. This provides a unique aspect to norms pertaining to human living, an aspect missing from the lives of other living beings.

Of course, this element of self-directedness, or self-governance, is controversial, but it does not directly bear on the issue of objectivity. Whether human beings possess free will, normally, is a matter pertaining to what kind of beings they are, so it will concern what behavior they can cause. It will also bear on the precondition of self-responsibility, including the kind of political framework within which they would live most in accord with their nature. (This is where natural-rights theory is said to come into play.) But the behaviors that will be good for them to engage in – what they ought to (choose to) do – are as much of an objective matter as what will be best for a redwood tree or a bumble bee or a baboon.

We might, then, have the following:

1   "X is not living well," a truth claim that can be established objectively.
2   "In order to live well, X ought to do (only) Y (as one possibility)," which is also possibly true and can be established objectively.
3   "If X does Y, he or she will live better than by doing Z," another truth claim that can be established objectively.

IDIOSYNCRATIC CAN BE OBJECTIVE

It seems, then, that there is good reason to think that no problem of subjectivity afflicts the sphere of (ethical, political) norms and that these norms pertain to sometimes rather complex yet nonetheless objective facts. When applied to human beings, of course, there will be much evidence of conduct that is divergent from these norms, but that does not alter their objectivity. One thing that makes ethics even germane is that human beings can initiate conduct that fails to accord with the norms they ought to live by. Unlike in the case of, say, a redwood tree or a giraffe, what makes for a good state of affairs in human life is often within the power of the individual person to bring into being or fail to bring into being. Thus, if being thoughtful is right for human beings but whether one will be thoughtful is largely up to the individual agent, the norm amounts not only to the claim that "human beings are best off being thoughtful," but also to the claim that "human beings ought to be thoughtful." As such, they could fail to be thoughtful, fail to abide by this objectively true norm of their existence.

Furthermore, there can be a good deal of variation in the way moral norms become soundly instantiated. Given the diverse identities and circumstances of human beings – the sorts of factors that tempt one ever so powerfully to embrace economic, technological, historical, cultural, or other kinds of relativism – what is objectively right to do can vary a great deal.

It seems to me that this way of understanding the objectivity of norms escapes many problems and solves others not adequately solved by the subjectivist approach. Since uniformity is not a requirement here,[23] not all norms must apply to all persons (some can apply to just a few or even just one). Diversity, too, would make clear enough sense, so some of what cultural relativism stresses could be true without conforming to the cultural relativist explanation of norms.

LAST WORDS ON OBJECTIVITY

I have not addressed the broader issue of epistemological objectivity here, although I have tried that elsewhere.[24] My point was to indicate that certain features of subjectivity depend upon a misunderstanding of what objectivity requires. In order to facilitate getting across my position, I would like to finish with a point in epistemology that was made by Barry Stroud in the context of discussing Wittgenstein's ideas about logic:

> Logical necessity . . . is not like rails that stretch into infinity and compel us to always to go in one and only one way; but neither is it the fact that we are not compelled at all. Rather, there are the rails we have already traveled, and we can extend them beyond the present point only by depending on those that already exist. In order for the rails to be navigable they must be extended in smooth and natural ways; how they are to be continued is to that extent determined by the route of those rails which are already there. . . . [W]e are "responsible" for the ways in which the rails are extended, without destroying anything that could properly be called their objectivity.[25]

Objective knowledge does not demand impossible, unchangeable, perfect, timeless truth; it demands only support that establishes the truth of something beyond a reasonable doubt.

5

A DEFENSE OF PROPERTY RIGHTS AND CAPITALISM

The superior freedom of the capitalist system, its superior justice, and its superior productivity are not three superiorities, but one. The justice follows from the freedom, and the productivity follows from the freedom and the justice.

(Henry Hazlitt, from an address by before the Chamber of Commerce of the United States in Washington, DC, April 30, 1962. It appeared in *The Freeman*, August 1962.)

The concept of freedom, in its socially relevant sense, means the condition of individuals being free from aggression by others.[1] This is the political freedom of the unique American political tradition. It rests on the recognition of every individual's equal moral nature as a self-determined and self-responsible agent, regardless of admittedly enormous circumstantial differences.[2]

By "political freedom," I mean that no one is an involuntary master or servant of any person or group, including a government. In short, when the consent of the governed is the reigning principle, political freedom exists; when the consent is compromised, political freedom is in peril. Economic freedom implies freedom of trade, in the classical–liberal tradition of political economy.

A moral case for a system of community life needs to make clear that such a system supports the ethical life of its members instead of thwarting it. Ethics are principles by which human beings can *choose* to guide themselves to live properly, in line with what is the good life for them. There are competing ethical systems, of course, but not all can be sound. The best ethical system is the one that most consistently and completely fulfills the purpose for which it is intended, namely, to guide human living toward success in the case of any particular person. A political system is ethically sound if it is in accord with those virtues that bear on community life, that is, if it is just.

So the main issue facing someone who considers a political–economic system, such as capitalism, is whether this way of organizing a community, including its economic life, is conducive to justice. Here I will touch on only a few of the more widely voiced moral questions raised about capitalism, hoping to show that at least from a commonsense ethical framework (one that embraces such virtues as honesty, courage, prudence, justice, generosity, and decency), capitalism is morally defensible – more so, probably, than its competitors, such as socialism, fascism, the welfare state, and communitarianism.

To understand capitalism, one must understand free trade. The nature of free trade is best grasped by noting, first of all, that it is logically dependent on the principle of the right to private property. One cannot trade if one does not own anything. Oddly, Karl Marx clearly identified the function of property rights: "the right of man to property is the right to enjoy his possessions and dispose of the same arbitrarily, without regard for other men, independently from society, the right of selfishness."[3] Marx focused on the worst-case scenario, but one should not do *only* that when considering the characteristics of a system of principles. Of course, the right to private property makes free trade possible and thus leaves one free to dispose of one's possessions irrationally. But it also leaves one free to act and trade in accordance with the best judgments one can form – something Marx did not mention. Marx gave us just a fraction of the story. Private property enables one to dispose of one's belongings either responsibly or irresponsibly, so trade can yield both worthy and unworthy results. Yet precisely because it is private property, acting in a fashion that brings unworthy results will be less likely, since the harm will first of all befall the owner, not others. A system of private property discourages irrationality and encourages rationality.

It bears noting that most prominent and articulate contemporary defenders of capitalism are economists. This creates a false impression. Economists study the way the free market satisfies human desires, but they do not question the merits of those desires. Nor do they concern themselves with whether the market may be morally justified, whether it is an institution basically in line with human moral values. Economists focus on explaining, describing, and predicting the ways of a free market. They insist that economics is value free.

When the most prominent advocates of capitalism are economists, it appears that nothing other than efficiency matters about the marketplace. This leaves understanding of the system incomplete, since efficiency must always be judged by reference to some goal, and the goal of prosperity, which economists worry about, is itself controversial. (This lies behind the oft heard charge that life in capitalist countries is too materialistic and not spiritual enough.) There are, thus, various ethical features of the free society that an economic analysis leaves unexplored. This would not be a problem if economists were not the virtually exclusive defenders of capitalism.[4] But their approach does not stress that the market rests on ideas and institutions that are ethical in nature.

For example, freedom of trade presupposes personal property rights. If no one owned anything, people could just take from others what they want and would not need to wait for agreement on terms. Or, alternatively, if everyone owned everything, everyone's permission would be required for every transaction. To set terms of trade, individuals and voluntary associations, such as corporations and partnerships, must have the authority to make decisions about property. That is indeed a moral feature of a free market, not a purely "descriptive" one.[5]

66

The moral nature of property rights can be made clear simply enough: If I own something, that means that others *ought to* refrain from thwarting my choice of what to do with it. I am the one who is authorized to set terms, not others. (This is why theft is morally wrong!) This is a moral issue because it involves considerations of how persons ought to choose to act, of what is right and wrong for them to choose to do.

And not surprisingly, critics of a free society seem to know all this. They exploit the fact that economists are reluctant to discuss ethical issues by suggesting that something is amiss in their free-market theory. Yet what critics should realize is that precisely because of this value component at the base of free-market economic theory, the system is demonstrably sound and much of what economists say about it gains support not just from technical economic analysis but also from ethics.

If economists defending the free marketplace would admit that at its base we find certain assumptions as to how individuals ought to act and what governments should uphold, they could still proceed to carry on with their technical analysis of how such a system works and why it produces more efficiently than all others. They would simply not address the question as to whether those basic assumptions are ethically sound – let us say, in the spirit of the division of labor. The economist could insist that the job of economics is to study market processes and that others should take on the task of figuring out whether a market economy is morally preferable to other systems.[6]

Let us now return to just that task. I have noted that the principle of personal property rights underlies the market. These rights are necessary preconditions of genuine free trade and thus of a free market, specifying moral and legal authority for making decisions about socially valued items.

Certainly there are numerous societies in which conditions resembling a structure of private property rights are evident – we might call them a structure of property privileges. In these societies persons are *permitted*, within certain limits, to individually hold and trade goods and services, although the government – the local Coastal Commission, the Federal Communications Commission, the king, or some other powerful group or person – is legally authorized to revoke the privilege. In such societies there is no genuine free market. They have what resembles free markets in the same way a sophisticated zoo can resemble the actual wilds, or the way some children enjoy limited personal responsibility that resembles what is enjoyed by adults but is granted by parents. And of course, the more such privileges become entrenched and depended upon, the more the market will exhibit the tendencies we expect in a free marketplace. But such a structure is not based on the right to private property, the bedrock of economic freedom.

THE RIGHT TO PRIVATE PROPERTY

In order to be moral agents, to make choices about what to do in their lives, people need to have sovereignty, personal authority, liberty. Such liberty, as understood within the Western, particularly the American, (classical) liberal political tradition, is inseparable from economic freedom and the principle of the right to private property. Why is this so?

Political freedom, as we have seen, means not being aggressively intruded upon by any others. This is not the restricted freedom of taking part in politics, but the broad liberty to live freely among other persons in one's community. Such liberty is a crucial requirement of human dignity, the opportunity to make moral choices and to aspire to moral excellence. What has not yet been made clear is that any opportunity must have a concrete sphere, or realm, where action can take place. Making effective moral choices in one's life requires, to use Robert Nozick's term, "moral space."[7]

Very plainly put, the principle of the right to private property serves the purpose of always translating the freedom of personal responsibility into real-istic, concrete policies. To the extent that a human polity must be focused on securing either individual or general welfare – and insofar as general welfare must be achieved by individuals – a good human community must secure for all individuals a realm of personal jurisdiction.

The law of property is that branch of jurisprudence that develops the method for securing for all their proper domain of authority within a highly complex society, one in which what belongs to someone can range from a horse to a sophisticated chemical formula to a musical arrangement. To the extent that the law of property is not guided by the principle of the right to private prop-erty, it departs from this objective. Once this is grasped, the next crucial question that faces us in this connection is how to determine the parameters of the domain of personal authority and thus to justly assign protection to property someone lays claim to.

This is a very complex issue indeed. John Locke's well-known labor theory of property is not adequate as an answer, because it is not clear what can count as "mixing one's labour" with nature. Ideally, if we were to start from scratch, it would be best to use the entrepreneurial theory of property described by James Sadowsky: "The owner of property performs an entrepreneurial function. He must predict the future valuation that he and others will make and act or not act accordingly. He is 'rewarded' not primarily for his work, but for his good judgment."[8]

This is consistent with the very basis of personal moral responsibility. That basis lies in one's fundamental choice to think, to exercise one's rational capacity, one's faculty of reason. The Aristotelian idea that the basic virtue of human life is right reason suggests this, as do several other analyses of what lies at the basis of human morality. In general, since morality presupposes choice, and since all persons are free primarily in their use of their minds, the source of moral merit is, as Sadowsky put it, good judgment. A rational creature would be expected to excel precisely in proportion to his willingness to live by good judgment, and when this good judgment is made with reference to matters of prosperity, it is no less meritorious than when it is made with reference to hygiene, truth seeking, family matters, career, or politics.[9]

Economic freedom is a necessary but not sufficient condition of human excellence. It is a prerequisite of human dignity. It is indispensable for moral agents who must make their way in a world whose various parts may be controlled by different individuals. To make certain that each individual has a reasonably clear idea of what parts of reality are within his or her jurisdiction – so that he has, as it were, his moral props in clear focus – a system of private property rights is necessary. Such a system preserves the moral independence – though not, as caricatured by Marx and many others, the social autonomy – of everyone.

CAPITALISM AND MORALITY

Statists of all stripes have been very eager to undermine the moral legitimacy of capitalism. Economic defenders of the system have tended to avoid the argument, maintaining that on the whole, the capitalist system produces greater wealth than other systems, a result that everyone seems clearly to prefer.

But this defense is inadequate. We can easily think of circumstances when considerations of prosperity must be traded off to achieve other values. We know that no expense must be spared when aiming for some goals. Some economists duck this fact by engaging in economic imperialism, holding that since all values are reducible to wealth, all trade-offs are economic. But this is not so. Friendship is not mainly an *economic* value (that is, something with a price) – if one were to trade it for, say, a rise in pay, one would be acting unethically, not simply losing some valued items. A betrayal will not qualify as an exchange of economic values.[10]

Because the economists have tied their hands about morality, capitalism has been under fire from all sides. It is really something of a tragedy that the most humane, most productive, and most benign system of human economic arrangements would be the target of some of the most morally reprehensible critics – terrorists, Marxist–Leninists, fascists, and others. But, to quote Shakespeare, "Wisdom and goodness to the vile seem vile: Filths savour but themselves."[11] Consider some typical and oft repeated charges against capitalism:

1 Capitalism is anarchic.
2 Capitalism produces waste and trivia.
3 Capitalism caters to the base within us.
4 Capitalism neglects the poor.
5 The workers under capitalism are exploited.
6 Capitalism favors the wealthy.

7   Capitalism destroys the fine arts.
8   Capitalism abuses the environment.

One could go on, especially if one included charges that are leveled with a particular ax to grind, for example, inequality of wealth and the disparity of wages paid to different segments of society. But these charges presuppose the moral priority of human economic equality, something that rests on intuition rather than argument.[12]

Let us take some time here to respond to some of the moral criticisms of the capitalist, or free-market, system. We will see, I think, that in preserving human freedom, especially in the context of commerce, capitalism not only escapes being responsible for moral shortcomings but actually facilitates moral excellence throughout a culture.

CAPITALISM AND HUMAN EXCELLENCE

The alleged anarchism of capitalism rests on the view that when free trade reigns – that is, when producers can freely attempt to interest consumers in their wares and consumers can freely choose to spend their earnings on items they wish to have – this must result in reckless disregard for what is really important in human life. The charge is plausible, because in a free marketplace, there is ample opportunity for producing and consuming trivial and even morally odious goods – for example, pet rocks and pornography. The charge, made by Marxists and conservatives alike, is strengthened by the fact that the alternative is always offered as some vision of perfect order – for example, humanity fully matured in some distant future (Marx) or society well governed by wise leadership (Plato).

But the reality is that markets are not anarchic but merely reflect the human situation. We are not guaranteed the company of wise and virtuous fellows. We can only choose what we will do about their presence in the neighborhood. We can trust in some future paradise on Earth or the guaranteed, long-range superiority of certain persons, both of which are fantasies. Or we can try to make sure that the effects of other people's foolishness and vice will be limited to their own domain. A system of private property rights can do this better than anything else.[13]

As for the second objection, capitalism does at times produce waste and trivia. But it produces immensely useful items as well, more so than any other system. From the mass production of stereo equipment and prints of the best of humanity's artistic achievements, to hospital instruments and special nutrition for those with health problems, capitalism serves both the ordinary and the unique, because its system of production – guided by prices and other information made available via market transactions – informs producers of needs and wants better than any sort of planned system could.

70

Moreover, what may seem trivial to some people can be of immense value to others. The reason this is overlooked is that even today, many people fail to accord proper standing to individual differences. Thus, while most of us may find the various items in tourist traps useless, there can be individuals to whom these can be of value.

As to the pornography and prostitution that could exist in a pure capitalist system, they need not be rationalized as good things on the ground that there is a demand for these and the consumer is king. Professor Walter Block's book *Defending the Undefendable*,[14] which argued from a free-market perspective, makes it appear, quite mistakenly, that nothing but coercion constitutes evil conduct. Clearly, however, one can betray friends, debase an ideal, lack courage, act imprudently, and do all kinds of moral wrongs without coercing anyone. Even some of the practices that may appear to be justified rebellion, such as littering, could turn out to be mere slothfulness or at least lack of civility.

The defense of human liberty does not require abandoning moral standards – quite the contrary: It is in part so as to enable us to invoke moral standards freely, without the regimentation from others that would rob us of our moral sovereignty, that freedom is vital to every adult. Moral wrongs are no doubt going to be present even in a free society, but it is imperative and clearly possible to combat them on the personal, social, and cultural levels (through comic arts, editorials, pulpits, and so forth).

Capitalism protects not just the freedom of the base but also that of the noble. It is a prejudice to hold that the market caters to our baser desires. Capitalism, by encouraging the rational and responsible use of property, actually encourages virtues such as thrift, industry, and prudence and discourages vices such as greed, envy,[15] and dishonesty. It is in planned economies that those vices are rife.[16]

As for the poor and the workers, it is true that England at the end of the eighteenth and the beginning of the nineteenth century was hardly in an ideal state, but there would have been even greater misery had capitalism not been introduced. And the extent of the misery under early industrial capitalism has been grossly exaggerated.

Preindustrial England was far from idyllic, and many of the problems under early capitalism were a legacy of the system it replaced. While most of the worst restrictions on economic action were removed, many of the enormous feudal landholdings were left untouched in the name of respect for private property. As we know, these holdings were mostly the result of either conquest or state land grants. It is extremely doubtful that these holdings could ever have attained their size on the free market. Justice would have dictated the division of these lands among the agricultural workers. Unfortunately, this was not done. The result was that a few individuals had votes in the market far beyond their due and were thereby enabled to determine the course of events.[17] With this power at their disposal, it is not surprising that "capitalists" enjoyed special advantages. But to mistake this for a typically capitalist situation is a serious confusion.

There is another error underlying the charge that capitalism leads to worker exploitation. Contrary to the fallacy that workers are helpless creatures, the market makes it possible for workers to improve their lot. Marx was influenced by Thomas Malthus's view that the working class would multiply far more rapidly than the income it could generate would support, and therefore would become more and more exploitable as the number of workers increased. Malthus has been refuted both in theory and by history – enormous numbers of working people in the world have found themselves very productively employed, usually when markets were more rather than less free, and when governments did not distort the principles of free trade by domestic and international violation of individual rights.

In addition, Marx had little confidence in human creativity and entrepreneurship. Thus he did not allow sufficiently for a sustained rise in the supply of and demand for goods and services, based on what human beings could both invent and learn to enjoy or use. The workforce in a capitalist society is, therefore, far from easily exploited. Indeed, it is insulting to workers to think otherwise; Marx (and later Lenin) had a low opinion of ordinary human beings.

Finally – and this is most difficult for some to accept – many of those who are allegedly exploited have actually placed themselves in a position of weakness. Having failed to develop their skills and talents, they must take what they can get of the limited number of jobs available for the unskilled. Under these circumstances, it could be argued that instead of protesting that they are being mistreated, they should be grateful that capitalism has made it possible for even people with few skills to live better than people who were considered wealthy in the past. To proclaim that workers are always exploited, as a class, is to demonstrate an ideological prejudice that ignores the actual characteristics of the different people making up the labor force.

The next charge against capitalism is that it favors the wealthy. In a free society where no special legal privileges are permitted for anyone and where the government is constitutionally restricted from regulating economic affairs, the wealthy would have only those advantages that come from wealth. These involve the greater ability to purchase various goods and services offered on the free market, an advantage that in a constitutionally limited government does not include political power. Furthermore, wealth is only one type of advantage. Personality, character, talent, good will, perseverance, and hard work can often result in far greater success than wealth.

Marx tried to discredit the claim that it was governments in the past – feudalist, mercantilist – that gave lopsided advantages to select people. When the large joint-stock companies began to be established, governments clearly favored them, so that nations might gain wealth, although this proved to be a rather frail strategy. But contrary to Marx, this is not inevitable. Wealth need not become politically influential, unless the legal system opens itself up to this by way of giving governments inappropriate powers. Moreover, in democratic societies, governments get those inappropriate powers when people are legally empowered to vote for politicians who promise to seize assets from the rich so as to transfer them to the poor, regulate big businesses, provide protection against unforeseen adversities, even self-inflected ones, or do whatever else the voters want to wrest from others who may not voluntarily comply with their desires.

In any case, without exploring the historical reasons why some firms managed to exercise undue power in the marketplace – namely, their special legal privileges – we can point to some matters that could secure general agreement. For one thing, we can note that in the United States, which has had the greatest degree of capitalism in human history, the positions of the wealthy and the poor are not held by a select few. Rather, these positions are in constant flux (at least this has been so in the past, prior to the onset of the massive welfare state), far more than under any other system. This suggests that the wealthy have less political power under capitalism than under other systems.

The charge that capitalism destroys the fine arts because it makes mass culture dominant is also unfounded. Because of the "noise" of popular culture, the fine arts may not be so visible. But in total quantity, never have so many listened to, viewed, and otherwise experienced great artistic achievements as in capitalist or near-capitalist societies. The mass production of the arts, including the finest of them, proves this beyond any reasonable doubt.

As to capitalism's impact on the environment, there is no other system that makes a better effort to avoid the tragedy of the commons, the source of all environmental problems. The tragedy stems from common ownership of resources, which will be overused by all those who are convinced that their goals and purposes may be served by using these resources without restraint. Under capitalism, property is privately owned, so any use of private resources is costly and thus limited. And when property is used to the detriment of neighbors, this could be legally actionable as a form of dumping, trespass, assault, invasion, and so forth. In situations where privatization is impossible or technically difficult, there could be personal-injury provisions against pollution. Any activity that is damaging or violates the rights of persons in this sense would have to be prohibited, no less than assault is now. Indeed, the most effective environmentalist public policy flows from a system of private property rights in which both persons and property are supposed to be protected from invasion.[18]

FINAL REFLECTIONS ON THE VALUE OF FREE MARKETS

It is true that human beings are not perfect. To try to force them to be perfect is futile. Herbert Spencer was right when he observed, "The ultimate result of shielding men from the effects of folly is to fill the world with fools."[19] A sign of our imperfection is that we keep returning to the failed effort to perfect one another by means of coercion.

To ask that government, for example, attempt to cure us of our imperfection is to show that one is not willing to live by one's own evaluations: If the world needs improving, the proper approach is to use whatever skill one has to remedy matters. Censors should try their hands at writing better literature. Critics of waste should produce things of value. Those who fear the base within us should turn to moral education as a way to help out. Those who sympathize with the "exploited" workers might help by becoming one and seeking remedies.

Capitalism is the political manifestation of the human condition: We are free to do good or evil, and in society we need to keep this in mind. The free market, through the principle of the right to private property, helps us keep this in mind – indeed, institutionalizes it through the law of property.

Democracy itself, which is so much prized even by outspoken critics of the free market, would be impossible without meeting the requirements of a free market. This is because democracy requires some secure realm of personal juris-diction for those who are asked to make their political views evident. They need to know that if they are a minority, they will not be at the mercy of vengeful victors who may deprive them of their lives, liberty, or property. In short, a democratic polity cannot function without capitalism, the system in which private property rights are protected.

Thus we can conclude that the free-market, or capitalist, system of economic life, provided it is not compromised and, thus, corrupted, is indeed supported by morality and supportive of the ethical life of human beings. To fully appreciate this, however, it is necessary to forgo utopian politics, whereby the supposedly perfect (community) becomes the enemy of a realistically best system. Unfortunately, this habit too often dominates, and humanity has suffered serious political and economic failings as a result. Perhaps there will be a chance to improve matters in the future, should the defenders of capitalism draw atten-tion to its moral merits.

6

AMERICA'S FOUNDING PRINCIPLES AND MULTICULTURALISM

AMERICAN INDIVIDUALISM

My purpose here is to argue that the multiculturalist position often embraced by contemporary academics and school administrators is best served within a country that is founded on the principles of political individualism, principles pretty much distinctive of America's political tradition, if not always its actual public policy.

The United States of America is known across the globe mostly for its tradition of individualism. Not that most scholars or diplomats hail this aspect of America. In fact, as we will see shortly, the mainstream academic community has few nice words and many nasty ones to say about individualism. Oddly enough, many who promote multiculturalism join the ranks of the naysayers about individualism. I would caution them not to carry on that way, lest they rob themselves of the only legal–political framework that can be reasonably hospitable to great varieties of cultural practices within one another's vicinity.

Let me first consider what individualism is and what can be said in its support. This is needed so as to indicate why, in the last analysis, individualism best suits human social life. To begin with, individualism is not an entirely clear-cut position. It is a mix of elements that are psychological, political, ontological, and normative, amounting to the idea that human individuals are politically most important. This is the feature of American political life captured by the authors of the Declaration of Independence when they wrote that

> all men are created equal, that they are endowed by their Creator with certain unalienable Rights [to] Life, Liberty and the pursuit of Happiness [and that] to secure these rights, Governments are instituted among Men, deriving their just powers from the consent of the governed.

These sentiments pretty much capture the basic principles of political individualism.

As such, individualism is a position that distinguishes America and, by now, many other Western societies with legal systems that give some attention to individual rights and due process of law. Yet we ought to keep in mind that, as Colin Morris observes, "Western individualism is ... far from expressing the common experience of humanity. Taking a world view, one might almost regard it as an eccentricity among cultures."[1]

Individualists claim that individual human beings, not some collection of them, are most important, indeed, irreplaceable, where public policy and law are concerned. They believe that a person is not for others, including governments, to use without that person's consent. Each person is a sovereign being, by nature entitled to self-government, not subject to the rule of others – that is, not subject to mastery, oppression, paternalism, tyranny, coercion. Individuals must have the final say in what happens in their own lives, within the limits of their possibilities and the rights of other individuals.

WHAT IS THE MAIN ALTERNATIVE?

In contrast to individualism, even loosely conceived, collectivism amounts to the view that some *grouping* of individuals is of primary – though by no means exclusive – value in politics and law. Here family, tribe, clan, neighborhood, religion, race, sex, nation, and humanity are candidates for what takes political priority. Collectivities do things, cause what is worthwhile in human life, are to be blamed for what is wicked, and, most of all, require loyalty from us at every turn. Within this framework, the individual is, basically, a cell in the larger whole of, for example, society or humanity – which Karl Marx called an "organic whole" or "organic body."[2] Or, as Auguste Comte, another advocate of collectivism, put it:

> Every one has duties, duties towards all; but rights in the ordinary sense can be claimed by none. . . . The only principle on which Politics can be subordinated to Morals is that individuals should be regarded, not as so many distinct beings, but as organs of one Supreme Being.[3]

Karl Marx thought individuals are but "specie-beings," bits of the above-mentioned organic whole, the way one bee is but a bit of the whole beehive or one ant is but a bit of a whole ant colony. Marx said:

> The further back we go into history, the more the individual, and, therefore, the producing individual seems to depend on and *belong to* a larger whole: at first it is, quite naturally, the family and the clan, which is but an enlarged family; later on, it is the community growing up in its different forms out of the clash and the amalgamation of

claims. It is only in the eighteenth century, in 'civil society', that the different forms of social union confront the individual as a mere means to his private ends.[4]

(My emphasis)

ANTI-INDIVIDUALISM

Many of those who have an important role in leading the discussion of political ideas in America are anything but individualists. Indeed, one of the most prominent intellectual movements today is communitarianism, a social philosophy whose advocates make a special point of criticizing individualism at every turn. As Harvard political theorist Michael J. Sandel puts it in an article for the *Atlantic Monthly*, the issue for us should not be so much concern for individual liberty and freedom of choice but concern for "belonging, a concern for the whole, a moral bond with the community whose fate is at stake." It is not securement of individual rights that is vital for a good community. It is government's task to promote "formative politics, a politics that cultivates in citizens the qualities of character that self-government requires."[5] This is a central tenet of communitarianism.

The movement is led by Robert Bellah and colleagues, authors of *Habits of the Heart: Individualism and Commitment in American Life*,[6] and, especially, Professor Amitai Etzioni, who wrote *The Spirit of Community*.[7] Such notable American political figures as Vice President Al Gore and Secretary of Labor Robert Reich are communitarians. And the bulk of English-language academic and popular books dealing with basic political philosophy champion not individualism but some kind of communitarianism or even collectivism.[8]

Of course, until very recently half the world was openly committed to developing and advancing perhaps the most overtly collectivist ways of community life: socialism and communism. We will return to this in a moment. For now, let us notice that even many who claim to be upholding American ideals actually promote not individualism but the primacy of the family – something clearly evident in election campaign rhetoric. There is little doubt that on many fronts, the idea embodied in the Declaration of Independence and the Constitution is now dwindling in importance; that is, prominent folks across the United States no longer hold that the general welfare is secured by securing the welfare of individuals. Instead, there is a lot of talk about private *versus* public welfare or individual *versus* social purpose. Accordingly, some associate individualism with outright bad things. As one prominent scholar, John N. Gray from Oxford University, recently put it, "[I]ndividualist cultures devour their own moral capital and slide into debt-ridden stagnation as individualism corrodes family life and long-term planning and investment."[9]

Individualism is often seen as making people careless, thoughtless pleasure seekers. Furthermore, some critics of individualism see it as a recent *invention*.

77

Major political theorists across the world, working at prestigious colleges and universities, have argued that in the sixteenth century or so, some human beings, who were members of or mouthpieces for ruling classes, decided that thinking of ourselves as basically individuals – sovereign citizens, consumers, producers, voters, lovers, scholars, and so forth – was *useful*. Supposedly, believing – that is, entertaining the myth – that we each matter individually served the purpose of getting us to work harder, to seek greater prosperity for ourselves and in this way to build up the society's wealth. Individualism is seen by these critics as a kind of temporarily useful delusion, a fiction we needed so as to advance society's prosperity, but a fiction nonetheless.

Accordingly, individualism is but a relic of the modern era, to be superseded by what is being called the "postmodern, postliberal age." It is predicted, by John Gray, for example, that "as individualism corrodes, ... the nonindividualist market economies are likely to achieve an ever greater comparative advantage over the declining individualist cultures over the coming decade." As Gray sees it, "the East Asian economies have achieved their spectacular success without accepting any of the Western liberal shibboleths of constitutionalism, individualism, cultural pluralism, universalism, fundamental rights, the idea of progress, and other relics of the Enlightenment."[10] And Gray and others note all of this with glee, not dismay, because they do not value these "shibboleths" and do not believe that they deserve to be valued – for a great variety of reasons (in Gray's case because he is a skeptic and does not believe that anything can be shown to be of real value or that any moral principles can be shown to be binding on us).

According to this line of thinking, we ought to abandon the idea that individualism applies to all human beings everywhere and content ourselves with its temporary role in our narrow corner of the globe. Thus we should not think that Ghanaians ought to revise their practice of subjecting ten-year-old virgins to slavery under the guise of having them atone for sins of their parents or other family members, since, as the *New York Times* reported, the Ghanaian priests who support it "say the practice stems from a world view that sees justice and punishment in communal rather than individual terms; an individual who has no connection to a crime may be punished to spare others."[11]

MULTICULTURALISM

What is the currently prominent sentiment about individualism among prominent academic and popular thinkers? At worst, that individualism is bad, divisive, corrosive, anticommunity, and unfit for human social life. At best, that individualist societies are only one of several equally valid types of human communities. And this is part of the theme of multiculturalism.

Broadly put, multiculturalism holds that every culture, however unusual, however offensive to members who do not belong to it, is worthy of respect.

This respect is to be granted regardless of the fact that many cultures embrace mutually exclusive social and political principles. Accordingly, it is wrong to condemn some culture as flawed, barbaric, or otherwise unworthy, since such condemnation must stem from the perspective of the culture the critic hails from. And no one can escape hailing from some culture – even the so-called internationalist viewpoint, embraced by human rights organizations such as Amnesty International, is not free of cultural biases, so when such organizations make various moral and political criticisms of certain countries, they are, in fact, practicing a form of cultural imperialism (as representatives of Third World governments made clear at the Human Rights Conference in Vienna, Austria, in 1993).

From this multiculturalist perspective, what we must develop is a social–political framework that can make room for all varieties of culture. No preference must be shown to European, African, Latin, Russian, Chinese, American, Greek, Arab, or any other political or cultural components in such a truly just society. Every culture must be treated fairly, without exception. For example, the educational institutions of a society should, then, treat these different cultures neutrally, with no preference given to the products of any of them.

I do not wish to go into the multiculturalist thesis in detail – it is now part of the intellectual atmosphere of academic life, so what it entails is common knowledge. In education it was made the centerpiece of Stanford University's well-known controversy about the role that studies in Western civilization should have in higher education. It was the subject of controversy at Yale University, where a large grant specifically designed to promote studies in Western civilization was returned to the donor because faculty found prominently featuring Western ideas objectionable. And many administrators of elementary and secondary schools grapple with what they regard as multicultural issues – as when multilingual instruction is proposed. Even in sports, the matter of whether one needs to stand for the national anthem calls forth multicultural, multireligious issues. The debate over creationism versus evolutionary biology does no less.

Precisely because of its nature as a kind of amalgam of various traditions, there is no easy way to define multiculturalism. We usually mean by the term the idea that every culture is owed equal respect, especially as we try to educate students in a society with a citizenry hailing from families that reach back into a great many different cultures or embrace varied religions. What concerns me here is just how such multiculturalist objectives may or may not square with or relate to individualism. The reason is plain enough: America has a distinctly individualist political heritage, and many multiculturalists have found it inhospitable to various cultural traditions.

Our first clue as to the relationship between the American polity and multiculturalism comes from the fact that cultural diversity has, in fact, always been part of individualist American society. From the start, America was comprised of people from widely different cultures. As J. M. Holley, a college student in 1788, wrote to his brother who also lived in the United States,

> the diversity of dress, manners, & customs is greater in America, than in any other country in the world, the reason of which, is very obvious. It is considered as a country where people enjoy liberty and independence; of course, persons from almost every nation in the world, come here as to an asylum from oppression; Each brings with him prejudices in favor of the habits of his own countrymen.[12]

Clearly, over the more than two centuries of its existence, even while the administrators of the American system have not been uniformly vigilant about welcoming and making room for members of all cultures, there is hardly any doubt about the diversity of American society, as compared to other societies. In this connection, consider that nearly every town and village in America is home to diverse races and cultures, whereas in other countries, this is true only in the cosmopolitan centers – London, Paris, Rome, Vienna. Once out in the countryside, in most societies there is evidence of a good deal of homogeneity and, indeed, cultural exclusivity.

WHY IS INDIVIDUALISM IMPORTANT?

If individualism had nothing much going for it as a sound way to understand human life, there would probably be nothing much to say for it apart from certain matters of interest to intellectual historians. Its influence might be noted, but we note the influence of Nazism and Satanism without pretending to like these. I want to make the point here that individualism is actually a quite sensible way of understanding human social life.

The first thing to note is that individualism in human life is actually quite inescapable. Even to argue about it presupposes it: anyone who advances ideas, makes arguments, criticizes others for their arguments, or acknowledges that human beings do some original things in their lives has to admit to a significant measure of individualism.

It is the creativity of a human being that is the first major clue to our individuality. We make things happen; they do not simply happen *to* us. We bring novelty into the world, with our artistic, philosophical, commercial, technological, scientific, poetic, literary, and other contributions. These are all evidence of the fact that we individually, even if but minimally, make things happen as (in part) independent beings with minds of our own. Even when we do not actually do so, we *can*; thus we have the essential capacity for individuality, even though we may not exercise it all the time and everywhere.

In one sense, our individuality is given, at the basic, factual level – each person is one being, one who most often is born alone and dies alone, with a unique brain, personality, temperament, history, and so forth. What we might call our ontological individuality is clear from the way we cannot make good sense of our identity without reference to the "I" about us, about our personal responsibilities, guilt, achievements, and so forth. In another sense, individuality is an option that, arguably, we *ought* to choose, not simply a static fact. Individualism is, in this second respect, a normative issue, just as democracy and friendship are normative – we are free to select or reject them. Our actions, especially at the very personal levels, show that we do often choose individuality over conformity. Moreover, doing so seems to be imperative, generally, if we are to flourish as creative, productive, imaginative living beings.

IS INDIVIDUALISM DISPENSABLE?

What should we say, however, of the fact that in many societies, little individuality is evident and individual lives are valued, at least officially and in written records, much less than ethnic groups or the nation? What about the widespread absence of institutional acknowledgment of individuality?

The individualist response was nicely put by the late David L. Norton. He noted that individualism is everywhere *in potentia*:

> Beneath the accretions of contemporary epochs and cultures a vestige of the original ... intuition endures today ... in the individual's conviction of his own irreplaceable worth. But this small conviction is wholly unequipped to withstand the drubbing it takes from the world, and from which all too often it never recovers.[13]

So, despite all the anti-individualism, there is for many of us, in our day-to-day proceedings, the basic idea that the proper way for us to live is to strike out on our own initiative, with others who choose to join us on theirs, so as to live as decent a human life as we can.

In addition to seeing that individuality is basic to our lives, it can also be shown that people's crucial activities, those that flow from their essential humanity, depend upon their individuality. If so, then we have gone some way toward establishing the significance of individualism for our conception of justice, a conception we can associate with the founders of the American polity.

Indeed, the capacity people have for thinking and for guiding their lives by means of practical reason – which is something distinctive about human beings – is something they alone can begin to actualize. That this is so is once again affirmed by the manner in which human beings hold each other responsible, from the most minuscule to the most complicated bits of conduct – from whether they keep holding on to a glass of water or drop it, to whether they take their factories overseas where they can hire low-wage labor or leave them at home to give jobs to highly paid domestic workers. From economic management to international diplomacy, from our discussions about Jack Kevorkian to those about Saddam Hussein, there is this inescapable element of fixing personal responsibility.

I could go on to list other examples and show that what appears to diverge from my point also fits the case. But let me just mention that the point holds, as well, when one evaluates a public address, a philosophy paper, or the piloting of an airliner. The practice of looking to individuals for assessing human conduct is global – the leaders of mainland China blame the president of the United States for granting visas to Taiwanese leaders, and the members of Greenpeace denounce executives of American companies for polluting the environment.

INDIVIDUALISM AND MULTICULTURAL SOCIETIES

Having examined what makes individualism a very plausible candidate for the best way to understand ourselves and, therefore, to conceive of the basic features of a just human community, let us now turn to the central question of this chapter. What kind of legal, political, and economic order is likely to be most hospitable to a society in which some of the saner attitudes toward widely varying cultures are to prevail? I wish to propose that such an order would be far more individualist than most multiculturalists suspect. The reason multiculturalists do not generally accept this point is that they tend to look upon individualism as just another cultural perspective, a product of Western culture. According to them, to admit that individualist political systems are really best for preserving cultural diversity is to sanction cultural imperialism.

One place where the soundness of my proposal is clearly suggested is in the terms and activities of what are called human rights watch organizations, such as Amnesty International. These find that the near-individualist framework of human rights they invoke is well received across the globe, especially among ordinary people, if not governments.

It is, furthermore, the underlying notion of individual human rights that has excited ordinary folks across the world about the United States of America for more than two centuries. Political leadership of America is understood to consist mostly of championing the protection of the basic human rights of all individuals to life, liberty, and pursuit of happiness (which is understood to include legally acquiring private property). As most people seeking to emigrate to America know well enough, even when they do not fully articulate the point, in a system with such principles, there would be a chance for any individual, from nearly any culture, to embark upon living a reasonably successful life and pursue a great variety of human objectives. It is this legal setting, in which basic negative human rights are protected, that has been referred to, by the philosopher Robert Nozick, as "the framework for utopias,"[14] experiments of all kinds in how men and women can and should ideally live.

COLLECTIVISM AND MULTICULTURAL SOCIETIES

In contrast, what do we get from collectivist systems? Well, we have seen two such systems, National and Soviet socialism, demonstrate just how miserable life is when the individual is officially dispensed with and, instead, the welfare of some collective is placed before us as the most important objective to serve. Hitler was an explicit collectivist, championing the German *Volk*, or people, as a whole, not the individuals who comprised the citizenry of Germany. Marx, as we have already noted, championed humanity as a whole, with individuals comprising little more than the parts of this whole. In an essay written for the *New Republic* magazine shortly after the fall of the Soviet Union, Tatyana Tolstaya observes:

> According to [collectivists] "the people" is a living organism, not a "mere mechanical conglomeration of disparate individuals." This, of course, is the old, inevitable trick of totalitarian thinking: "the people" is posited as unified and whole in its multiplicity. It is a sphere, a swarm, an anthill, a beehive, a body. And a body should strive for perfection; everything in it should be smooth, sleek, and harmonious. Every organ should have its place and its function: the heart and brain are more important than the nails and the hair, and so on. If your eye tempts you, then tear it out and throw it away; cut off sickly members, curb those limbs that will not obey, and fortify your spirit with abstinence and prayer.[15]

What about smaller collectivities? Do these fare any better? Bosnia-Herzegovina is only a more recent example of what happens when the welfare and success of ethnic groups are placed at the top of the list of priorities for people to serve. In the African country of Burundi, as in Somalia, people have been sacrificed by the thousands for the sake of tribal supremacy. In South Africa until recently, white Afrikaners, as a group, placed themselves above members of other races and treated them with nearly total disregard for their well-being and sovereignty. In the Northern Irish conflict, children and innocent bystanders are sacrificed for the greater good of a religious or regional group or some other collective.

Even in the United States, the heritage of individualism is giving way to a clamoring for collective identity. Blacks are told to live for African American emancipation, and individuals who do not conform are denounced. Women, especially in the academic community, are told to toe the line of certain versions of feminism, lest they betray their sisterhood. Native Americans are lumped into one horde by many shallow historical references, as if there never existed individual, diverse persons in the region Columbus encountered when he sailed west to look for Asia. In addition to groups that demand loyalty based on ethnic or sexual identification, there are labor unions; associations of professionals such as teachers, artists, lawyers, and farmers; and hundreds of other groups identifying themselves as some super-entity deserving of special loyalty and service. So whereas initially the U.S. government was supposed to serve sovereign individuals, these days it tends more in the direction of distributing some mythical collective wealth among all these special-interest groups.

Diverse communities – linked culturally, ethnically, racially, religiously, and so forth – are still more likely to flourish and coexist peacefully in the United States and other Western countries than in countries that do not have an individualist tradition. But the increasing collectivism is dragging Western societies into a lobbying war of all (special-interest groups) against all.

CULTURAL IMPERIALISM

One major English political philosopher who has worried a great deal about the compatibility of individualist Western classical liberalism with multiculturalism is Sir Isaiah Berlin. He and others are concerned about how one can promote the political system of individual liberty, which makes value pluralism more likely than any other polity, even while no conception of the good human life is given superior status in the society. They are concerned that the soundness of classical liberalism may be undermined by its political neutrality about different, often culturally bound, approaches to living a good human life. They pose the question, "How could one system be valuable for so many others without contradiction, namely, without elevating classical liberalism to a higher level than other value systems – that is, without the dreaded cultural imperialism?"

The individualist answer is that we may have to give up on political cultural *egalitarianism* in order to retain the possibility of cultural *pluralism*. Maybe what is important to cultural diversity is not political. Maybe what makes cultures what they are is their music, art, religion, styles of cuisine and dress, language, and other nonpolitical matters. It is not crucial, therefore, to maintain egalitarianism about coordinating legal systems, or making them all harmonious, even while the commitment to cultural pluralism is sound.

In his critical assessment of this issue, Professor Michael Walzer of Harvard University observed,

> If value pluralism is true ... and if only liberal minded men and women can fully recognize this truth, then liberalism may just possibly have a different status than other values and ways of life. And how can we say anything about this status if we are committed to value pluralism? Perhaps, if we can't say anything, we had best be silent.[16]

Actually, we need not remain silent. We can hold, with the American political tradition and the founders of the American republic, that there is a superior way of political life, namely, one in which individuals have the right to pursue their happiness while respecting the equal rights of all other individuals to their lives, liberty, and pursuit of happiness. A given mode of political life can be seen as superior to others at the same time that all personal, social, professional, religious, and other modes are free to be pursued provided those who pursue them do not impose them on unwilling others. The issue of which among these is best need not be of general concern, only of concern to the individuals who are making their day-to-day decisions about what to do.

Accordingly, for example, the Amish people in the United States manage more or less to pursue their own version of happiness – a life devoted to religious pursuits – as do the Hare Krishna, the followers of the Reverend Moon, and, indeed, the members of the approximately 1,200 different religious denominations and several hundred more secular groups. Actually, since the United States does not fully embody individualist principles, most of these different religious and cultural groups are somewhat imposed and intruded upon, but comparatively, they enjoy greater freedom than would any such groups in a country such as Iran or Iraq.

The one common requirement by which all of those in an individualist system must live is to also let others live. That is by no means something simple. In a multicultural society, one may have to put up with some practices on the part of one's neighbors that are difficult to tolerate, let alone accept. But acceptance is not the issue, only tolerance. If a group of Americans hailing from Spain want to purchase a park where they will practice bullfighting, the neighboring animal rights folks will have to tolerate it even if they do not accept it. The only means available for them to bring about change are (a) to exhort, and (b) to demonstrate in common terms, if that is possible, that animals, like humans, do indeed have rights, thus bringing about a change of the basic principles of the multicultural society such that animal abuse no longer counts as a culturally variable practice.

This individualist approach to sociopolitical arrangements will not, of course, suit everyone. The animal rights people, for example, will be unhappy with the situation as described above. And there will be others who follow certain doctrines about political life and therefore cannot be appeased this way. If they act on their convictions, their conduct will have to be treated as criminal because it constitutes an infringement of individual rights.

Take socialists, for example. They could live in a voluntary commune, share the wealth, follow the principle "from each according to his ability, to each according to his need." Many of them, however, would find this quite unsatisfactory. They hold, as we have already learned from Tatyana Tolstaya, that "'the people' is posited as unified and whole in its multiplicity." Accordingly, they could well take it upon themselves to attempt to forcibly unify the people, something that an individualist society would rightfully construe as illegal, criminal.

Indeed, in Western democracies, all of which permit encroachments upon individual rights if there is sufficient interest and support for doing so on the part of the majority of the actual voters, cultural imperialism is widespread enough. As an example, in education, from kindergarten all the way through college, a good measure of political power wielding occurs. USA *Today* reported on a number of these; for example,

> A poem in Marietta, GA., HIV, written by a middle-school student Meliass Grander to accompany a school report about AIDS, offended assistant principal Diana Ray, who objected to the words 'queer' [and] 'dyke.' She banned it from the school's literary journal.

As another example,

> The award-winning documentary, Eyes on the Prize, which chronicles the civil rights movement of the 1960s, was shown to a class at Joseph Lee Elementary School in Dorchester, Mass. A teacher complained it was racist and too confusing. Principal Maria Iglesias prohibited the future screening of any film from the school's media collection.[17]

It may be noted here, in passing, that government-run schools necessarily treat minorities disrespectfully, if only because there is never enough money, nor enough personnel, to provide all minorities with suitable treatment. Large groups of Americans, including some minorities, such as those whose ancestors hail from Italy, Ireland, Germany, Africa, England, certain disabled persons, women and so forth may gain special attention that addresses their special circumstances and background. But others will not – the ones whose ancestors hail from Korea, Finland, Hungary, Albania or Costa Rica. This is one reason that the objective of providing everyone with proper multicultural education must be a failure and tends to engender a good deal of resentment among those not picked for special treatment.

Of course, in private schools such decisions can be made selectively because they are not bound, in the spirit of the 14th Amendment of the US Constitution – "equal protection under the law" – to serve all pupils equally. Such schools are attended at the discretion of parents, not because all citizens are forced to pay and send their children to them (unless they can afford to attend private schools which, however, are also scrutinized by government agencies.) If taxpayers were not forced to pay for government schools, they would be more able to fund private schools (for their children or the children of others). There would still be some disagreements over policies, but there would be a great variety of schools to choose from. Families and teachers who were unhappy with a school could more easily switch to (or create) one that would better reflect their values, and parents could withhold their children from school until they were ready to attend and obtain full benefit from such attendance. Just as with a free press, it is not that all publications are equally fair and wise, but that there is a choice for citizens to subscribe to the ones they have come to regard as fit to read. The model of education in an individualist system would be much closer to what the United States presently enjoys *vis-à-vis* the press and religion, rather than, say, a conscript military.

We can perhaps put the matter along these lines: If there is anything at all that unites the various ideal ways of life, regardless of the particular ideals in question, it is the requirement that the person who lives in line with them does so to a significant degree on his or her own initiative. The creative aspect of human existence is so central that before anything else, individuals need to have a say in their lives, lest their very humanity – their capacity to act upon their moral nature – be seriously impeded. This is why individualism – and classical liberalism, its political expression – are better candidates for being *universal* frameworks for human association. They are basic norms of interpersonal social living. As Douglas Rasmussen and Douglas Den Uyl put it:

> Liberalism, then, is not designed to either promote, preserve, or imply one form of flourishing over another. It is not thereby completely open ended, however. Liberalism does prevent "forms of flourishing" which inherently preclude the possibility of taking place along side of other diverse forms of flourishing.[18]

That is, individualist systems insist on an "exit option," the condition of freedom of association. Apart from that, men and women in voluntary cooperation are free in such systems to pursue their own conceptions of happiness. And the founders of the American republic seem to have been pretty much aware of this, probably because they knew of the great differences, justified or not, in the ways citizens of America, hailing from different cultures as they had from the start, would pursue living as human beings. Any and all of the limitations placed on cultural diversity in the American type of political framework – that is, a framework consistent with the founders' vision, in which cultural imperialism is kept to the minimum – are, arguably, inescapable ones for any community that would enhance the morally good life for human beings as such.

INDIVIDUALISM IS THE BEST HOPE FOR ALL BENIGN CULTURES

Let me end by reiterating a point I made earlier. The individuality of human beings is undeniable – even as we debate the matter, it surfaces relentlessly in the form of our creative thinking, the way we forge new or reworked arguments in discussing any issue. This is not, of course, recognized or acknowledged by everyone, so the dispute will continue. But those who advocate some anti-individualist perspective have some bizarre footwork to perform to deny the fundamental individuality of human life.

The way this is usually done is to argue that if one is an individualist, one must give short shrift to community, fellowship, generosity, gregariousness, and friendship and that, in fact, communities that are governed by an individualist legal system foster antisocial tendencies, crime, and so forth.[19] But the individualism that is at issue in political systems is not necessarily even an ethical type, so the charge is misplaced. Furthermore, a well-conceived form of ethical individualism does not imply isolation or some kind of fake self-sufficiency for individuals. Values like cooperation, sociability, fellowship, and generosity are fully compatible with it, provided nothing is coercively imposed on any citizen.[20] These values are, after all, just as much a part of human life as is individuality.

Some individualists forget this and make the mistake of issuing hyperbolic slogans, such as "Each person marches to a different drummer," that are literally false, although perhaps understandable as ways to call attention to the often overlooked importance of the individual human being. The Marxian idea that "the human essence is the true collectivity of man" has pretty much swept the halls of academe, from departments of philosophy to departments of social psychology and criminal justice. And in response, some have given voice to individualist ideas with few of the nuances spelled out. Ayn Rand is often perceived along such lines. She and other individualists make clear, however, that no one can march to his or her own exclusive drummer – drumming, to carry on the metaphor, emerged in the context of human social life, with other performers also playing along.

And the mistakes of the overly enthusiastic individualists are not nearly so harmful and tragic as those of people who would compromise the individuality of human life by lumping us all into some group, whether we choose this or not, who would treat us as just parts of a hive, not as beings with a unique requirement, namely, our requirement to be able to choose and initiate our conduct, including our associations with other human beings.

I want to stress that however much individualism is dismissed by some as just another bias of Western culture, it is actually more of a fully humanistic philosophical discovery and ethical–political affirmation that happens to have been made, although not exclusively, in the Western world. Every human being, anytime and everywhere, would do (or would have done) better if his or her community embraced the insight of individualism and paid attention to every person's sovereignty and possession of the right to freedom and independence.

Only if this is fully realized can human beings begin to embark on a truly self-responsible form of life, including in each other's company, and continue to practice and further develop their unique cultures and customs in peace. While such full realization is not highly probable, it is certainly within our power to clearly articulate it and strive for it with greater vigilance than we are doing.

The fears that many have about individualism, namely, that it leaves the sociability of human life neglected and that it encourages crass self-centeredness, should not be allowed to squelch the essential truth of the doctrine, which is that in human life, the initiative and, thus, the liberty of the individual are central ingredients of decency and flourishing.

7

RADICAL FEMINISM AS UNIFORMITARIANISM

We can now consider some of the public policy matters that need to be addressed by any comprehensive system of political ideas and ideals. Not that any society has ever simply implemented such a system – in fact, most legal orders evolve slowly, with only a few being implemented in what comes close to a deliberate fashion (for example, the United States of America has been, more or less, "invented," to use a term Stanley Cavell has applied to America's origins). In an effort to demean the role of rationality in politics, conservatives often make note of the fact that few, if any, regimes throughout human history have arisen by deliberate design. While they are correct, the inference they draw is mistaken – the rationality that goes into the day-to-day decisions human beings make ultimately shapes all traditions, practices, and habits of thought and action. The error is to think that reasoning must always address only the global tasks, that it must be architectonic, and that the small steps that produce the overall structures could be taken without it.

Systematic thinking, in turn, often shapes the small steps we take. This is what has come to be called "the vision thing" in U.S. politics. Even if comprehensive systems of political ideas and ideals are not ever (peacefully) implemented deliberately, they do mold public policy by means of electoral decisions, legislative and executive choices, and judicial opinions. So we do need to study such systems and attempt to establish which is best.

In any case, an issue that bears considering in light of some of the matters discussed in previous chapters is just how well the individualist approach can manage some public policy issues that people in society may face. For example, an interesting conflict has arisen among those who advocate what is loosely called the "pro-choice" position. The crux of the dispute is whether we ought to be pro-choice on grounds that women and men have the negative, Lockean right to privacy and the state ought to remain outside the decision as to whether pregnancy is to be terminated, or on grounds that women ought to have the same power status as men do and the state ought to ensure that they have it.

Of course, the pro-life versus pro-choice controversy is surrounded by several questions. Among these is whether a fetus is a human being with corresponding human rights (at least as a child has them, namely, to be protected within the context of parental authority). Also, what are a pregnant woman's rights if she is carrying a human being or a potential human being? Should those opposed to abortion be forced to fund them? Should these matters be the concern of the federal government, or should the states deal with them? There may well be other questions, more or less fundamental.

One concern not widely discussed has been brought to light by certain feminist supporters of the *Roe v. Wade* decision. Catherine A. MacKinnon (a colorful figure in legal circles, whose career has been enmeshed in controversy over whether, in terms of her professional work, she is really a good legal scholar or, rather, a social philosopher and advocate) has argued that the pro-choice position should be advanced not in terms of the right to privacy, but as a matter of public policy aiming for gender equality. In her book *Feminism Unmodified*, she states that "the privacy doctrine reaffirms and reinforces what the feminist critique of sexuality criticizes: the public/private split."[1] She is concerned that if the *Roe v. Wade* decision on abortion remains the law as it has been argued, the "analysis makes *Harris v. McRae*, in which public funding for abortions was held not to be required, appear consistent with the larger meaning of *Roe*."[2]

One practical issue that arises from this is that if one has a right to abortion, one may still not have a right to have it funded by the state. The right to privacy – with its constitutional expressions in the First, Ninth, and Fourteenth Amendments – could cut so deep that while abortions could not be prohibited, neither could taxation for purposes of government funding of abortions be tolerated.

What is the basic issue that MacKinnon is bringing to light? It is that her version of feminism is not concerned with choice at all. It does not concern itself mainly with a woman's right to freedom of conduct or whether a fetus is a child or merely a potential child.

What worries feminists like MacKinnon is more political and, they would contend, more basic. As MacKinnon puts it, "The abortion choice must be legally available and must be women's, but not because the fetus is not a form of life."[3] What concerns MacKinnon is that "women get pregnant . . . as a consequence of intercourse under conditions of gender inequality."[4] She holds, in effect, that the basic condition of male/female sexuality that now exists is a violation of the ideal of full human uniformity – whereby women and men have a uniform status and standing with respect to all the relevant issues. This is a political issue.

To put the matter bluntly, MacKinnon wants men and women to enjoy the same powers in all areas of life, and she does not want any supposed right to privacy to stand in the way of the government's accomplishing this goal once the government has come to agree with her. If one defends the right to privacy, one has not yet guaranteed that men and women enjoy the same status in life – politically, sexually, and in numerous derivative respects.

Indeed, if one has the right to privacy, one has a negative right, namely, the right not to be interfered with by others, including the government. Thus the government may not, morally and legally, make and enforce some determination of how burdens and benefits ought to be distributed among men and women. So the uniformity desired by MacKinnon would have to be implemented voluntarily, by persuasion, advocacy, and social action, not by way of the coercive power of the law.

MacKinnon wants it to be public policy, for example, that men and women experience equally the impact of sexual burdens now experienced only by women. Her view suggests that she does not merely want what nature elsewhere – though rarely – provides, namely, for males to be pregnant. (Sea horses, for example, are set up in that way – the male carries the little ones and cares for them, with the female roaming around free of this burden.) For MacKinnon, that would be unacceptable because it would simply switch roles and would not impose uniformity of conditions.

Is there anything wrong with wanting such uniformity? Why would any decent person resist MacKinnon's viewpoint? There are two reasons.

First, even if the ideal MacKinnon is aiming for has merit, there is no justification for demanding that it be forcibly imposed upon all of us. Ideals are moral objectives we ought to pursue, and "ought" implies "can," so if the ideals are imposed upon us, we certainly cannot make a moral choice to pursue them. Our moral agency is undermined by that kind of public policy. The reason why the right to privacy is vital even if MacKinnon's ideal is sound is that we are moral agents who require what Robert Nozick called our "moral space."

Second, MacKinnon's ideal plainly implies a denial of the diversity of life, including human life. It is actually a protest against this diversity and, ultimately, individuality. There are sounder moral ideals to pursue, namely, personal excellence just as one is, regardless of how this compares with other people's goals in life. Uniformity among members of a community of human individuals is plainly an impossible and therefore dangerous dream – it can produce lives of hopeless aspiration and, ultimately, cynicism. The human species is distinctive precisely in the large role that individuality plays in the lives of every human being. Contrary to Karl Marx, who, as noted earlier, said that "the human essence is the true collectivity of man,"[5] the human essence is actually the true *individuality* of man.

Human beings are different from other forms of life in large part because once they are born, they begin to give shape to their lives, indeed, are self-determined. This is a controversial point, but it is rather simply illustrated by philosophical argumentation itself – in the process of putting forth criticism, one is shaping oneself, placing oneself in a position that one has chosen. However much the bulk of human life is interwoven with the rest of humanity – that is, however much we all have a public life – there is an irreducible private aspect to it, namely, one's determination of what one will do and, largely, what one will be, based on the choices one makes in one's thinking about the wide range of options facing everyone. This is clearly illustrated by

MacKinnon's own vigorous intellectual activity and is evident in practically every conscious human being's life.[6]

This human trait can lead to major differences, based in part on facts of nature, in part on effort, in part on taste, and in part on circumstances. A person is not the result of some manufacturing process that follows some blueprint, with occasional major or minor variations on the design. If people were such beings, we could make it a matter of public policy to change them.

Certain trends in ethics and political philosophy seem clearly to be headed in this direction – for example, John Rawls's denial that one's moral character is one's own achievement,[7] a position from which a certain version of political egalitarianism may reasonably be said to flow! MacKinnon seems to be taking this trend into the province of law. Contemporary Marxism, following Marx's own lead, is also emphatic about denying a significant place to individuality and diversity in human social life. Marxists lament that the capitalist, free-market system rests on the ideal of "capitalist acts between consenting adults," as Robert Nozick put it.[8] Such stress on consent, just as the stress on privacy, ignores the supposed merits of the uniformity of members of society and instead acknowledges – if only implicitly – that diversity is morally acceptable and that even the more accidental individual differences (looks, talents, conditions, prospects, luck) are not matters that should be addressed by public policy. With such self-developed traits as the virtues, individuality is deemed to be an indispensable and splendid thing indeed.

Uniformitarianism rests in part on another old-fashioned idea, one that appears in much of Western and Eastern social philosophy – the oneness of all, especially of the human family, the "brotherhood" of mankind (which has not been read with any gender emphasis and could easily have been the "siblinghood" instead). The supreme virtue of fairness, too, has been an underlying ideal in this kind of social philosophizing. It is unfair for the poor to be poor, the rich to be rich, the crippled to be crippled, the beautiful to be beautiful, the lucky to be lucky, and so forth. And to Rawls it is even unfair for the virtuous to benefit from their virtue, since moral character is also accidental. The implication is clearly that ideally, all these differences would be eradicated and that in human social life, there is an option to do so. If justice actually requires it, then it is legally mandatory, not merely a matter of moral aspiration.

But the option to do things right or do them wrong makes the most important source of human differentiation impossible to overturn. Differences in our social lives are produced by our making choices about ourselves and the world around us and mingling these choices in innumerable varieties – for better and for worse.

Thus, as I hinted at before, even if it became technologically feasible for men to take over women's sexual functions, that would still leave us without what MacKinnon wants. For her, what justice seems to demand is that we are all the same, that no one look, feel, or, most of all, be better than another!

But, MacKinnon might respond, this is a distortion – she merely demands full equal opportunity. However, even if this point is granted, we must immediately take note of the fact that for MacKinnon, full equal opportunity translates into uniformity, since she wants the opportunity for women to enjoy the same privileges and exercise the same powers that men do. What this seems to mean for her is that women ought to be able to say no to the role of motherhood, to pregnancy, even when they want a child, and to innumerable other features of their lives that now come with being women.

It needs also to be noted that MacKinnon does not do full justice in her analysis to what men face. They suffer burdens that women do not suffer. Women do not have to carry the suspicion of being rapists, the stigma of being the coercers in the sexual act (except perhaps *vis-à-vis* minors), or the imperative to protect their spouses. And as far as the history of their respective advantages in life is concerned, women have some that men clearly lack – for example, the emotional freedom to be self-expressive, especially as regards showing feelings of sadness, hurt, distress, and ambivalence.

MacKinnon might, of course, argue that it is male-dominated society that has denied men emotional freedom. Yet that line of argument pretty much destroys the notion that men have arranged the world to benefit themselves, including at the expense of women, which is certainly a theme of radical feminism. This theme extends way beyond politics and law all the way to the idea that men have biased our view of nature, that even the principles of science reflect not truth but a male version of reality. If all this ends up hurting males, robbing them, for example, of their emotional freedom, one is hard put to figure what is the point of it all.

Given that MacKinnon sees the matter so lopsided to start with, even if equal opportunity is the issue, it cuts so deep that it becomes uniformitarianism in the last analysis. She is advocating placing identical burdens on men and women, and since she takes it that women have greater ones, this now would come to placing numerous limitations on men. In short, MacKinnon finds it terrible that in life some people have burdens or benefits that others do not share uniformly. She regards this as unfair.

But isn't MacKinnon mostly in favor of women's liberation? Would that not put her on the side of the right to privacy and, derivatively, on the side of the right to choose freely?

No. Or, rather, this is misleading – MacKinnon and those who join her in her version of feminism do not mean by "freedom" or "liberty" what is meant in the context of the American political tradition, namely, being free of others' forcible intrusions into one's life. They seem to mean by "being free" having the full ability to do what is deemed best for them. This, of course, implies being provided whatever is necessary to achieve this ability – including government support for abortion and government redistribution of powers and privileges (mostly those that have to do with sexual differences).

Men obviously have burdens and benefits in human life that are different from women's, and this is what in MacKinnon's view needs to be ended. What she wants is a reregimentation of society. As MacKinnon puts it, "the right to privacy is not thought to require social change. It is not even thought to require any social preconditions, other than nonintervention by the state."[9]

The abortion debate occurs within a community of persons with some very similar basic ideas. Both sides agree that persons should have their rights protected. The pro-choice people deny that fetuses or zygotes or embryos are persons, and the pro-life groups insist on the opposite. But once they leave that matter aside, they agree that individual rights make one something of a sovereign authority about one's life. One is in charge if one has a sphere of privacy.

Much of this is denied by radical feminists such as MacKinnon. (They are indeed radical, championing, as they do, a sort of tribalist solidarity among women.) They claim that in marriage, for instance, women are a subjugated party. This is insulting to the intelligence, savvy, and moral initiative of women in most Western societies – as distinct from societies where women are politically kept subservient. Once that political subservience is gone, women can and often should take their lives into their own hands – which, of course, runs the risk that they may want to get married, have children, and even, heaven help us, be housewives.

By calling for the government to establish uniformity between the sexes, MacKinnon is actually renovating political subservience. As long as women's choices are seen by MacKinnon as placing women into a position of not having powers identical to those of men, she disapproves of them and would wish to have public policies enacted that would eradicate them. She seems to think that women are somehow too weak to determine whether to enter a contract of marriage and agree intelligently to some of the conditions of that contract – for example, that they will carry to full term if they become pregnant, or that they may, at least temporarily, lack some powers or privileges that their husbands possess, due to the division of roles in their mutually agreed to and cooperative lives. They are too weak, MacKinnon appears to believe, to make such decisions for themselves, so long as men are this forceful, threatening group who want nothing other than to make women into pleasure slaves for themselves. As MacKinnon so directly puts it, "Just as pornography is legally protected as individual freedom of expression – without questioning whose freedom and whose expression and at whose expense – abstract privacy protects abstract autonomy, without inquiring into whose freedom of action is being sanctioned at whose expense."[10]

MacKinnon evidently believes that all these freedoms – the negative kind that so many people in oppressed countries keep hollering for – really make it possible for men to run roughshod over women, nothing else. Never mind that since the institution of such negative political liberty – the freedom of individuals to determine their own lives within the context of their own identities and others' equal right to liberty – women have made it evident that they can choose plenty as far as their lives are concerned. MacKinnon does not trust them to do this well and is determined to have the government get back into the saddle and order all of us around for the ideal of uniformitarianism. I think we can safely say that this is classic reactionary politics, taking us back past the feudal era to the period when clans and tribes ruled over individuals.

Don't get me wrong, I am not insensitive to the fact that some things women face are tough and it is often desirable to ease their burden. Yet this is nearly always an interchangeable situation – there are and have been nearly equivalent burdens that men carry but women are free of – and even when it is not, there tend to be benefits not enjoyed by men that are associated with women's burdens. If that is intolerable, then life is intolerable – there are special burdens and benefits for the tall as well as the short, the beautiful as well as the homely, and so forth. In that respect, a kind of uniformitarianism is already prevalent.

And even if some burdens are really unique to certain persons, what is so horrible about that? Nothing. Life is not mainly about everyone sharing burdens uniformly, but about doing the best with the burdens and benefits we each have in our lives. MacKinnon is like those who cannot accept that their picnic was rained out while someone else's came off without a hitch. She does not realize that life is not fair, that fairness is relevant only where individuals have voluntarily taken on some mutual burdens. Life is not fair, but it can be better or worse, which is an issue far different from sharing burdens and benefits uniformly.

There are, of course, complicated issues of politics and law that are not discussed here, some of which would involve clear disadvantages for women in the public sphere – lack of full property rights, lack of full citizenship status in many cultures, economic and educational disadvantages that men have not had to experience. These are often the result of traditional roles that may have made sense at one time but have run their course and still invade the fabric of most societies. Habits of law and custom are no less difficult to adjust to new understanding and possibilities than are personal habits.

Yet if men really had been so clever and shrewd as to arrange human communities to benefit them at women's expense over many centuries, that would be something rather discouraging for feminists – why would the males of the species suddenly become less adept at manipulating matters to their advantage? Would this not mean that all the political, legal, and economic changes that women have experienced are but a ruse, a clever deception designed to keep women in a subservient position?

A more sensible explanation of the maladies that feminists call attention to is that women and men have, together, mismanaged much of their lives and have experienced various obstacles to their respective full development. Some members of each group have exacerbated their problems through indulging personal vices such as obstinacy, stubbornness, and exploitation of the other group's vulnerabilities. But neither group is innately better or worse at dealing with humanity's tasks, more rather than less inclined to be unjust, unwise, cruel, or insensitive. There is no natural viciousness or virtue involved in being either a man or a woman. If there were, things would be intractably unbalanced and it would be futile to attempt to remedy matters.

The point of this chapter is to make clear one thing: the resolution of the problems that feminists call attention to is far more promising in terms of individualism than in terms of collectivism. Indeed, if anything has hurt the cause of feminism, radical or otherwise, it has been to think of women as having a uniform nature, as being all of a piece, instead of individuals who have the capacity to develop by their own lights and vigilance. Indeed, it would appear that the individualist idea of basic human rights to life, liberty, and property has made more of a contribution to advancing human welfare than has any other idea in recent political history.

8

HUMAN RIGHTS REAFFIRMED

One aspect of individualism is, of course, the Lockean natural-rights legacy. According to this school of political thought, the purpose of civil government is to protect the basic negative individual rights of citizens, the rights to life, liberty, and property – in Locke's terms, "person and possessions." I will not dwell at length over the precise interpretation of Locke. (Elsewhere I have made a case for a Lockean conception of individual rights.[1]) For our purposes it is important only to note that it was he who developed the theory of individual rights into a full-fledged political system, although there were intimations of such a theory in nearly all of recorded history.

The idea of natural human rights has always been criticized, most famously by Jeremy Bentham, who called the idea "nonsense upon stilts." It is under scrutiny no less in our time, on various political and diplomatic fronts, as well as in the literature of political philosophy.

The criticisms, though, do not always distinguish between Lockean, negative rights and more recent ideas of positive rights. For example, at the 1993 summer Conference on Human Rights in Vienna, Austria, some diplomats raised such questions as "When we speak of human rights, are these conditions that everyone everywhere ought to enjoy?", "Should these same basic conditions be protected by governments everywhere in the world?", and "Is it perhaps the case that human rights are one thing for people in one part of the globe and another for those in another part?" Such questions were raised mostly about rights spelled out in the United Nations Declaration of Universal Human Rights, both negative and positive – for example, the rights to freedom of expression and to public education, respectively. Many Third World leaders claim that human rights cannot be understood the same way when applied to their societies as in the context of Western liberal democracies.

In political philosophy, questioning the concept of natural human rights is familiar. After John Locke developed the idea that everyone, by virtue of possessing a human nature, has certain fundamental, unalienable rights, the view suffered philosophical assaults at the hands of empiricism, scientism, skepticism, holism, and so forth.

Yet the idea, now designated as "human rights," is certainly resilient. It parallels ideas elsewhere that aim to identify certain broad, unifying, comprehensive principles.[2] Such ideas about universalism go back at least to the time of Socrates, and each generation will probably continue to reconsider the matter.[3]

I want here to address recent criticism about the possibility of developing any sound idea of "human rights."[4] Among these critics we find some, such as Richard Rorty and John Gray,[5] going very deep, while the objections of others, such as Ernest van den Haag,[6] are based on a belief in the comparative superiority of another system. And some, such as John O. Nelson,[7] criticize the idea of human nature, the basis of the idea of human rights.

CONSERVATIVE–UTILITARIAN CRITICISM OF THE IDEA OF HUMAN RIGHTS

A prominent conservative–utilitarian criticism of the natural-rights position begins with the point that although it may be true that there are various necessary conditions that are required for human existence and flourishing or excellence, it does not follow at all that from these (or from knowing these) it is possible to infer norms or virtues or principles of human conduct. (This is plainly a restatement of the "is–ought gap" thesis of David Hume and the subsequent empiricist/positivist movement in epistemology and metaethics.[8]) From this it would seem both hopeless and undesirable to forge and sustain a society by relying on natural human rights. One such critic of the natural-rights stance, van den Haag, argues that utilitarian ethical or political theory provides us with better results, because utilitarianism is not metaethically flawed and is, for purposes of ethics and public policy, more successful than the latter when it comes to handling difficult problems. Some, following Karl Popper, also object that liberty itself, which natural-rights theorists claim to be concerned about, is at risk with a theory that relies on some stable conception of human nature. Finally, van den Haag adds that anomalies are handled more adequately in utilitarian theories than in natural-rights theories.

SKEPTICAL CRITICISM OF THE IDEA OF HUMAN RIGHTS

The criticism of the skeptics has three main parts. First, naturalism has been invalidated by contemporary empirical science.[9] (This is because naturalism depends on some type of teleological thesis.) Second, no liberalism can succeed, contrary to what some claim, based on an ethics of individual flourishing drawn from Aristotle. John Gray writes:

> Writing in an age of mass democracy and wage-labour, Aristotle's latter-day liberal followers prescribe a life of bourgeois virtue – of thrift,

industry, prudence, and creative work. However one assesses these ideals, the salient point is that in each of them the content given to human flourishing is taken wholly from the conventional norms of the theorist's local culture. It is far from clear what is the claim on reason attributed to these ideals.[10]

He adds: "The attribution to Aristotle of a belief in the moral centrality of choice-making . . . is all the more incongruous in that the belief plainly presupposes an affirmation of the freedom of the will which Aristotle does not make."[11]

Third and last, the skeptical critics doubt the relevance of the ideals of classical liberalism to different cultures, thus denying their self-proclaimed universality. They claim that the individualism involved in the West's political legacy will probably not – and certainly need not – apply to a tribal culture. Therein the freely chosen goals, projects, tastes, desires, and preferences of individuals are not seen as important.

This is similar to what some historicists say about the natural-rights position:[12] Western liberal political thought rests on the fallacy of seeking some stable, transhistorical foundation for political justice, but standards of justice, of goodness, and so forth are going to have to be relative to given stages of human(ity's) historical development.

These historicists object, for example, to the natural-rights theory's reliance on an individualism implicit in the Lockean doctrine and claim that such individualism is merely an invention (ideology) of a certain historical period.[13] This criticism, reminiscent of Marxian objections to bourgeois ethics, politics, and law, contends that the self, or ego, is something certain intellectuals created so as to rationalize certain public institutions and policies. Based on what we have learned from the history of ideas, political history, and cultural anthropology, we can see, the argument goes, that the idea of the individual self, the autonomous or sovereign person, is a modern contrivance, instead of a successful identification or true discovery of some fact about the human species.[14]

CRITICISM OF THE IDEA OF HUMAN NATURE

Central in this criticism is the challenge of a crucial premise in the argument for human rights: it states what human nature is. John O. Nelson responds that "human nature is not in fact simple or regular or even consistent in its components. It is much more like a crazy quilt than a triangle."[15] So, while the argument may be valid, it is *unsound* because human nature is not anything determinate. In particular, certain neo-Aristotelian efforts fail when claiming that human beings are rational beings or rational animals.[16]

Locke and his neo-Aristotelian natural-rights followers argue[17] that in every human community, the same *kind of* beings, namely, rational animals, reside and require certain conditions to embark upon a fully human life (flourishing by their own wits). The human rights to life, liberty, and property – that is, negative, or freedom, rights – amount to these conditions and need to be secured. If there is not a consistent, noncontradictory human nature that can be identified in universal and stable terms, these rights amount to myths.

RESPONSE TO THE CONSERVATIVE–UTILITARIAN CRITICISM

The is–ought gap troubles moral philosophy only if we accept a questionable, albeit prominent, theory of what it is to be and to know something, as well as the belief that a rational argument must have a deductive form. The empiricism underlying the alleged gap begs the question of what there can be. Supposedly, only beings capable of being sensed can exist. This rules out not only *a priori* but also *ad hoc* any type of existence that could involve characteristics we associate with values and morality. Since the empiricist view is open to serious doubt and there is reason to believe that a more pluralistic ontology would be more sound – based on ordinary awareness and its integration into a logically coherent order of existence – the is–ought gap suggested by empiricism need not be accepted as binding on a serious effort to inquire into the issue of values and rights. Furthermore, the view assumes that the formation of valid concepts could proceed only by way of *deducing* ideas from others that already fully contain them. This denies the evident growth and improvement of human knowledge. So accepting the sting of the is–ought argument cuts much too deep – it undermines not just morality but all substantive (nontautological) claims to knowledge.[18]

There is, of course, an additional problem with the positivist approach to understanding values. It leaves undecidable whether to embrace that theory, which is a normative question. The positivist – in economics or in law, not to mention in ethics – is advocating something, advancing the proposal that *we ought to* embrace a theory about values and virtues that states that values and virtues are subjective. The positivist's own theory comes to no more than something we should embrace if we like it but should not embrace if we do not like it.

Does the framework of natural law and rights (that is, objective morality and politics) pose a threat to human liberty? That is a justified concern only with an *intrinsicist* conception of values and moral goodness. This view has it that by virtue of certain innate properties, some beings are good and command support from those capable of seeing their goodness. The stress is on an enforceable, obligatory command that may be acted on by anyone, including someone who understands the command as it bears on another and can coerce this other's adherence.

The crucial difference between this intrinsicist conception of goodness and the naturalist view is that the former omits from consideration *the relational element of choice* involved between a human individual and the values appropriate for that person to pursue.[19] Intrinsicism holds that regardless of choice, only behavior that furthers a goal counts as morally adequate, since that will satisfy the implication that the good should be pursued. Yet, of course, if "ought implies can," as it must, this intrinsicist view stumbles very badly. Having made someone behave so that this behavior promotes some goal has not succeeded in producing *moral* value (for example, justice), since moral value is dependent on *choosing* the appropriate behavior, that is, on acting rightly.

What about ethical and political anomalies facing natural-rights theories? Some utilitarians seem to think that these sorts of cases cannot be handled by the natural-law/rights position, an evident failing since they evidently occur. If a moral/political/legal framework cannot guide us in this task, that framework is seriously flawed.

There are peculiarities about anomalous cases. To begin with, each anomalous case in ethics or politics involves an emergency; that is to say, it places people in unique circumstances that no ethical theory is able to render *easily* manageable. Typical are desert-island or lifeboat examples so often raised in judging ethical theories, or new problems for which solutions are yet to emerge. Ethical principles are *general* guidelines to human conduct, based on a supposedly sound comprehensive ethical theory. So if they cannot handle the emergency or new cases, they must fail.

In the neo-Aristotelian support given to natural human rights, the rigid-rule ethics vulnerable to the criticism based on anomalies is rejected; for example, industriousness may be a virtue, but sometimes one should first practice courage, and moderation is secondary to justice. Very fundamental moral imperatives, however, such as right reason, or *phronesis*, will enable one to rank these virtues for particular cases and make it possible to manage anomalies, accordingly. It is not possible to find any kind of specific conduct, outside of following the very general policy of being rational, that will always be the right one for the situation, especially when it is extraordinary.[20]

Natural rights, furthermore, are supposed to guide the formation of law and government, not personal conduct. Natural rights apply only in circumstances where *public* life is possible. Specifically, libertarian natural-rights theorists have taken their clue from John Locke, who distinguished situations "where peace is possible"[21] from those where it is not.

But there is also the consideration that past moral wrongs might produce a case that now seems to present a dilemma. In such a case, one might be persuaded that someone's rights should be violated so as to correct a previous wrong, thus accepting the view that natural rights are not compossible – that is, capable of mutual respect.[22] However, if no individual can be found to be prosecuted for the rights violation, there is no remedy and any effort to provide one would turn out to be unjustified, a violation of the rights of someone who is to be burdened with some disadvantage. Mandated affirmative action policies are of this type of sham remedy.[23]

In summary, the purpose of ethics, or moral systems, is to provide for the guidance of human living, with political ethics and law to provide for the guidance of human living in the company of other human beings. To the extent that an ethical and/or political system helps achieve this natural purpose – which is presupposed in the asking of the question that gives rise to it – it is a sound system. But even a sound system of ethics and/or politics can face difficulties, so the question is whether one or another faces them more successfully – more comprehensively, with greater integrity, and so forth.

RESPONSE TO THE SKEPTICAL CRITICISM

A normative naturalist would indeed have to invoke a teleological conception of human behavior. The standards of right and wrong, good and evil, come from considering the natural end of human life. If by nature it would not be more healthy or suitable or fitting for human beings to be doing one thing rather than another, what would show that doing it is right? The only alternative is a theistic doctrine, but it, too, embraces some variety of teleology and would face similar fire from empiricists.

However, empiricism is no decisive blow against teleology. One would have to be rather steeped in a discredited logical positivism to think that teleology can be dismissed so cavalierly, thus easily sweeping away normative naturalism (that is, natural-rights ethics, law, and politics).

Furthermore, antinaturalists are also suspicious of free will, once again because of their scientism – thinking that somehow the belief in free will is antiscience, antiempirical, anticool! Poppycock! It is no more so than many other fully functional ideas – for example, moral obligation, justice, and due process. Science – though not scientism – is fully compatible with the idea of free will.[24]

Aristotle addresses the issue of choice making in his distinction between the intellectual and the moral virtues. The latter require choice – naturally, since morality involves self-responsible conduct or neglect, which could not exist without the capacity for choice. Aristotle had a doctrine of free will, although it was not a major aspect of his moral theory; he located free will in deliberation. As Jaeger notes, "Aristotle's notion of free will is the exact complement of the notion of most perfect deliberation in the *Epinomis*."[25] David Ross puts it this way: "On the whole we must say that [Aristotle] shared the plain man's belief in free will but that he did not examine the problem very thoroughly, and did not express himself with perfect consistency."[26]

Regarding the universality of human rights, Aristotle is the first to admit that not everything that is morally right and wrong is universal, even though fundamental virtues are. In my own position, as well as the positions of others, *rationality* is the central virtue – just as *right reason* fills that role for Aristotle. Other virtues are bound to a narrower context. Moreover, all the virtues spelled out by "latter-day liberal followers" can be conceptually related to the original virtues spelled out by Aristotle. (Universality is discussed further in the next section.)

Most of those who are skeptical about rights theories do not bother to investigate these issues at great length.[27] Suffice it to conclude, therefore, that many of the skeptical claims advanced directly against natural-rights theory are unsupported, and some are evidently false.

HUMAN NATURE EXISTS

Let me begin my response to the criticism that human nature cannot be consistent by recalling a point made by Laszlo Versenyi some time ago:

> If human nature is unknowable then so is human good and it is impossible to talk about human excellence in general. Indeed it is impossible to talk about man as such, since man as such could not even be identified. Barring all knowledge of human nature – that which makes a man a man – the word man would mean nothing and we could not even conceive of man as a definite being distinguishable from all other beings. Consequently anything we might say about man would be necessarily meaningless, including the statement that human nature as such as unknowable to man. Thus the postulate of the strict unknowability of man is self-contradictory. To the extent that we talk about man we obviously hold that his nature is, in some respect at least, knowable.[28]

Natural-rights theory does not presuppose a Platonistic type of essentialism or the timelessness or finality of definitions or natures. All it requires is the most comprehensive, consistent statement of what something must (for now) be to be human, a point that deflates the objection based on the charge that the idea of human rights "conflates temporalities with timelessness."[29] A contextual conception of natures, including human nature, avoids the problem of having to identify human nature as something unalterable.[30]

What of the claim that human nature is a crazy quilt? It is unclear. One reason one might so characterize human nature is that with their capacity for rationality – which entails, of course, their freedom not to exercise reason, to do so sporadically, to apply it to extremely diverse situations, and so forth – people are likely to live highly diverse lives, develop diverse cultures, and generally defy many simple categorizations.

Yet this does not deny the presence of precisely the kind of nature that human rights theorists, who stress the function of choice in human affairs, have identified as human. Quite the opposite. Just that source of immensely wide diversity needs to be taken full account of, its existence given a paramount

103

place in understanding what it is to be human. And some human rights theorists have done just that.

For example, many cultural differences can and need to be honored. But they do not have to do with human rights, which are sound basic principles of human community life anywhere, at any time, allowing for variations based on certain advances in conceptual development.[31] And we are well aware of this fact in how we view other cultures – even as we may be mistaken in our judgments and evaluations. We know, for example, that cultural differences are morally acceptable only where they include peaceful practices, customs, mores, etiquette, styles, tastes, and so forth. This is because we know that peace (and the conditions that secure it) is required for humans to flourish. But beyond this, different cultures often exhibit the fact that people possess distinct styles, temperaments, tastes, habits, customs, and so forth. Accordingly, there will be diversity in things such as the arts, cuisine, sports, and the creative and productive orientation of different cultures, based on different personalities, histories, climates, and other factors.

The validity of certain cultural differences may be established by reference to facts about the cultures that influence behaviors that are optional. Whether one should wear a turban or a hat, kilts or pants, whether one ought to dance the Csardas or the mashed potato, and whether it is pasta, paprikas csirke, or tacos that should comprise one's menu are optional because one's human nature alone gives no guidance for how to act in these realms other than to, say, protect oneself against the elements, partake in the performing arts, undertake nourishment, and so forth. But within these broad limits, the climate, the prevailing temperament, or the surrounding sounds and sights will be decisive.

When it comes to the sacrifice of the firstborn son or virgin daughter, the subjection of a child to a religious ritual involving poisonous snakes, the refusal of medical care for one's infant child, the murder of one's wife so as to obtain a new dowry, the enslavement of conquered neighbors, and the like, there human nature itself is being violated.

Human rights are based on universal human attributes. Indeed, universal human rights concern the basic freedoms that people ought to have protected so as to make peaceful choices for themselves in all walks of life, including whether to follow various cultural mores.[32] It is only if such rights are given full protection that the valuable (as distinct from destructive) differences based on the highly diverse circumstances in people's lives can be fully experienced.[33]

9

DO ANIMALS HAVE RIGHTS?

ELEVATING ANIMALS

Although the idea that animals have rights goes back at least to the eighteenth century, it has only recently become something of a *cause célèbre* among numerous serious and well-placed intellectuals, including moral and political philosophers. Jeremy Bentham, for example, seems to have suggested legislation requiring humane treatment of animals, but he did not defend animal rights *per se* – not surprisingly, since Bentham was not impressed with the more basic (Lockean) doctrine of natural rights. John Locke's idea of natural rights has had enormous influence, however, and even where it is not respected, it is often invoked as some kind of model for what it would take for something to have rights.

In recent years the doctrine of animal rights has found champions in important circles where the general doctrine of rights is itself well respected. For example, Professor Tom Regan, in his important book *The Case for Animal Rights*,[1] finds the idea of natural rights intellectually congenial and extends this idea to cover higher animals. The political tradition that Regan works in appears to be Lockean, but he does not agree that human nature is distinctive enough, in relevant respects, to restrict the scope of natural rights to humans alone.

Following a different tradition, namely, utilitarianism, the idea of animal liberation has emerged. This can lead to roughly the same conclusions as the natural-rights tradition, but the argument is different because for utilitarians, what is important is not that humans or other animals must have a specific sphere of dominion, but that they be well off in their lives. So long as the bulk of the relevant creatures enjoy a reasonably high living standard, the moral and political objectives for them will have been met. But if this goal is not reached, moral and political steps are required to improve on the situation. Animal liberation is such a step.

Before answering the question of whether animals have rights, I want to note that rights and liberty are certainly not the only things of moral concern to us. There are innumerable other moral issues one can raise, including about the way human beings relate to animals. In particular, there is the question of how people should treat animals. May they be utilized for nonvital human purposes? May their pain and suffering be ignored in the process of their being made use of for admittedly vital human purposes?

It is clear that once one has answered the question of whether animals have rights or ought to be liberated from human beings, one has by no means disposed of these other issues. I will be dealing mostly with the issues of animal rights and liberation, but I will also touch briefly on the other moral questions just raised. I will indicate why they may all be answered in the negative without it being the case that animals have rights or should be liberated – that is, without raising any basic political issues. One could address, for example, the issues of whether animals may be hunted, used for sport, domesticated, and so forth. But these are mainly issues of ethics, so they are beyond the scope of the present discussion, which focuses primarily on matters of politics and law.

So, then, in this chapter I will argue that animals have no basic rights to life, liberty, or property. Now, this is a task that needs to be approached obliquely since it is not possible to straightforwardly prove a negative proposition. That is one reason why in the criminal law, it is the prosecution that must prove its case, with the defense merely needing to refute what the prosecution advances instead of having to make a case for a negative proposition, a denial. (There are some metaphysical considerations that underlie this matter, but we will skip these.)

Let us put it this way, then: the concept of "rights" is inapplicable to considerations of how animals ought to be treated. I will argue that to think otherwise is to confuse categories – it is, to be blunt, to unjustifiably anthropomorphize animals, to treat them as if they are what they are not, namely, human beings. Rights and liberty are political concepts applicable to human beings because human beings are moral agents, in need of what philosopher Robert Nozick called "moral space," that is, a definite sphere of moral jurisdiction where their authority to act is respected and protected so that it is they, not intruders, who govern themselves and either succeed or fail in their moral tasks.

It was to spell out the crucial difference between moral agents, such as human beings, and nonmoral ones, such as other animals, that the topic of free will was discussed earlier in this work. Defenders of animal rights make their case, first and foremost, by denying this difference and claiming that no fundamental faculty distinguishes humans from other animals. If, however, this is wrong, if human beings are fundamentally distinguished from other animals by virtue of possessing the capacity for moral agency, for initiating conduct that can be good or bad and for taking responsibility for that initiative, then we have here a sphere of uniqueness that can give rise to concepts that will not be applicable to other than human animals.

Oddly, it is clearly admitted by most animal rights or liberation theorists that only human beings are moral agents – for example, they never urge animals to behave morally (by, for example, standing up for their rights by leading a political revolution). No animal rights theorist proposes that animals be tried for crimes and blamed for moral wrongs. If it is true that the moral nature of human beings gives rise to the conception of basic rights and liberties, then by this alone, animal rights and liberation theorists have made a fatal admission in their case.

WHY MIGHT ANIMALS HAVE RIGHTS?

To have a right means being justified in preventing those who have the choice from intruding on one within a given sphere of jurisdiction. If I have the right to use a community swimming pool, no one is justified in trying to prevent me from making the decision as to whether I will use the pool.

When a right is considered natural, the freedom involved in having this right is supposed to be justified by reference to the kind of being one is, one's nature as a certain kind of entity. The idea of natural rights was formulated in connection with the issue of the proper relationship between human beings, especially between citizens and governments.

Since Locke's time, the doctrine of natural rights has undergone a turbulent intellectual history, falling into disrepute at the hands of empiricism and positivism but gaining a revival at the hands of some influential political philosophers of the second half of the twentieth century. Ironically, at a time when natural-rights theory had not been enjoying much support, the idea that animals might also have rights came under increasing discussion. Most notable among those who proposed such a notion was Thomas Taylor. His anonymous work *Vindication of the Rights of Brutes*, published in 1792, discussed animal rights only in the context of demeaning human rights. More positive (though brief) was the contribution of Jeremy Bentham, who, in his *An Introduction to the Principles of Morals and Legislation* (1789), argued that those animals capable of suffering are owed moral consideration, even if those that molest us or we may make good use of may be killed – but not "tormented."

In the latter part of the nineteenth century, Henry S. Salt devoted an entire work to the idea of animal rights.[2] And in our time, numerous philosophers and social commentators have made attempts to demonstrate that if we are able to ascribe basic rights to life, liberty, and property to human beings, we can do the same for many of the higher animals. Their arguments have two essential parts. First, they subscribe to Darwin's thesis that no difference of kind, only a difference of degree, can be found between other animals and human beings.[3] Second, they claim that even if there were a difference in kind between other animals – especially mammals – and human beings, since they both can be shown to have interests (for example, the avoidance of pain and suffering), for certain moral and legal purposes, the difference does not matter; only the similarity matters.[4]

Now, I do not wish to give the impression that no diversity exists among those who defend animal rights. Some do so from the viewpoint of natural rights, treating animals' rights as basic limiting principles that may not be ignored except when it would also make sense to disregard the rights of human beings. Even on this matter, there are serious differences among defenders of animals' rights – some do not allow any special regard for human beings,[5] while some hold that when it comes to a choice between a person and a dog, it is ordinarily the person who should be given protection.[6]

Others choose to defend animal rights or obligations we owe to animals (including abstaining from hurting them) on utilitarian grounds: to the extent that it amounts to furthering overall pleasure or happiness in the world, animals must be given consideration equal to what human beings receive. Thus an animal that is capable of experiencing pleasure or happiness may be sacrificed to further some human purpose only if that demonstrably contributes to the overall pleasure or happiness on earth. Barring such a demonstrable contribution, animals and humans enjoy equal rights.[7]

One advocate of animal rights began his argument with the rather mild point that "reason requires that other animals are as much within the scope of moral concern as are men" but then moved on to the more radical claim that therefore "we must view our entire history as well as all aspects of our daily lives from a new perspective."[8]

Of course, folks have usually invoked *some* moral considerations about how animals should be treated – think about disapproval of the proverbial kids' play of pulling off the legs of flies. I personally recall such cases from living on a farm in Hungary when I was eleven. I got all kinds of rebuke about how I ought to treat the animals, receiving severe scolding when I mistreated a cat and lots of approval for taking the favorite cow grazing every day and establishing some kind of bond with it over time. Hardly anyone can have escaped one or another moral lecture from parents or neighbors concerning the treatment of cats, dogs, or birds.

I recall that when a young boy once tried out an air gun by shooting a pigeon sitting on a telephone wire before the apartment house in which he lived, there was no end of rebuke in response to this wanton callousness. Yet those who rebuked the boy were not implying that "we must view our entire history as well as all aspects of our daily lives from a new perspective." Rather, they seemed to understand that reckless disregard for the life or well-being of animals shows a defect of character, lack of sensitivity, callousness – without denying, at the same time, that numerous human purposes justify our killing animals and using them in the various benign ways they have been used throughout human history.

And this really is the crux of the matter. But why? Why is it more reasonable to think of animals as available for our sensible use rather than owed the kind of respect and consideration we ought to extend to other human beings? It is one thing to have this as a commonsense conviction; it is another to know it as a sound viewpoint, in terms of which we may confidently conduct ourselves.

WHY WE MAY USE ANIMALS

Before returning to the arguments for animal rights, I would like to present a classical–individualist case for the use of animals for human purposes. Without this case reasonably well established, it will not be possible to critically assess the case for animal rights. After all, this is a comparative matter – which viewpoint makes better sense and therefore is more likely to be true? Moreover, it was from a roughly classical–individualist stance that the idea of basic rights was developed, by John Locke and others.

One reason for the propriety of our use of animals is that we are more important or valuable than other animals and some of our projects may require the use, even killing, of animals so as to succeed. Notice that this is different from saying that human beings are "uniquely important," a position avidly ridiculed by Stephen R. L. Clark, who claims that "there seems no decent ground in reason or revelation to suppose that man is uniquely important or significant."[9] If man were uniquely important, that would mean that one could not assign *any* value to plants or nonhuman animals apart from their relationship to human beings. The position I am defending is that there is a scale of importance in nature and among all the various kinds of being, with human beings *prima facie* the most important – even while some members of the human species may indeed prove themselves to be the most vile and worthless as well.

How do we establish that we are the most important or valuable? By considering whether the idea of lesser or greater importance or value in the nature of things makes clear sense and applying it to an understanding of whether human beings or other animals are more important. If it turns out that ranking things in nature as more or less important makes sense, and if humans qualify as more important than other animals, there is at least the beginning of a reason why we may make use of other animals for our purposes – for instance, when a trade-off is unavoidable.

That there are things of different degree of value in nature is admitted by animal rights advocates, so there is no need to argue about that here. When they insist that we treat animals differently from the way we treat, say, rocks – so that we may use rocks in ways that we may not use animals – animal rights or liberation champions testify, at least by implication, that animals are more important than rocks. They happen, also, to deny that human beings rank higher than other animals, or at least they do not admit that ranking human beings higher warrants our using animals for our purposes. But that is a distinct issue. What matters for now is that variable importance in nature is at least implicitly admitted by defenders of the high moral status of animals.

Quite independently of this acknowledgment, there simply is evidence through the natural world of the existence of beings of greater complexity *and* of higher value. For example, while it makes no sense to evaluate as good or bad such things as planets or rocks or pebbles – except as they may relate to human purposes – when it comes to plants and animals, the process of evaluation commences very naturally indeed. We can speak of better or worse oaks, redwoods, zebras, foxes, or chimps. While at this point we confine our evaluation to the condition or behavior of such beings without any intimation of their responsibility for being better or worse, when we start discussing human beings, our evaluation takes on a moral component. Indeed, none are more ready to testify to this than animal rights advocates, who, after all, do not demand any change of behavior on the part of nonhuman animals and yet insist that human beings conform to certain moral edicts as a matter of their own choice. This means that even animal rights advocates admit outright that to the best of our knowledge, it is with human beings that the idea of moral responsibility enters the universe.

Clearly, this shows a hierarchical structure in nature: Some things – rocks, comets, minerals – do not invite evaluations at all; it is of no significance, except in relationship to the well-being of some living entities, whether they exist or what condition they are in or how they behave. Some things – zebras, frogs, redwood trees – invite evaluation as to whether they do well or badly but without any moral or ethical implications. And some things – namely, human beings – invite moral evaluation in light of the fact that they exercise choice regarding good and bad things they can do.

The level of importance or value may be noted to move from the inanimate to the animate world, culminating, as far as we now know, with human life. Normal human life involves moral tasks, and that is why we are more important than other beings in nature – we are subject to moral appraisal; it is a matter of our doing whether we succeed or fail in our lives.

Now, when it comes to our moral task, namely, to succeed as human beings, we are dependent upon reaching sensible conclusions about what we should do. We can fail to do this and too often do so. But we can also succeed. The process that leads to our success involves learning, among other things, what it is that nature avails us with to achieve our highly varied tasks in life. Clearly, among these highly varied tasks could be some that make judicious use of animals – for example, to find out whether some medicine is safe for human use, we might wish to employ animals. To do this is rational for us, so as to make the best use of nature for our success in living our lives. That does not mean that we can do without guidelines for how we might make use of animals – any more than we can do without guidelines for how we use anything else. In a discussion of ethics, such guidelines would become essential, but they are not the topic of politics or law in a free society (except when animals or plants become the subject of contractual agreements and their enforcement or when there is an issue of violating rights by invading or depleting natural life support resources such as the ozone layer or, if the example fits, the rain forests. These would amount to actions comparable to depriving another of the air that surrounds us all.)

The above line of reasoning also counters a frequently raised objection to our use of other animals: Could not the same argument be used within the human species, giving better people the right to make use of worse people? The answer is that making choices is a precondition for determining who is better or worse among human beings, and using people against their will squelches their choice – at least with respect to what they ought to do next – so those who are better have the obligation to leave those who are worse to continue to make choices that may well reverse the situation. It isn't over, as the saying goes, until the fat lady sings, so, as we have learned from Aristotle, the comparative assessment of human beings must await the completion of their lives, at least in principle.

Of course, we do in fact "make use" of some very bad people – those who have been duly convicted of having exempted themselves from human community life. We banish – usually by imprisonment – those who violate others' basic rights. We punish them at times by forcing them to work – for example, to produce license plates in the United States. Personally, too, there are limits to tolerance: if someone threatens us with serious harm, with taking our lives or property, we act to remove the threat, to subdue the aggressor. This is not outright "using" of someone, but it does show that for self-defensive purposes, human beings are not immune from being killed or maimed, akin to how we might treat animals if they stand in the way of our flourishing.

WHY DO HUMANS HAVE INDIVIDUAL RIGHTS?

Where do individual *human* rights come into this picture? The rights being talked of in connection with human beings have as their source, as noted earlier, the human capacity to make moral choices. We have the rights to life, liberty, and property – as well as more specialized rights connected with politics, the press, religion, and so forth – because we have as our central task in life to act morally. And in order to be able to do this throughout the scope of our lives, we require a reasonably clear sphere of personal jurisdiction – a dominion where we are sovereign and can either succeed or fail in living well, doing right, acting properly.

IS THERE ROOM FOR ANIMAL RIGHTS?

We have seen that the most sensible and influential doctrine of human rights rests on the fact that human beings are indeed members of a discernibly different species, in which the members have a moral life to aspire to and must have principles upheld for them in communities that make their aspiration possible. Now, there is plainly no valid intellectual place for rights in the nonhuman world, the world in which moral responsibility is for all practical purposes absent. A few would want to argue that some measure of morality can be found within the world of at least higher animals, such as dogs. For example, Rollin holds that "[i]n actual fact, some animals even seem to exhibit behavior that bespeaks something like moral agency or moral agreement."[10] His argument for this is rather anecdotal, but it is worth considering:

> Canids, including the domesticated dog, do not attack another when the vanquished bares its teeth, showing a sign of submission. Animals typically do not prey upon members of their own species. Elephants and porpoises will and do feed injured members of their species. Porpoises will help humans, even at risk to themselves. Some animals will adopt orphaned young of other species. (Such cross-species 'morality' would certainly not be explainable by simple appeal to mechanical evolution, since there is no advantage whatever to one's own species.) Dogs will act 'guilty' when they break a rule such as one against stealing food from a table and will, for the most part, learn not to take it.[11]

Animal rights advocates such as Rollin maintain that it is impossible to clearly distinguish between human and nonhuman animals, including on the grounds of the former's characteristic as a moral agent. Yet what they do to defend this point is to invoke borderline cases, imaginary hypotheses, and anecdotes.

In contrast, in his book *The Difference of Man and the Difference It Makes*, Mortimer Adler undertakes the painstaking task of showing that even with the full acknowledgment of the merits of Darwinian and, especially, post-Darwinian evolutionary theory, there is ample reason to uphold the doctrine of species distinction – a distinction, incidentally, that is actually presupposed within Darwin's own work.[12] Adler shows that although the theistic doctrine of radical species differences is incompatible with current evolutionary theory, the more naturalistic view that species are superficially (but not negligibly) different is indeed necessary to the theory. The fact of occasional borderline cases is simply irrelevant – what is crucial is the generalization that human beings are basically different from other animals, by virtue of "a crucial threshold in a continuum of degrees."[13] As Adler explains:

> [D]istinct species are genetically isolated populations between which interbreeding is impossible, arising (except in the case of polyploidy) from varieties between which interbreeding was not impossible, but between which it was prevented. Modern theorists, with more assurance than Darwin could manage, treat distinct species as natural kinds, not as man-made class distinctions.[14]

Adler adds:

> Without the critical insight provided by the distinction between superficial and radical differences in kind, biologists [as well as animal rights

advocates, one should add] might be tempted to follow Darwin in thinking that all differences in kind must be apparent, not real.[15]

After Locke's admittedly incomplete – sometimes even confusing – theory had gained respect and, especially, practical import (for example, in British and American political history), it became clear enough that the only justification for the exercise of state power – namely, law enforcement – is that the rights of individuals are being or have been violated. But as with all successful doctrines, Locke's idea became corrupted by innumerable efforts to concoct rights that governments must protect, rights that were actually disguised special-interest objectives – values that some people, perhaps quite earnestly, wanted very badly to have secured.

While it is no doubt true that many animal rights advocates sincerely believe that they have found a justification for the actual existence of animal rights, it is equally likely that if the Lockean doctrine of rights had not become so influential, they would now be putting their point in another way that might secure for them what they, as a special-interest group, want: The protection of animals they have such love and sympathy for.

MORALITY AND RIGHTS

As with most issues on the minds of many intelligent people, as well as innumerable crackpots, a discussion of whether there are animal rights and how we ought to treat animals cannot be concluded with dogmatic certainty one way or the other. Even though many of those who defend animal rights seem certain almost beyond a shadow of a doubt, all I claim to be is certain beyond a reasonable doubt. Animals are not beings with basic rights to life, liberty, and property, whereas human beings, in the main, are just such beings. Yet we know that animals can feel pain and can enjoy themselves, and this must give us pause when we consider using them for vital human purposes. We ought to be humane; if we kill them, rear them, train them, hunt them, or otherwise use them, we should do so with care about them as sentient beings.

Is it wrong to use animals for nonvital purposes? Quite likely, ethically, but that is not the same as holding that animals have rights. Should there be laws against certain kinds of cruelty to animals? This is not something I am willing to address fully here. It is not an issue I have fully thought through. Suffice it to say that in my opinion, it would be morally unexceptionable for someone to rescue an animal that was being treated with cruelty, even if this amounted to invading someone's private property. If one were to spot a neighbor torturing his cat, albeit on his own private property, one could well be morally remiss in failing to invade the place and rescue the animal. A court, however, would probably correctly consider this illegal trespassing but might, nonetheless, pardon the transgressor as a matter of judicial discretion.

Exactly where this leaves us with the matter of whether laws should exist to ban cruelty to animals I am not sure – I would have to address that elsewhere, more carefully, after a good deal more thought.

In a review of Tom Regan's provocative book mentioned above, *The Case for Animal Rights*, John Hospers makes the following observations that I believe put the matter into the best light we can shed on this topic:

> As one reads page after page of Regan's book, one has the growing impression that his thesis is in an important way "going against nature." It is a fact of nature that living things have to live on other living things in order to stay alive themselves. It is a fact of nature that carnivores must consume, not plants (which they can't digest), but other sentient beings capable of intense pain and suffering, and that they can survive in no other way. It is a fact of nature that animal reproduction is such that far more creatures are born or hatched than can possibly survive. It is a fact of nature that most creatures die slow lingering tortuous deaths, and that few animals in the wild ever reach old age. It is a fact of nature that we cannot take one step in the woods without killing thousands of tiny organisms whose lives we thereby extinguish. This has been the order of nature for millions of years before man came on the scene, and has indeed been the means by which any animal species has survived to the present day; to fight it is like trying to fight an atomic bomb with a dartgun. . . . This is the world as it is, nature in the raw, unlike the animals in Disney cartoons.[16]

Of course, one might then ask, why should human beings make any attempt to behave differently among themselves, to bother with morality at all?

The fact is that with the emergence of the human species, a new problem arose in nature – basic choices that other animals do not have to confront had to be confronted. The question "How should I live?" faces each human being. And that is what makes it unavoidable for human beings to dwell on moral issues and to see other human beings as having the same problem to solve, the same question to dwell on. For this reason we are very different from other animals – we do terrible, horrible, awful things to each other and to nature, but we can also do much, much better and achieve incredible feats nothing else in nature can come close to.

Indeed, then, the moral life is the exclusive province of human beings, so far as we can tell for now. Other – lower(!) – animals simply cannot be accorded the kind of treatment that such a moral life demands, namely, respect for and protection of basic rights to life, liberty, and property.

This argument may not have convinced everyone that animals do not have rights. For some people, the only thing about this subject they are sure of is that it hurts them to think of animals feeling pain or fear or grief. And it appears to them that without ascribing rights to animals, the treatment of animals that induces pain or fear or grief cannot be adequately discouraged. Assuming that we are, indeed, more important than other animals because we have moral tasks they do not have, that might be a reason why we have rights that *supersede* theirs. Yet couldn't the logic of the argument for human rights be used to show that animals (and even plants) have rights as long as their rights do not interfere with those of beings that are more important? For example, they might have some rights to property because, as human rights theory proposes, to flourish as the beings they are, they need part of Earth to be preserved as their natural habitat. And of course, they would also need to be alive and free to flourish.

The sentiments expressed here are powerful and have certainly engendered a widespread movement in favor of ascribing rights to animals. If there were no other way to address this attitude toward the treatment of animals, one might have to conclude that the normative conceptual framework of basic rights to life, liberty, and property would have to include animal rights. The notion that no ethical concerns arise *vis-à-vis* animals is just too obviously off base to be convincing. While our intuitions may not suffice to make adequate sense of the moral landscape involved here, they do suffice for us to be attentive to an area of our lives wherein they are so powerful. To claim, for example, that it is neither here nor there whether one tortures an animal, abuses it, or even, under normal circumstances, lets it starve would seem to contradict too much of our lives to let it go. Our children are brought up to heed the welfare of their pets, of domesticated animals, of livestock, and of wild animals. Wanton killing of birds or field mice is naturally deemed morally objectionable. So clearly, there is need for a moral analysis of this realm of human conduct.

Yet it is confusing, as I have argued above, to introduce the idea of rights, since what distinguishes them in moral discourse is that they are the framework for the treatment of beings with a moral nature, beings who can make moral choices, which is not the case with animals. Humane treatment, compassion, lack of cruelty, and similar moral concepts will have to be developed for our adequate understanding of how animals ought to be treated by human beings. When enlisted to handle this area of our moral concerns, the concept of rights simply cannot be made use of smoothly enough without watering it down as a clear concept within politics and law.

LAST THOUGHTS ON ANIMALS, COMPUTERS, AND HUMAN MINDS

Proving a negative is, of course, impossible. That animals do not qualify as rational beings and, therefore, basic rightsholders[17] is something we know not from a syllogistic proof but from reflecting on the evidence and putting forth an explanation that makes better sense than any other. For example, as far as we can tell, no animal raises the question of whether animals are thinking beings. Animals, furthermore, appear to have no central, crucial need of thinking, whereas without thinking, human beings cannot begin to survive. Thinking for us is the mode of survival and flourishing – we cannot count on our instincts to get on with our lives. Other animals, in contrast, can handle their lives by means of their instincts, and for them their minimal abstract thinking is an aside, brought on usually by human beings, scientists who induce thinking in them while they are in captivity. From this we can conclude, sensibly, that it is valid to conclude that human beings are rational animals. That is what distinguishes us from other living things.

Let me just address very briefly the issue of whether machines can be rational. For example, what about Deep Blue, IBM's powerful chess machine, and the accompanying claims of the artificial-intelligence community? This will be but a brief comment, but it needs to be included here to round out the discussion of whether animals and, perhaps, other nonhuman beings may have basic rights to life, liberty, and property.

Computing machines are good at very rapid calculation, mainly because that is how human beings have designed them to be useful to humans in various tasks. Even calculators are faster than most of us when it comes to adding, subtracting, and so forth, and computers are faster at figuring out the best strategy for winning at chess. Except for a few human beings, such as Gary Kasparov, who have devoted the bulk of their lives to it, most of us are pretty pedestrian about figuring out how to win at chess. So Deep Blue is not really big news. What humans do that no machine, as we ordinarily understand them, can do is to start thinking at will, on their own initiative. Human thinking, as I have repeatedly argued in this book, is self-generated, a matter of one's own free will, something machines are not up to, plain and simple. That is why *we* can be mentally lazy, but animals and machines cannot. That is why when a machine misbehaves, it makes no sense to blame it – any more than it makes sense to blame or praise animals for their deeds. That is why believers in rights of animals and artificial-intelligence machines address their arguments and appeals not to nonhuman animals or powerful digital computers but, simply, to us. They know well enough that it is human beings who have the capacity to choose to think in certain ways and to stop thinking in others – to change their minds, in other words.

A thinking being is free to supervise its impulses, drives, and inclinations and is responsible for the outcome. This is what makes us unique and what puts us into the position of worrying about who and what we are, something other animals and machines evidently do not do. Whether this is wonderful or not is not the issue here. All that needs to be noted is that our humanity does leave us with certain unique attributes, and it is pretty much pointless to constantly attempt to deny it.

Now, when computers and nonhuman animals begin, all on their own initiative, to put on conferences about human intelligence, animal rights, or other controversial topics, when they start up what for them would be the equivalent of laboratories and scholarly journals exploring these issues just as human beings do now, perhaps then we can begin to seriously consider that they have come to be pretty much like us and that our uniqueness in nature has disappeared.

10

POLITICS AND GENEROSITY

What are the political prerequisites of the flourishing of the virtue of generosity? Many seem to believe that a society in which generosity flourishes would need to be a rather robust welfare state. I want to show, however, that to the contrary, it is an individualist, libertarian legal order that is most conducive to the exercise of this virtue. Furthermore, such an order is more conducive to the flourishing of all the moral virtues. But I single out the virtue of generosity because it is of the greatest concern to those – among them the formerly libertarian political philosopher Robert Nozick[1] – who finds such a legal lacking in compassion.

GENEROSITY

To start with, we need to see what generosity is. First, a generous person is not fighting to restrain some stingy inclination, needing to withstand the temptation to be greedy. Rather, such a person is acting, as it were, from second nature, spontaneously. Generosity would, then, be a trait that either is "bred into" someone – for example, by parents – or is cultivated by a person. Under appropriate circumstances and without much effort, such a person would engage in conduct that is helpful (but not by right due) to others.

Generosity is a character trait, not a matter of proximate deliberate choice. Perhaps more than other traits with possible moral ramifications, it comes close to retaining the sort of status that for Aristotle all the virtues had. They were supposed to be part of one's personality, or deeply ingrained character traits, albeit the result of deliberation at some prior point in time. Generous, honest, temperate, or courageous conduct was supposed to occur as a matter of course, as a routine element of the good human being, even though it had to be cultivated through right reason. Even now we view generosity and other virtues along such lines.

GENEROSITY IS NOT A DUTY

A generous person is not doing others good because duty requires this. Morality is often construed in terms of duties, especially duties toward other persons. But duties are the sort of moral prescriptions that place one at odds with one's inclinations. When people act fairly, for example, they act from duty to make sure all get the same from goods they may have to distribute, especially when they would rather keep all or indulge in prejudice. Fairness is closer to a duty than to a virtue, involving quite elaborate calculations and discipline at the time of its practice so as to decide who gets how much of what.

GENEROSITY AS A MORAL VIRTUE

How can generosity be both a trait of personality and a moral virtue? I take it here that virtues can exist; that is, I will assume a framework for understanding human life that does not rule out virtues as habituated and cultivated traits that guide the life of the agent toward its own excellence. If virtues can exist, then generosity would be that trait, or inclination toward action, that steers one to benefit other persons, or indeed anything that is capable of being benefited. (One could be generous toward animals.) Generosity can be a virtue if its cultivation is something over which the agent has significant control.

But why would generosity be such a trait? Why would being inclined to benefit others amount to a trait that steers one toward one's own excellence? Is there not a paradox in this? To enhance one's own excellence, one might want to be prudent, even self-interested, but why generous? Would that not be precisely a trait that steers one away from one's own enhancement of life and toward someone else's?

To be able to appreciate that generosity is at once a trait guiding one toward benefiting others and a mode of self-enhancement, or striving for one's own excellence, it is necessary to consider human nature. The following section is a summary of more detailed discussions in previous chapters, particularly Chapters 1 and 4.

HUMAN NATURE

The nature of something is the attributes the thing must have to be what it is. One of the attributes of humans is that they are thinking animals. To function well as human beings, they must think. This could change, but simply because a change *might* occur, it does not follow that it will.[2] It is possible that human nature has been roughly the same for very long indeed and that no good reason exists to expect that it will change. (The notion, found in the Sartrean version of existentialism, that human beings lack a nature but can create one for themselves is, I think, misguided: it rests on a conception of the nature of something as necessarily determinate or petrified, not capable of consisting of the capacity to develop on its own. In contrast, Aristotle's conception of humans as rational animals clearly allows for creative development, self-directedness.)

GENEROSITY AND HUMAN NATURE

Since humans are thinking animals, they can greatly enhance their lives through interaction with others. Generosity is doing what is helpful to other persons, mostly in those circles in which others are reasonably well known to the generous person. The beneficiaries of generous conduct are not benefiting from some fulfillment of obligation – for example, the obligation that parents have to care for their children or that parties to a contract have to honor the terms of the contract. Rather, the beneficiaries are benefiting from a respect bearing on their individual circumstances – what they might enjoy, need, want, and so forth. To know that another person enjoys, needs, or wants certain things, one must know the person reasonably well. The more institutional forms of generosity have acquired the distinct designation of philanthropy or humanitarianism.

Generosity, then, is a good trait because with it we are more at home with the world, given what we are and ought to choose to become. By bestowing upon some others – ones we know well enough to benefit as a matter of our second nature, almost "on the run" or automatically – various goods, such as time we have to spare, skills they could use, some article of value, or money, we contribute to the positive upkeep and improvement of our community. We may not be making extreme sacrifices by being generous, but we are going beyond the call of duty. We contribute with this to an atmosphere of congeniality.

VIRTUES AND GOOD ACTIONS

Does what has been said thus far imply that generosity is always going to be something worthwhile, something that invariably vindicates or merits its habituation or cultivation? No. Generosity can be extended indiscriminately. Since it is an inclination, there can be unusual circumstances for which a generous person may not be prepared. In those cases, one could be "generous to a fault." Of course, if we are indiscriminate, negligent, or reckless in how we extend ourselves toward others – if we keep giving or helping with what harms others or give to or help bad people – then our trait can no longer qualify as a virtue at all. We will be regarded as gullible, foolhardy, irrational, albeit perhaps generous. This is why generosity is not always a virtue.

This suggests that for generosity to be a virtue, it needs to be accompanied by some other virtues that will give generosity its needed limits. And from a moral perspective that concentrates on virtues, it is clear enough that generosity will not by itself ensure a successful, good human life. We all require other virtues, or moral characteristics. Furthermore, quite possibly it is insufficient for a successful, good human life to rely entirely on our virtues, since once they have been cultivated, these are more or less automatic in the way they guide us. To deal with novel or surprising situations, we need to cognitively monitor our nearly automatic actions flowing from virtuous traits.

INDIVIDUALITY AND THE VIRTUES

To conduct oneself morally, to follow the dictates of the virtues and other ethical principles, is to choose to live well. This choice may gain much from community supports – parents, neighbors, idols, leaders, ministers, friends. But in the last analysis, it is morally significant only if *it is the choice of the agent who is engaging in the moral conduct at issue.*

While in many spheres men and women live by other than total self-reliance, in their moral lives – as it is put at times, in their soul of souls – they are alone. Here is where they come off as better or worse human beings. For this to be possible in society, there must be a certain "distance" between individuals, at least once they have reached adulthood. There must be individual sovereignty. It does not require physical separateness or isolation, as some might imagine, only a knowledge of where one's sphere of moral jurisdiction lies. Within that sphere, one is responsible for one's choices and the ensuing conduct and its consequences – such notions as liability, accountability, and culpability testify to our familiarity with this fact about human beings. And if that sphere is invaded, moral responsibility gets very confusing – a type of tragedy of the commons is generated, just as when people do not know where the physical limits of their jurisdiction lie and start getting in each other's way, even without actually choosing to. Cooperation, friendship, neighborliness, and so forth all gain their human quality from being in part a product of ever so subtle yet individual choice, of ever so tacit yet personal decision.[3]

Basic individual human rights spell out the conditions for cooperation (and needed mutual compliance) among nonintimate adults. They are principles that spell out the basic, most fundamental moral requirements of human community life. (They are, of course, derived from more basic moral principles that spell out how human beings ought to live as individuals in or out of society.)

RIGHTS AS SOCIAL GUIDELINES

Individuals have rights to life, liberty, and property – which is to say, no one in society may murder, kidnap, assault, or steal from another. These are negative rights – they impose on others the enforceable duty, or legal obligation, not to

121

act in certain ways, not to invade other people's private domains. Positive rights, in turn, are supposed to spell out duties to provide some service to the rightsholder. But positive rights are not basic rights. They arise from the explicit or implicit consent of individuals – for example, contract or reproduction.

This is not the place to defend the claim that basic human, individual rights are all negative – I have addressed the topic elsewhere more fully than can be done here.[4] But a few points need to be offered to explain the position since there is in our time considerable sympathy for the view that basic rights ought to include some positive rights, for example, the right to health care, social security, or education. The point of these remarks is to stress that these are benefits but not basic rights, since they limit personal jurisdiction in the sphere of choosing or neglecting to choose to do what is right, exactly what basic rights exist to enable us to preserve in a social context.

The reason basic rights are negative is that their function is to provide adult persons with a sphere of moral jurisdiction. This is due them because of their moral nature, because they have moral tasks in life that they ought to fulfill. Intruding on their sphere of moral jurisdiction would amount to thwarting their moral agency. And basic rights spell out where the conduct of others would or would not amount to intrusion. That is why the "border" analogy is useful, even if it runs the risk of giving a physical image of a person's sphere of moral authority. Moral agents require borders around them so as to know what their responsibilities are and where others must ultimately leave decisions up to them.

Now, the above position is one that many philosophers find controversial. And since the claim plays a vital role in my argument, it deserves some development. Let me note first that if someone is forced to behave in a way that morality would require, that person cannot take credit for the conduct involved. One might argue, of course, that the person would have chosen the behavior, so credit may be taken. But this kind of counterfactual claim is not defensible in this case unless there is a history of the person having chosen to behave in the fashion at issue; that is, any credit due to forced behavior is parasitic on prior credit due to unforced behavior.

If one's negative rights – for example, the right to private property – are violated, one's sphere of jurisdiction is diminished. One has to engage in conduct that others have a decisive influence upon – one may require permission, support, resources, and so forth from some group or from the society. The explanation of the action is not oneself but oneself plus all these others. Of course, one often finds oneself blamed or praised for conduct taken in others' company – for example, an orchestra misinterprets a composer's music, a corporation misinvests stockholders' funds, a team plays out a wonderful strategy, or a military squadron is victorious over a vicious enemy. Members of these groups are often blamed or praised.

Yet the members usually join these groups or are assumed to share the groups' objectives or commitments. Indeed, when this is in doubt – as, for example, with drafted soldiers who belong to the squadron – so does the blame or praise become doubtful. In the most extreme case, slaves simply cannot be blamed or praised for the order they carry out (unless, of course, they are not *de facto* slaves at all and were at least *de facto* free to avoid those orders).

It seems, then, that if one does not enjoy sovereignty in the moral realm – in the sphere of both reaching moral conclusions and implementing these in action – the notion that one may be morally appraised seems to be undermined. Since negative rights – to life, liberty, and property – secure the sphere of sovereignty for each person (in that they are the "borders" around a person within which he or she is sole ruler) and since such sovereignty is essential to full moral agency, the virtues that depend on moral agency would seem clearly to require respect for such negative rights.

Private property rights are, of course, the most controversial case in point. Such rights exclude others from sharing in the wealth they might be able to make very good use of and may well need for their very survival in some circumstances. At times, then, private property rights can be contributory to situations that seem morally repugnant. With private property rights intact, someone can freely choose to be callous, insensitive, heartless, ungenerous, and uncharitable.

Yet private property rights are also the concrete expression – the practical manifestation – of the rights to life and liberty. If I have the right to be free to worship but not the right to own what we might call the props for worship (or use some that other people own), what does my freedom to worship come to in practice? Nothing. If I have the right to express myself in print – as in reference to a free press – but lack the right to own a printing press, paper, distribution facilities, and so forth, again, what is the practical import of my right? Nothing. (This seems to be quite evident in such systems as the former Soviet Union, where the state, or the collective, owned the major means of production and individuals were dependent on the authorities representing the collective when they wished to publish something.)

Let me just spell out a possible scenario in which the above points would be manifest. If Sam has a sphere of moral authority, and this sphere is indeed respected and protected, it will be Sam's task to do what is right and abstain from doing what is wrong in his life. For example, if Sam should, morally, develop his artistic talents, it needs to be left up to Sam whether to do this or not. It must be Sam's decision to do or not to do the act. If Judy were to force Sam to enter art school, say by threatening to harm Sam, then even if Sam became a successful artist, he could not take credit for the decision to pursue art. It might seem that Judy could, although it is not she who became the great artist but Sam. It is, first of all, wrong for Judy to thwart Sam's chances for doing the morally right act (even though Judy also prevented Sam from losing the credit or gaining blame for a bad decision).

Judy's basic moral responsibility toward Sam, a stranger to whom she is not bound by other moral considerations, such as contract, parental obligation, or fraternity, is to refrain from intruding on him. Sam has basic rights to life, liberty, and property, and it would be wrong for Judy to violate these rights, even if she has a correct view of the objectives Sam should pursue. It is a denial of Sam's moral agency by Judy, an assault on Sam's dignity as a human being and moral agent, to substitute Judy's decision for Sam's in these kinds of matters.

To put it another way for my purposes, there can be many ways for Sam to benefit from Judy. But here, again, whether Judy will impart them or not is a matter for her to decide, even if it is evident enough to others that she ought to impart them. Sam has no right to such benefits, only to Judy's abstaining from intruding upon him.

Now, if Sam's sphere of sovereignty is unspecified or indeed does not exist at all, Judy will not be able to know what limits of action apply to her *vis-à-vis* Sam. Is Sam's body at Judy's disposal to use? Sam's skill for producing music? A chair that Sam made out of wood he found in a wilderness where no one had laid claim to any of the raw materials? (It is possible that the famous tragedy of the commons results largely from this indeterminacy of a person's sphere of sovereignty; with everyone eager to attain various worthy goals, it is no wonder that without borders there is overuse of resources.)

I do not wish to suggest by this example something Marx focused on, namely, that "the right of many to property is the right to enjoy his possessions and dispose of the same arbitrarily, without regard for other men, independently of society, the right of selfishness."[5] Persons with the right to private property do indeed have the right to "dispose of [property] arbitrarily," but by no means need to do so. Indeed, if they do so, they may soon be rid of the property they have a right to – it may go to waste.

There is much more that could be said in support of basic rights, including whether they can be positive. (For more on private property rights, see Chapter 5.) Suffice it to add here that no more than the requirement to observe the negative individual human rights (the rights to life, liberty, and property) may be forced upon strangers as they relate to each other. That is because the rest of what they should do must lie within their own jurisdiction if they are to enjoy their full moral agency. It pertains to them, to their own moral space, whereas respect of everyone's negative rights is required for the preservation of the moral space of everyone. And to avoid the problems that stem from the occasional recalcitrants, institutions to secure the rights in question should be established – ergo, government. (The "should" here comes from the imperative that one ought to do what makes it possible for one to flourish as an individual human being. To be prudent about the debilitating harm others can do to one is a clear example of a kind of virtuous conduct, namely, prudence.)

RIGHTS AND GENEROSITY

How does all this apply to our topic, generosity? We must note, first of all, how respect for rights is not in the same moral category as the practice of the virtues.

When another is owed something by right – for example, not to be killed or kidnapped, or the fulfillment of the terms of some special relationship, such as a contract or parental guardianship – granting what is owed is not a matter of generosity or, indeed, a matter of practicing some other virtue. While there is an element of goodness toward others involved in respect for their rights, it is the acknowledgment of the other as a person. Furthermore, it is also the kind of conduct that may be compelled when it is not granted freely. The reason is that the very act of interacting with other human beings, who are rational moral agents, implies that one is committed to living by certain standards that respect their nature as rational moral agents – including the fact that they ought to protect their own moral sovereignty.

Respecting others' rights does not lack moral content, but that content must be traced back to the choice to be a peaceful participant in human community life. That content enters by way of a deliberate decision to do the right thing, to act in line with certain principles of human interaction. And when one is compelled to abide by that deliberate decision, the compulsion is justified because it is akin to the extraction of a debt that is due or the enforcement of a contract that is binding, in both cases by the explicit or at least tacit choice of the agent being compelled.

We may then put the point generally: generosity requires a kind of community life in which one's sovereignty is acknowledged – that is, where individuals have jurisdiction over themselves, including their belongings. Of course, while it may not be officially acknowledged, as long as one's sovereignty is recognized by oneself and one's fellows, even if only tacitly, the opportunity for virtuous and thus generous conduct exists. The point is that moral sovereignty[6] must be a fact that is taken to be a fact by the relevant parties – those who could act on that fact or act in defiance of it.

Furthermore, let us assume that moral sovereignty is impossible for us – that we relate to our society or to humanity as a whole in the fashion our arms, ears, and lips relate to each of us as we understand ourselves in commonsense terms. If that were true, we would possess no moral virtues at all, since morality is possible only where the possibility of and capacity for initiating some choices are also present. One does not praise one's arm for a good discus throw, except figuratively. One's eyes are not given moral credit for having correctly detected a disease, even if the eyes played a role in that detection. In short, if we were part of a collective whole, we could not be regarded as moral agents and our good traits would not be moral virtues.

Let us consider a person who is not a sovereign, who is merely a part of a tribe or a state. That person has nothing personal to give, to contribute for the benefit of another – including labor, time, property, and talents. If we were really merely elements of a larger whole – in Marx's terms, elements of the "organic body" of humanity[7] – there would be no opportunity for any of us to choose to give or to cultivate a giving character. We would have nothing of our own, and we would have no jurisdictional authority over anything of our own.

125

Some might consider this unfair – didn't Marx, after all, make room for at least personal property for everyone?[8] Given that we do have the right to personal property, would this not make room for generosity within a Marxist collectivist system? Was he not, in fact, more of an individualist than many give him credit for, thus making ample room for morality within his framework?

Two objections face this response. First, the line of demarcation between private and personal property is hopeless in Marxian theory. If the major means of production are public property, then human labor is public property. So the scope of public jurisdiction is in principle unlimited. An artist's life could not escape its borders, because what the artist produces could turn out to be major, depending on how people receive it.

Second, if one makes use of the standard idea that personal property is not a significant "means of production," which is why one could have an individual right to such property in the first place, its social uses are nil. So one would have no reason to be generous with such property – no one else could make any good use of it. And the second that personal property acquired social usefulness, it would change from personal property to society's property. Although it may appear that one is generous mostly with personal possessions, that sort of generosity – minor gift giving – is not what we are concerned with in exploring whether generosity is likely to make a difference in different kinds of sociopolitical systems. Philanthropy is a significant sort of generosity and certainly goes way beyond giving away one's used clothes or household appliances. Such generosity requires the entire range of private property associated with capitalism, not just what Marxists would allow as socialist personal property.

Furthermore, generosity is irrelevant in a community wherein everything important is to be shared, where it is a built-in obligation of human life to proceed along communitarian lines, ones that impose positive rights on all and do not leave the mutual benefiting from riches to personal virtue. Marx's conception of the human community follows closely the tribalist model wherein no individuality is accepted.[9] Marx globalizes tribalism. Generosity, however, assumes that individuals have lives of their own and should sometimes reach out toward others but are not obligated to do so.

INSTITUTIONAL GENEROSITY

In complex social circumstances, men and women will not engage in generous conduct the same way they would in simple social settings. When people who share goals and values live scattered about the country, connected only by complicated technology, their ways of acting generously will differ from those of people living in a medieval village. Just as giving some seed to a neighboring farmer in times of bad harvest could be an act of generosity, sending a copy of the phone numbers of prospective customers to a fellow merchant by way of one's modem could be an act of generosity in the twenty-first century.

But there is more to it than the technology. Institutional generosity emerges as a process of trust among persons interested in promoting ends that are of mutual value – some acting as donors, others as volunteers, yet others as professionals with the requisite skills. Philanthropy can be one outgrowth of this. After learning that there are deserving persons with whom one shares an interest in some political, artistic, literary, environmental, or other cause, one might elect to choose an intermediary to disburse some valued help. Contributing to a wildlife fund that will enable those most expert at the task to perform most effectively is an example of such extended, or institutional, generosity.

This may appear to contradict the nondeliberative, spontaneous character of generosity discussed earlier. Surely, writing out a check each month and mailing it off to some organization would seem to be (a) deliberative and (b) impersonal. Yet this is only an appearance. The choice to give to either an intimate or a remote beneficiary could well be something spontaneous, the result of one's second nature to be alert to opportunities that call forth one's help and support. And the knowledge of shared values would make someone remote more familiar than strangers whose values and goals one does not know.

THE GENEROUS COMMONWEALTH

Without (the recognition of) the moral sovereignty of human individuals, generosity would appear not to be possible. It could only manifest itself in occasional rebellion against the general social structure, as when in communism someone acts generously but thereby must break the rule of communal ownership. Even in voluntary communes, generosity – special benevolent outreach toward another person – would have to be viewed with suspicion since it might tend to undermine the disciplined prior obligation of all toward the whole! Whatever the merits of such communal moral living, this shows at least that generosity would not be a virtue under such a system. It is incompatible with any kind of actual collectivism – that is, a system where the sovereignty of the individual is effectively rejected in favor of total subservience to some common purpose – whether freely accepted or imposed. The lack of generosity would generate not so much particularized guilt but lack of self-esteem on the part of those who would not have opportunities to be generous.

All of the virtues require effective individual sovereignty, because they presuppose the moral initiative of the individual person who possesses or lacks them. But it is especially important for my purposes, which include stressing the appropriateness of a capitalist polity, that no room would be left for generosity – the choice to benefit others with one's skills, belongings, and so forth – without a system that secures one's sovereignty in choosing who will benefit from actions one undertakes. The very impetus for wishing to supersede or abolish capitalism seems often to be a belief that it fails to involve sufficient generosity and benevolence and cultivates, instead, greed and profit seeking. Yet if my argument is right, a capitalist system is actually required for generosity to flourish.

Both direct and extended generosity presuppose a human community in which a significant degree of personal sovereignty is extant. Such a culture would also have to include a significant degree of respect for a system of stable private property rights. The reason is that if one had no decisive control over some valued items from which others can benefit, one would have no way to make the personal decision to extend such benefit to others.

Such a system would have to be extensive enough to permit the development of habits of ownership of valued skills, items, time, and so forth on the part of individuals. Only with such a stable system of private property rights could generosity be expected to become part of the character of members of the community.

INTEGRITY AND GENEROSITY

Virtuous generosity requires support from a polity that does not usurp personal virtue and a community that does not expect such usurpation to take the place of personal virtue. As already noted, this implies that the neglect of generosity by someone would have to be politically but not morally tolerated – it is being generous to a fault to tolerate unexplained lack of generosity in many others. Morally, a lack of generosity is wrong unless it is justified by exceptional circumstances, such as illness or catastrophe.

Yet moral virtues are matters of volition – as they must be so as to constitute a source of moral credit or blame for a person. They can only be unforced attitudes, not regimented behaviors. So political tolerance of lack of generosity would be proper. This means that no one – no Robin Hood or government – would act properly by banning lack of generosity. This is so even as moral tolerance of this lack would be wrong. (This is well recognized in the case of journalism and intellectual conduct. Bad reporting should be morally criticized, from the position of journalistic ethics, but not censored. And bad arguments ought to be condemned but not legally forbidden.)

So it seems that a classical–liberal social order, one that recognizes individual sovereignty, is most conducive to the possibility of generosity. But is it unreasonable to focus exclusively on personal virtue when discussing the question of the possible generosity of a polity? It has already been noted that there is ample room for institutional generosity in a good human community. Firms, clubs, churches, schools, and other institutions may, by virtue of being managed by human beings themselves capable of virtue, institute more or less generous policies in the appropriate sphere of their organization's operations. Why not extend this possibility to government?

Here are some initial reasons why such extension might not be appropriate, although we will have to see whether these are decisive. One reason is that there is a serious danger to the integrity of a legal administration if its administrators yield to considerations of generosity in how they carry out their duties. The appropriate analogy would be the way a referee or judge behaves at an athletic event. When judging a diving competition or refereeing a tennis tournament, those who are entrusted with the responsibility for judging correctly and faithfully – that is, by strict adherence to the standards – have no option to interject some other consideration, such as generosity or kindness. The integrity of the role demands that only what is called for from the position being held – judge, referee, umpire – be taken as a guide to conduct. The same may be said for the role of teachers as graders, for the role of parents as fair-minded adjudicators of sibling disputes, and so forth.

GENEROSITY VERSUS FAIRNESS

Of course, if someone in an athletic contest is hurt, a referee who has first-aid skills might offer help. That could be a gesture of generosity that in no way compromises the role of referee. And when a doctor helps a patient in some issue unrelated to medicine, say, in providing financial advice or clues as to where one might find the best real-estate agent in town, there is generosity, but not at the expense of duty or professional responsibility. But if in the course of an operation the surgeon were to leave so as to help some other patient with some personal or even professional problem, it is very likely – barring some peculiar circumstances – that a breach of duty would ensue.

Similarly, when a police officer walking a beat is asked for directions by a lost person, a helpful and courteous response, provided no duty is being neglected or breached, would by no means involve anything inappropriate. And this gives us a clue as to the nature of generosity on the part of governments.

The central issue is what governments are for. For a government, there is an especially crucial issue at stake with extending itself in special ways toward some members of the public but not toward others. That is especially so if even a modicum of democratic theory of government is sound. Fairness is a vital virtue of governments, since these organizations are paid by the entire membership of the community. Any special treatment would very likely imply resources used for some citizens that would be taken from the resources of all citizens.

Consider, as a rather extreme case of this, deficit spending, a way to finance certain services for which no revenues have been found. This may be deemed a generous thing to do, but in fact, the act involves breach of duty to those who later will have to repay the debt and yet have had no say about how to allocate what they will be paying into the treasury.

EMERGENCY AND GENEROSITY

We have characterized the virtue of generosity as a kind of trait that inclines one to extend oneself toward benefiting others in a spontaneous fashion, except for some of its more remote manifestations – that is, through institutions. We have also noted that generosity is a virtue when its development and practice are a matter of human choice. As such, it requires the presence of a community in which the sovereignty of individuals is granted and respected. That sovereignty, in turn, implies the institution of the right to private property, since to make decisive and responsible choices, a person needs to act within a determinate realm of nature, a realm – great or small – within which that person alone chooses what will happen.

Unless there is widespread voluntary acknowledgment of such sovereignty and suitable conduct that accommodates it, a community must at least have this sovereignty of individual human beings vigorously protected. This is necessary for any virtue to flourish, but especially for generosity because of its involvement with the disposition of what persons own, including their labor, skills, property, and labor (or life) time.

Can governments themselves ever be morally obliged to be generous? Would this not undercut their own rather particular mission of maintaining and preserving justice? Would it not make them into wealth redistributors and thus instruments of regimentation of human action that would impede the possibility of individual and voluntary virtuous conduct? Furthermore, if governments need to remain scrupulously fair in the performance of their primary mission, how could they remain fair while also extending themselves generously toward some people in society? If the duty of fairness is so vital in government, and if generosity consumes resources and extending it would generally involve favoring some citizens over others, would not all cases of generosity involve some breach of duty?

No. This is because even for a government, there are possibilities for extending oneself without breach of duty, as spontaneously as this is possible for an institution. A voluntarily funded government could enter the picture in times of far-reaching catastrophes – earthquakes, floods, and so forth – when the resources of the private charitable institutions were stretched to their limits. But it would enter not as a matter of its primary obligation or job description, but rather as a gesture of good will toward persons in need of emergency services. (And provisions might be made in society that would render it superfluous for governments ever to leave their posts, as it were.) Just as a police officer would help an elderly person who has fallen down – though not, probably while in pursuit of a criminal – so a government could probably legitimately extend itself, temporarily, for purposes of assisting someone or some group in dire need.

The point here is not to describe in full the relationship between the virtue of generosity and the precise character of good government. What I wanted to do is to indicate how a conception of generosity as a vital human virtue would relate to a conception of a good polity that stands ready to preserve the conditions required for the development and exercise of that virtue.[10]

11

UNDERSTANDING EASTERN EUROPEAN DEVELOPMENTS

INTRODUCTION: TWO COMPETING PERSPECTIVES

I will consider here some of the ways in which we might understand recent developments throughout Eastern Europe, including the former Soviet Union. I will explore whether we might more sensibly see these developments within the framework of a kind of Marxian analysis or within that of a classical–individualist one.

To put the matter briefly, it could be argued that what has occurred can be best understood as a result of a mistaken view of the role of the Soviet Union in the development of humanity. Leaders of the Soviet Union, starting with Lenin, claimed that their society was instantiating the course of human history predicted by Karl Marx. The Soviet Union was supposed to have been the vanguard of the proletariat on the historically necessitated march toward communism. A more refined Marxian analysis, however, might dispute this and claim that in fact, the Soviet Union instantiated simply a disguised feudal system and was by no means ready to play the role claimed for it by Soviet Marxists. Accordingly, now that the feudal system of greater Russia has reached its culmination, the time has come for that society to turn itself into a largely capitalist society. Once this capitalist phase has played itself out, the time will come to change into a bona fide socialist system, one that will have the benefit of the previous capitalist productive phase on which to base its political and economic developments.

That is one scenario. The other is that whether socialism follows feudalism or capitalism is irrelevant – it is a hopeless political economy. In fact, the assumptions of Marxian analysis are wrong – humanity is not an "organic whole," as Marx claimed,[1] and it is not on a historical march toward its alleged maturity, namely, communism. Efforts to direct it along such a path must of necessity fail and result in the kind of tyranny that the Soviet Union exhibited, not because the capitalist phase was skipped and socialism was tried prematurely, but because socialism in any of its incarnations is an unsuitable political economy for human community life.

There is some evidence – to the extent that one can speak of evidence

132

within a historical discussion – for both ways of understanding current affairs in Eastern Europe. Nevertheless, this chapter will argue that the latter is the more rational perspective.

THE MARXIAN ANALYSIS OF EASTERN EUROPEAN DEVELOPMENTS

In 1882 Karl Marx wrote a new preface to the Russian edition of *The Communist Manifesto*, in which he answered a question posed to him by some Russian revolutionaries. Here is the question and Marx's answer to it:

> Now the question is: Can the Russian *obshchina* [village community], though greatly undermined, yet a form of the primeval common ownership of land, pass directly to the higher form of communist common ownership? Or, on the contrary, must it first pass through the same process of dissolution as constitutes the historical evolution of the West?
>
> The only answer to the possibility today is this: If the Russian Revolution becomes the signal for a proletarian revolution in the West, so that both complement each other, the present Russian common ownership of land may serve as the starting-point for a communist development.[2]

This may seem at first a rather straightforward passage from Marx. Yet there is controversy about it. The late Sidney Hook, for one, held that it was of no great significance.[3] Yet it seems that there is a great deal to this passage, and that possibility deserves some discussion.

Marx appears to be saying that a Russian revolution will not "serve as the starting-point for a communist development" unless it "becomes the signal for a proletarian revolution in the West." What may we understand by this? If we keep in mind that Marxian socialist revolutionary theory posited the need for an international revolutionary development – and if we also keep in mind Marx's emphatic insistence that prior to moving on to any new historical phase, the previous stage of development must be fully realized – it becomes clear that Marx believed that the Russian revolution must be exported to be successful.

Clearly, given Marx's own assessment that "the Russian *obshchina* [village community], though greatly undermined, [is] a form of the primeval common ownership of land," Marx could not have believed that communism could be realized within the borders of greater Russia. Russia simply was not ready – it had no prior capitalist system, which Marx deemed absolutely necessary for future socialist and communist developments. As Marx noted, "the economists have been proving for fifty years and more that socialism cannot abolish poverty, *which has its basis in nature*, but can only make it *general*, distribute it simultaneously over the whole surface of society!"[4] It is capitalism that abolishes poverty.

So unless Russia's revolution were to spread to those lands where capitalism had gained a solid foothold, its socialism and communism would not materialize in the benign fashion Marx had envisioned, as follow-up stages of capitalism. It is therefore clear that Marx did not see any justification for a Russian revolution that would attempt to introduce socialism without at the same time expanding the process throughout those portions of the globe that had already experienced substantial capitalist developments.

It is not so difficult now to see that once the attempt by the Soviet Union to spread its kind of political economy across the globe had not come to fruition – just witness the most recent failures in Africa, Latin America, and, especially, the West – the socialist experiment within its borders had to be construed as a failure in Marxian theory itself.

Thus current Eastern European developments need by no means strike a blow against a Marxian conception of human history. All they need to signify is that there really was no genuine Marxian revolution in the Soviet Union. Instead, what was labeled by Soviet Marxist wishful thinkers as Marxist–Leninist socialism has to be thought of, in authentic Marxian terms, as merely nominal. In fact, the Soviet Union amounted to only a somewhat modernized feudal system that, in Marx's own terms, could at best attempt to "distribute [poverty] simultaneously over the whole surface of society" and at worst use the term "socialism" as a cover for a kind of (albeit modernized) feudal rule.

Current developments in the former Soviet Union, involving substantial transformation toward a relatively free market economy, can thus be seen in Marxian terms as no more than the natural and necessary advance from feudalism to bourgeois capitalism. When Abel Aganbegyan, president of the Soviet Academy of National Economy, claims, "The old system was a bad system. Everyone knows that,"[5] it need by no means be taken as a rejection of Marxism. Quite the contrary. It can be taken as a realization that the past seventy years of Marxist–Leninist rhetoric had been wishful thinking, at best, or a hoax, more probably. Kings, caesars, pharaohs, czars, dictators, and similar tyrants have always needed some kind of ploy for deceiving the public. The "big lie" theory of tyrannical leadership had been spelled out and indeed rationalized by Plato, and it would be no major amendment of Marxian analysis to allow for it in recent Soviet history. Once religious calls for submission to tyranny had lost their plausibility, the more secular message and promise of Marxist–Leninist rhetoric would naturally come in handy to win some support from the peoples of the diverse Soviet republics in the effort to uphold the unity of imperial Russia.

But of course, this had to come to an end, as Marx could foresee very well, since without capitalism, socialism simply socializes poverty. And in the absence of a successful internationalization of the purported revolution, the

Bolsheviks could ultimately lay claim to nothing much more than a putsch, a violent change of the ruling group in greater Russia. There was very little that was genuinely revolutionary about the change – that is, it did not fundamentally alter the principles of political economy.

Furthermore, the willingness of the Soviet ruling elite to rid itself of its Eastern European satellites can also be understood in Marxian terms. This would be little more than a replay of the decolonization of many other world powers in the wake of bourgeois developments. Eastern Europe has experienced a bourgeois revolution – a turn toward democracy and away from the modern rendition of feudal rule. Its subsequent confusion, leaning toward a substantially market economy and parliamentary or constitutional democracy, parallels what occurred over a century ago in Western Europe. With the realization that the Soviet Union could not engineer a worldwide socialist revolution without a substantial capitalist development, there was no need to hang on to Eastern Europe in any political sense. Market developments will establish the kind of interdependence that characterizes the "world market," or economy of "civil societies," with their oppressive "world-historical activity."[6]

Finally, it could also be argued from a Marxian framework that the true "overthrow of the existing state of society by the communist revolution . . . and the abolition of private property which is identical with it"[7] are right on course. There is little doubt that the Marxian analysis has serious plausibility when one considers that most Western capitalist societies are transforming themselves into democratic socialist states; when it is recognized that the institution of the right to private property is nowhere intact any longer (what with all the regulations, at municipal, county, state, and federal levels); and when one understands that the law of contract has been nearly abolished and courts have usurped the authority of individuals and companies with doctrines of unconscionability, workers' rights, affirmative action, and environmental protection provisions – even as Eastern Europe is turning toward capitalism and privatization. Marx argued, in a speech given in Amsterdam on 8 September 1872, that in "America, England, and if I were more familiar with your institutions, I would perhaps also add Holland . . . the workers can attain their goal by peaceful means."[8] Certainly, there is not much in recent North American and Western European history that would count against the Marxian analysis.

Are we, then, to settle for the conclusion that Marx was, after all, correct, and that recent developments bode much less well for the ideas of classical liberalism than many today seem to believe?

THE INDIVIDUALIST ALTERNATIVE

If we consider the issue of political economy from a more philosophical than historical perspective, the individualist alternative becomes theoretically and practically much more attractive. The first matter to be touched on has to be the question of whether human individuals are in fact, as Marx believed, essentially "specie-beings." Marx held that the "human essence is the true collectivity of man."[9] His entire historical–materialist account of humanity's development is predicated on this conception of human nature. What this amounts to is the view that human beings are actually mere parts of what Marx saw as the "organic whole" of humanity.

In his collectivism, Karl Marx was not original. The idea that humanity is an organic whole, a concrete being, had its first major exposition in the writings of Plato. Plato's metaphysics posits two realms of reality: one ideal, the other visible (natural, actual, material). Those entities that occupy the ideal realm are superior in every way to those within the visible realm, although they are closely related. In particular, human individuals participate as copies in the ideal realm, where their perfect rendition exists. That perfect rendition in Plato is, of course, a universal intellectual entity, not something physical, as are all human individuals. And this concrete universal entity is far more important than all the individuals that participate in it and gain their imperfect identity through such participation.

Marx did not accept Plato's dualistic metaphysics, but he did retain the idea that humanity is a collective being and as such the locus of value. He said something very early in his life that seems never to have left his philosophy:

When we have chosen the vocation in which we can contribute most
to humanity, burdens cannot bend us because they are sacrifices for all.
Then we experience no meager, limited egoistic joy, but our happiness
belongs to millions, our deeds live on quietly but eternally effective,
and glowing tears of noble men will fall on our ashes.[10]

The collectivism we find in Marx shows, of course, the influence of Hegel and Feuerbach, the first providing the progressivist (dialectical) component, the latter the materialist (or naturalist). In short, Marx saw humanity as an organic whole on the march toward ultimate self-fulfillment, self-realization. This is what is unique in his philosophy and political economy. This is why he found the kind of bourgeois individualism evident in classical liberals such as Locke, Smith, Ricardo, and the American founding fathers a shallow worldview. To conceive of humanity as consisting in the individuals who comprise the human species instead of the whole species simply did not, for Marx, sufficiently comprehend the depths of the human condition. And the kind of individual liberty that came from such an "insipid" doctrine could not do justice to what humanity required in the way of political development and emancipation. Marx held that the classical liberals' version of "individual liberty is thus at the same time the most complete suppression of all individual liberty and total subjugation of individuality to social conditions which take the form of material forces."[11]

So before we can judge whether the Marxian analysis laid out earlier is sound, we need to ask whether this most fundamental aspect of Marxism is sound, for it is on this that the rest of Marxism rests. There is not much to the idea of the historical march of humanity toward communism, with capitalism and socialism as mere transitory stages, unless we can confidently hold with Marx that humanity is indeed the kind of organic whole that can be involved in a developmental process, somewhat as an individual living being can be said to be so involved, moving from infancy through childhood and adolescence, to young adulthood and maturity. Is humanity, in short, the collective whole that Marx thought it is?

I have examined this issue elsewhere and can only touch on it briefly in this chapter.[12] There are three main problems with the Marxian metaphysics.[13] First, the abolition of the human individual as an active choosing agent is unjustified and leads to results that are self-defeating even for Marxism itself. Marx was, after all, a very creative and original thinker who has managed to exert tremendous impact on the world. Even if we acknowledge that Marxism is not a sound worldview, we cannot deny that many human beings have read and been influenced by Marx's works and have gone on to make an impact on their world guided accordingly. Marx and his more inventive followers cannot be explained away solely by reference to economic determinants; they must be credited with individual initiative, the very capacity Marx denies to people when he sees them as captives of class consciousness and the forces of material production. It is interesting in this connection that most Marxists have tended to be intellectuals, not the workers who were supposed to be propelled to revolutionary action by their material circumstances. While Marx has never acknowledged entrepreneurial initiative in his political economy, in fact he himself – as well as many of his students – must be identified as perhaps one of the most brilliant political entrepreneurs.

Second, the metaphysical principle of the dialectic – even if applied only to human history rather than, as Engels would have wanted, to all of reality – is a species of that long hoped for but entirely elusive philosopher's dream, the philosopher's stone, the one key with which the secrets of the world may be unlocked. While it is undeniable that some major clashes in human history, such as the bourgeois revolutions and the ancient slave rebellions, have propelled subsequent generations of human beings in fruitful directions, to construe the principle of progress-through-dire-conflict as the sole motive force in human history is entirely unjustified. Many other principles – including many involving no conflict but negotiation and cooperation – have accomplished worthwhile goals for human beings. In short, the reductionism involved in Marxian dialectical analysis is not a sound methodology. History has shown that its assumptions about early human societies are not to be taken very seriously – for example, not even most early societies were ordered in economies of common ownership. Tribalism is by no means uniform throughout prehistoric human societies.

Third, the kind of materialism we find in Marxism is not justified as a satisfactory account of the nature of reality. Marx did not recognize that some natural beings had the capacity to cause their own actions. He saw human individuals as altogether too passive and thus could not imagine developments that did not follow a predictable course. Karl Popper was right to construe Marx's laws of history as invalid.[14] Human beings are not moved around by impersonal forces; they have the unique capacity to move themselves around, to judge and to fail to judge well, and to guide their conduct accordingly. This way, also, the progressivist bias in Marx's historical materialism has to be abandoned – it is, indeed, evident enough that human beings can have lives much worse than those of their forefathers, that human history does not always lead to improvements in the human condition.

It does appear that for at least the last three hundred or so years, human history has conformed closely enough to what Marx would have claimed and predicted. Does this mean that socialism is the wave of the future, that the developments in Eastern Europe and the Soviet Union do not at all contradict the Marxian analysis, even if we grant that the philosophical base of that analysis is unsound? This is just what some analytic Marxists – such as Jon Elster, John Roemer, and G. A. Cohen – might wish to say to those who believe that with recent global developments, Marxism must be consigned to the dustbin of defunct worldviews.

WHAT WE MAY SAY ABOUT THE FUTURE

A central feature of bourgeois philosophy, or "classical individualism," is that human life is not subject to predictions. This is because human individuals have the capacity to choose what they will do. Of course, one can estimate trends, based on well-established habits of mind and action, the constraints of nature and law, and so forth. But just how human beings will cope with the constraints, how they will come to terms with their own habits of mind and action, whether they will change their laws – those questions must not be answered prior to what they will actually do. Perhaps the most grievous fault of contemporary social science is to have built up expectations in us that ignore the above aspects of human life. Social engineering can go only so far – usually as far as the next person's intelligent way of preempting the engineers' plans.

Within these limits, what we can honestly say about Eastern Europe's future is the following: Many problems that were suppressed by the forty to seventy years of tyranny will come to the fore and will require management before this part of the world can be expected to catch up with the West. Of course, the West has its own share of problems to cope with. But there are many habits of mind no longer accepted as proper in the West – for example, racism, sexism, ethnic prejudice, and religious bigotry – that in the East tend still to be acceptable. There are also problems the East shares with the West, notably the disdain for commerce and the profession of business. The East can afford such attitudes far less than the West, where the momentum of the capitalist system still has some speed. As Janos Kornai notes, not even the limits imposed on capitalism by the welfare state can be tolerated in the Eastern countries, lest they slide into major economic decline.[15]

For a permanent social rejuvenation, the East needs to learn what the West has nearly forgotten, namely, that it is not enough to install capitalism as a utilitarian economic stopgap solution. What is needed is that the entire legal agenda of classical liberalism be enshrined within the culture. The classical–liberal concern for the fundamental rights of the individual to life, liberty, and property cannot be treated as a mere Band-Aid device to bail a society out of its past mistakes, only to be abandoned, once some measure of economic resurgence occurs, on the altar of the welfare state, with all of its wasteful, albeit at times well-intentioned, public policies in behalf of aspects of society that will not be upgraded without self-discipline, without the discipline imposed by the free market economy and the laws that uphold the principles of individual rights in all domains of community life.[16]

The most recent admission of the failure of economic collectivism – in the wake of the collapse of the Soviet bloc economy – comes from Professor Robert Heilbroner, one of socialism's most intelligent and loyal champions for the last several decades. As he puts it in his 1990 essay "After Communism":

> Ludwig von Mises . . . had written of the "impossibility" of socialism, arguing that no Central Planning Board could ever gather the enormous amount of information needed to create a workable economic system. . . . It turns out, of course, that Mises was right.[17]

But, not unlike previous thinkers who have seen various examples of the failure of some kind of perfectionist, idealist normative moral or political scheme, Heilbroner cannot quite say good-bye to his utopia. He notes that there are two ways it may remain something of a handy concept. First, it may leave us piecemeal social objectives to strive for – but these have always come in the context of essentially capitalist economic systems. Second, it may reemerge as the adjunct of the ecological movement. As Heilbroner puts it:

> [If] there is any single problem that will have to be faced by any socioeconomic order over the coming decades it is the problem of making our economic peace with the demands of the environment. Making that peace means insuring that the vital processes of material provisioning do not contaminate the green-blue film on which life itself depends. This imperative need not affect all social formations, but none so profoundly as capitalism.[18]

What is one to say about this new fear, a new problem allegedly too complicated for free men and women to handle? What kind of "insuring" does he have in mind apart from a strict protection of individuals against assault? What, besides insuring that no one assaults persons or property, via waste disposal and other types of dumping, is one supposed to embark upon for the sake of "the green-blue film on which life itself depends"? Certainly, no such insurance need involve abridging the principles of free trade or personal liberty. Certainly, to give these tasks to central planners or regulators is to insure nothing but mismanagement.

Has Heilbroner not heard of the "tragedy of the commons" so that he could imagine the environmental difficulties that face the collectivist social systems? It appears that he has not. Just consider how Heilbroner issues the "new" warning:

> It is, perhaps, possible that some of the institutions of capitalism – markets, dual realms of power, even private ownership of some kind of production – may be adapted to that new state of ecological vigilance, but, if so, they must be monitored, regulated, and contained to such a degree that it would be difficult to call the final social order capitalism.[19]

This somewhat new spin on what is essentially old-fashioned skepticism about free-market capitalism needs to be addressed. The first response is that there is no justification for any of this distrust of "the market," as opposed to trust in some scientific bureaucracy that is to do the monitoring, regulating, and containing that Heilbroner and so many other champions of regimentation are calling for. The market, despite how many employ the concept (as if it referred to some being that does this or that – for example, distributes goods, sets prices, allocates resources, and perpetrates failures), is simply a setting wherein human beings can embark upon various economic tasks without having bans, regulations, controls, or, in other words, prior restraints imposed upon them. To distrust such an arrangement betrays a habit of comparing the market system to some ideal and static construct developed in the mind of a theorist, an image of perfect order that is *somehow* being maintained. And it is postulated that government might manage to provide such maintenance, analogous to the way government is supposed to maintain equilibrium throughout the economy, the very thing von Mises and Hayek demonstrated cannot be done.

What Heilbroner and many, many others who are thus concerned seem to forget is that the problems of environmental degradation, as well as the ills in many other spheres of social life, stem from the tragedy of the commons. This is something Aristotle called attention to in his critique of Plato's limited communism, and it is also the thrust of Garrett Hardin's seminal essay on the subject.[20] Not surprisingly, the right answer to the question "How is the environment best kept safe?" is privatization on as large a scale as possible: individual moral responsibility, in a system of laws that encourages it, is the only rational hope one can have for taking care of any problem. The classical–individualist libertarian polity has the best chance of doing this. Collective ownership and responsibility are a hopeless gambit.[21]

Since, in fact, human community life is dynamic, all that can be done to make possible its optimum functioning is to identify and protect certain basic principles of law, or a constitution, that will keep the dynamics of the community within certain boundaries. Those boundaries are the ones that preserve and encourage individual responsibility, because human flourishing is predicated on the fostering of such responsibility. This is how the tragedy of the commons has the best chance of being avoided. (I use "has the best chance" advisedly: when human individuals are involved, even under the most suitable system, there is the real probability that some will fail to order their lives as they should. Yet this is true in spades for centrally run or regulated economies.) The central planning or even just regulating option will insure precisely the opposite, namely, the perpetuation of the tragedy of the commons, including the overuse and abuse of resources that are needed to protect the "green-blue film" about which Heilbroner is rightly concerned.

Put plainly, if men and women acting in the marketplace, guided by the rule of law based on their natural individual rights to life, liberty, and property, are incapable of standing up to the ecological challenges Heilbroner and many others in the environmentalist movement have in mind, there is no reason to think that those challenges could be met better by some new statist means. Why should ecologically minded bureaucrats be better motivated, more competent, and more virtuous than those motivated by a concern for the hungry, the unjustly treated, the poor, the artistically deprived, the uneducated masses, or the workers of the world? What is it that instills in Heilbroner – as well as other critics of the market, such as John Kenneth Galbraith, Robert Kuttner,[22] and William Greider[23] – the faith that those who wield the power of law making and enforcement are better men and women for purposes of taking care of whatever needs to be taken care of? Is a statist system's incentive structure more encouraging of human wisdom and decency than that of a system of rigorously protected individual rights to life, liberty, and property? Are its police less likely to be corrupted? Are its politicians and bureaucrats somehow innately more decent?

In fact, there is no reason to attribute to the members of any ecological politburo or central committee any characteristics more noble than those of the others who have made a try at coercing people into good behavior throughout human history. Any fair-minded, objective assessment of the relative success of free men and women – ones who act within the framework of what is often disparagingly referred to as bourgeois individualist rights, *vis-à-vis* the myriad tasks that face people in their communities – will have to conclude that the call for greater state involvement and the denigration of capitalism are based on idealistic visions, not on realistic appraisals of the comparative records of political systems.[24]

INDIVIDUALISM AND THE DEMISE OF MARXIST SOCIALISM

We have considered recent Eastern European developments from two very different perspectives, namely, Marxism and classical individualism (and classical liberalism). At first inspection, the former seems neater since it accords with what Marx himself identified as the scientific method.[25] Marx saw himself in the role of a "natural historian," someone who describes, explains, and predicts developments in a part of nature. In line with such an approach, it may appear that the most "scientific" approach to understanding Eastern European developments has to be Marxian.

But I have also argued that this approach is flawed – it rests on a collectivist metaphysics, denies human freedom of choice, and assumes progressivism. The alternative approach sees human beings as fundamentally individuals, not specie-beings or parts of an organic whole. Only a social order that does justice to their individuality is suitable for them. And the classical–liberal system, with its capitalist economy, based on personal property rights and motivated by prudence, makes better provisions for individuality than the socialist alternative.

Is such a system in accord with the common view of science as requiring that all events in nature are determined by abstract patterns of impersonal regularity? If we do not accept the quite unscientific thesis of reductionism – or, as some people have dubbed this, scientism – in which all human affairs must be fitted in with the mode of understanding derived from the physical sciences (even modified with the aid of the Hegelian dialectic), then this individualism, by doing greater justice to human nature than alternatives, is indeed scientifically sound. This does not yield a theory that may be used to prophesy social and economic developments. Instead, it gives us an approach that must leave open what will happen next in human affairs, including those in Eastern Europe. Human beings themselves, via their initiative or lack thereof, not historical laws, will determine the course of the future there and anywhere else.

This individualist approach, however, can say something about what course would be unwise to take. We have, accordingly, considered yet another suggestion for the adoption of socialist policies, this time in order to meet the challenges of environmental problems. I have argued that here, too, there is no reason to trust the coercive state in preference to the choices and actions of free men and women in the marketplace. That is as much as a science of human affairs can yield – some lessons from the past.

Most important, we need to note as a concluding point that the classical–liberal, capitalist system must not succumb to criticism based on the kind of morality that seems to drive much of social and political criticism in our time, namely, that human happiness on earth is somehow debasing and to be rejected in favor of self-renunciation, self-abnegation, self-sacrifice. Such a moral message can do nothing but damage the good turn of events in Eastern Europe and the former Soviet Union. It can only be hoped that sufficient thought will be spent on this issue so as to avoid such an eventuality.

12

INDIVIDUAL RIGHTS AND THE COMMON GOOD

The case of the environment

A TEST CASE FOR INDIVIDUALISM

It may be one of the most frequently cited general problems of political life in modern times, with traces of it found in every age: The supposed conflict between the rights of individuals and the welfare or good of the community as a whole. Examples of such alleged conflicts abound: Environmentalists stress that the power conferred upon individuals by the principles of the right to private property is extremely hazardous to the common welfare;[1] some criminologists stress that upholding the individual rights of the accused is threatening the good of the community by helping to leave criminals go unpunished; those who are concerned about the general moral climate of our society claim that upholding the individual's right to use harmful drugs will surely undermine public morals, while others, who are concerned about the ethics of the market-place, often express impatience with the right to freedom of commerce, claiming that such freedom unleashes the forces of avarice and greed at the expense of decency and harmony. No doubt, other examples can be cited. The curtailment of *individual* rights rarely occurs without claiming some *public* benefit from it. And the dominant political forces tend to claim for their agenda of such curtailment just that kind of public benefit.

But does it have to be thus? Must individual rights conflict with the common welfare? Certainly those who proposed the doctrine of individual natural rights didn't think so. It was precisely to show the congruence of the protection of individuals and the enhancement of the community that many advocated the protection of individual rights. John Locke would never have admitted that there has to be conflict in this area. Rather, the conflict, if there is any, stems from a basic misunderstanding. This involves thinking that the community is anything but *a community of human individuals who share certain community concerns which will best be served if each individual has his or her rights fully protected.*

The idea is that human nature unites us into one species and gives us standards by which community life may be fully harmonized, at least potentially.

143

And the natural rights tradition held that such harmony is best secured by granting every individual a sphere of personal jurisdiction. Within this jurisdiction each person is most likely to accomplish the best he or she can, giving rise to the least degree of mischief in the process, since by not granting persons the authority to intrude on others, the evil or harm they do is most likely to hurt only them.[2] This will certainly serve as a discouragement to wrong doing, which, in turn, confers overall benefit to the community.

Even many thinkers who believed that ideally the best course of conduct for everyone is to serve the community believed, also, along with Bernard Mandeville and Adam Smith, that public benefit could be procured *via* private vice, provided certain principles of liberty are upheld. And, even earlier, Aristotle believed that the right to private property would enhance public welfare, when he wrote:

> That all persons call the same thing mine in the sense in which each does so may be a fine thing, but it is impracticable; or if the words are taken in the other sense, such a unity in no way conduces to harmony. And there is another objection to the proposal. For that which is common to the greatest number has the least care bestowed upon it. Every one thinks chiefly of his own, hardly at all of the common interest; and only when he is himself concerned as an individual. For besides other considerations, everybody is more inclined to neglect the duty which he expects another to fulfill; as in families many attendants are often less useful than a few.[3]

One way to support the idea of the harmony of individual rights and the common good is to demonstrate the compossibility of individual goods and rights – i.e., that no one's objective good need obstruct another's objective good, which, in turn, suggests that the pursuit of individual goods within the framework of individual rights will bring about the maximum well-being of the community. But are the objective goods or values of individuals really compossible, that is, fully capable of being realized for all? Some argue that this isn't even conceivable, let alone possible. They believe that no common human nature exists so as to be able to identify some common standards of good or value. Or they argue that human nature is a myth, so any idea of compatible values is hopelessly futile. Then there are the more empirically minded critics who point to how history is replete with major and minor conflicts among human beings, so any belief in some kind of harmony is utopian, even if theoretically not entirely absurd.

Yet, of course, there is plenty that's problematic even with the idea of a common good, over and above individual goods. How are we to identify some transcendent specific common good in the first place?[4] Will any candidate not always be the candidate of some special group of human beings and thus by definition not the common good? Is there even such a being as humanity or society apart from the individuals who comprise it? So what else is there but the good of individuals?

But perhaps the more immediate issue that springs to mind under the heading "individual rights vs. the community" has to do with environmentalism. There are very few people involved in the international discussion of the environment who do not believe that some inherent conflict between the individual and the common welfare faces us here. Consider the alleged problem of the ozone layer. It seems that in the long run the right of individuals to secure for themselves, for example, refrigeration and air conditioning simply cannot help but conflict with the prospects of a healthy (current and future) human race. Free trade, the freedom to pursue one's happiness, even the freedom to express oneself freely seem to some not to be rights but occasional, highly circumscribed privileges that can and ought to be revoked by government whenever the environment or some other value is being threatened by them.

So there are a few who would protest and argue that, in fact, environmental well-being and other values not only are compatible with but entirely depend on the respect for individual rights.

ECOLOGY: A NEW EXCUSE FOR STATISM?

As we noted in the previous chapter, in the early part of the twentieth century Ludwig von Mises observed the same principle identified by Aristotle. Mises, as Heilbroner has reminded us, argued that collectivist management of resource allocation can simply never work.[5] Effective information dissemination and communication of what something is worth to whom and how much they want requires that individuals enjoy the freedom to buy and sell, which, in turn, requires the protection of their right to private property.

More recently, Professor Garrett Hardin, in his famous essay "The Tragedy of the Commons," argued that the difficulties first noticed by Aristotle plague us in the context of our concerns with the quintessentially public realm, namely, the ecological environment. Here over-usage is most likely because the realm seems to be inherently resistant to privatization. Hardin did not draw optimistic conclusions from this. Nevertheless we can conclude that the collectivist system, which rejects individual rights, does not appear to solve problems very well.

These various indictments of collectivism, coupled with the few moral arguments against it, didn't manage to dissuade many intellectuals from the task of attempting to implement various forms of the idea. Our own century is filled with enthusiastic, stubborn, visionary, opportunistic but almost always bloody efforts to implement the collectivist dream. Not until the crumpling of the Soviet attempt, in the form of its Marxist–Leninist internationalist socialist revolution, did it dawn on most people that collectivism is not going to do the job of enabling people to live a decent human social life. Although most admit

145

that in small units – convents, kibbutzes, the family – a limited, temporary collectivist arrangement is feasible, they no longer look with much hope toward the transformation of entire societies into collectivist human organizations.

Heilbroner, who was for a long time sympathetic to socialism, admitted, finally, that "...Ludwig von Mises...was right..."[6] But, unlike previous thinkers who have seen various examples of the failure of idealist normative moral or political schemes, Heilbroner does not abandon the hope for government regulation of some essentially peaceful areas of human life. He notes that there are two ways central regulation may remain something of a handy concept. First, it may leave us piecemeal social objectives to strive for.[7] Second, it may reemerge as the adjunct of the ecological movement. And just as we noted earlier that the planned economy is misguided, we need now to examine in that light Heilbroner's suggestion that coping with the challenges of environmental problems must involve considerable government interference. Heilbroner tells us that:

> The ecological crisis toward which we are moving at a quickening pace has occasioned much scientific comment but surprisingly little economic attention. [Professor Heilbroner does not follow the burgeoning literature of free market environmentalism; e.g., the works of John Baden and Richard Stroup.] Yet if there is any single problem that will have to be faced by any socioeconomic order over the coming decades it is the problem of making our economic peace with the demands of the environment. Making that peace means insuring that the vital processes of material provisioning do not contaminate the green-blue film on which life itself depends. This imperative need not affect all social formations, but none so profoundly as capitalism.[8]

To this idea, that a new problem faces us that is too complicated for free men and women to handle, we may respond by recalling that since this is not in principle different from other problems, Heilbroner's call for more meddling from government is unjustified. As we have already seen Heilbroner issues the "new" warning that capitalism needs to be restrained, now so as to secure environmental objectives. As Heilbroner put it, the system needs to be "monitored, regulated, and contained to such a degree that it would be difficult to call the final social order capitalism."[9] Despite already having attended to such objections to the free market economic, this recast skepticism about individualism needs to be addressed, if only because it is time that the technique it exhibits of undermining confidence in human freedom needs to be exposed.

THE POTENCY OF INDIVIDUALISM

First, none of anyone's bona fide, reasonable environmental worry justifies distrusting "the market," as opposed to some scientific bureaucracy that is to do the monitoring, regulating, and containing Heilbroner and so many other champions of regimentation are calling for. Put plainly, if men and women acting in the market place, guided by the rule of law based on their natural individual rights to life, liberty and property, were incapable of standing up to the ecological challenges Heilbroner has in mind, there is absolutely no reason to believe that those could be met better by some new fandango statist means. Why should ecologically minded bureaucrats be better motivated, more competent, and more virtuous than those motivated by a concern for the hungry, the unjustly treated, the poor, the artistically deprived, the uneducated masses of the world? There is no reason to attribute to any ecological politburo or central committee nobler characteristics than to the rest of those who have made various failed attempts at coercing people into good – prosperous, generous, prudent, courageous, wise, moderate, and other kinds of virtuous – behavior. In short, if free men and women will not manage the ecology, neither will anyone else. But there is much more to be said than this.

Again, put plainly at first, more optimism is warranted about the prospects of managing environmental problems in a legal framework of individual liberty than is expressed by Heilbroner and numerous others. This is the result, first, from examining just what are the sources of our ecological troubles. Given, especially, the fact of collectivism's far greater mismanagement of the environment[10] than that of the mixed economies we recklessly label individualist or capitalist, there is already some suggestion implicit here about what the problem comes to, namely, too little individualism. What Heilbroner and friends fail to realize or reveal – for it is no secret and takes no genius to discern – is that the environmental problems that can be clearly identified rather than merely speculated about are due to the tragedy of the commons,[11] not due to the privatization of resources and the implementation of the principles that prohibit dumping and other kinds of trespassing. With more attention to protecting individual rights to life, liberty and property, there would have to be fewer human-created ecological problems.

Let me put the argument I wish to advance in its most general terms first. The natural rights defense of the free market rests on the realization that it is the nature of human beings to be essentially individual. This can be put, alternatively, by saying that the individual rights approach is most natural – i.e., it most readily accommodates human nature and, therefore, the natural ecology.[12] If there is a crisis here, it amounts to the history of human action that has been out of line with ecological well-being, health, flourishing. But how do we know what kinds of human action might have been more or less conducive to ecological well-being? We need to know about human nature – what it is that human beings are and what this implies for their conduct within the natural world. If, as the natural rights tradition has intimated, human beings are individuals with basic rights to life, liberty and property, that also means that this is how they are best fitted within the natural world. This is how they fit best within the rest of nature.

The market is, after all, merely the result of the implementation of the principle of private property rights – the recognition that each person must have a sphere of individual jurisdiction within which to effectuate his or her choices, decisions, plans, purposes, etc. As noted, Aristotle and others have discovered that such an arrangement of a community, into individual realms of authority, tends in the main to facilitate responsible conduct. There can, of course, be exceptions – irrationality is not preventable even by the establishment of the most natural and useful organizational social principles. Even at great cost to themselves, people will sometimes misbehave.

Yet it makes good sense that when this cost does not affect individual agents, or affects them so remotely that the connection between their actions and the consequences that follow is very difficult to observe, confusion and mismanagement are more likely. And what is a human-created ecological crisis but the macro-result of such individual confusion and mismanagement – individual persons dumping their potentially harmful waste onto the lives of others, apparently costlessly. It means people using up difficult to secure resources as if they were free goods, etc., etc.

THE PROBLEM OF INDIVIDUALISM *VIS-A-VIS* ENVIRONMENTAL PROBLEMS

Clearly, the ecological realms mostly affected adversely by human agency are public realms – the air mass, lakes, oceans, many parks and beaches, and, of course, the treasuries of democratic states (for what is deficit spending but a tragedy of the commons?), etc. The ultimate harm, of course, befalls individual human beings – now or in the future – and other living things upon which human life often depends or from which it gains a great deal of benefit and satisfaction. Yet the injury occurs not in a way that is judicially manageable – namely, where victim and culprit can be linked and the crime may be dealt with.[13]

Let us for the sake of argument understand Heilbroner not to be advocating out and out collectivism but rather something of a compromise between an individualist-capitalist and a collectivist system, namely, what we have come to call the welfare state. After all, he admits that he envisions an ecologically prudent socioeconomic system to be substantially individualist – i.e., the institution of private property has not been entirely abolished in such a system – but one that is also "monitored, regulated, and contained to such a degree that it would be difficult to call the final social order capitalism."

Do we really need once again to abandon the individualist alternative for

148

some such regimented order? Let us take the environmental problem as a test case and ever so briefly present the case for why an individual rights approach will more likely solve it and, thus, be more conducive to the common good – as understood within a framework that acknowledges the ontological priority of human individuals to their various groupings – than alternatives that proposed to violate individual rights. While this may appear to be question begging – by denying at the outset any meaningful non-individualist sense of the common good – it will turn out not to be, once the individualist environmentalism that emerges comes to full light.[14]

First of all, we need to stress the individual rights position on pollution: Wherever activities issuing in pollution cannot be carried out without injury to third (non-consenting) parties, such activities have to be prohibited as inherently in violation of the rights of members of the community. (This would not include trade in pesticide-treated fruits, for example, where the risk of harm from eating such fruit is lower than or equal to normal risks encountered in everyday life.)

When pollution occurs along lines of thresholds, such that only once so much emission has occurred could the emission be actually polluting (i.e., harmful to persons) rather than simply defiling, a system of first come, first served might be instituted, so that those who start the production first would be permitted to continue, while others, who would raise the threshold to a harmful level, would not. This may appear arbitrary, but in fact numerous areas of human life, including especially commerce, make good use of this system, and human ingenuity could well be expended toward making sure that one's firm is not a latecomer.

A word about thresholds. The earth – as well as any part of the universe where life support is reasonably imaginable – can often absorb some measure of potentially injurious waste. (This can be expected, since life itself produces waste!) Most toxic substances can dissipate up to a point. Arguably this is no different from the simple observation that within a given territory only so much life can be supported, after which the quantity and quality of life must be lowered. Barring the privatization of such spheres, where they can be kept apart and separated from others, a judicially efficient management of toxic substance disposal must take into consideration how far disposal can continue before the vital point – whereby the waste is harmlessly absorbed and dissipated – is reached. Technical measurements would need to be employed and correlated with information about the levels of human tolerance for the toxic substance in question. Risk analysis would need to be performed so as to learn whether the risk of falling victim to toxic substance disposal corresponds with or exceeds expected risks not produced by human pollution.

It is important to state that the natural rights individualist standard of tolerance might very well be far lower than even those who support it would imagine. Many free market advocates favor a social cost–benefit approach here, based on the utilitarian idea that what ultimately matters is the achievement of some state of collective satisfaction. This is not the approach that flows from the idea that individuals have natural negative rights to life, liberty and property.

Assuming the soundness of the natural rights stance, it may be necessary to prepare for some drastic life style changes, so that some past abuses can be rectified. For example, whereas automobile wastes have been poured into the atmosphere with an understanding that from a utilitarian perspective it is worth doing so (based on social cost–benefit analysis), from the natural rights individualist-capitalist viewpoint it would be necessary to insist on the full initial cost being borne by automobile drivers/owners, thereby at least temporarily prompting a considerable rise in the prices of vehicles. (That the overall cost may be borne wider, since more expensive manufacturing and transportation processes will prompt more expensive goods and services, is not relevant here. The issue is what persons can choose to do or avoid doing in light of their understanding of what may harm them.)

Certainly, the government of an individualist political economy would not have the authority to rely on the utilitarian notion, used by many courts today in their refusal to enforce "public nuisance laws," that those harmed by pollution have to "pay" since the benefits of industrial growth outweigh such costs in health and property damage as are caused by pollution. Instead the principle of strict liability would apply: The polluter or others who are bound by contract with the polluter, such as nuclear utilities which may have a pact to share insurance premiums and liability resulting from accident at one member's plant, would be held liable. Benefits not solicited cannot be charged for if one respects the individual's right to choose, as the individualist system is committed to do.

TREATING UNCERTAINTIES AND COMPLEXITIES

Of course, there are environmental problems to which solutions are difficult even to imagine. Even if one particular country has managed to institute the legal/constitutional measures that would best handle environmental problems – ex hypothesis, a system of strictly observed and enforced basic private property rights – the international arena will still remain unmanaged. Various problems of judicial inefficiency, the tragedy of the commons, public choice based deadlocks, and the like will continue to permeate the international public realm.

The destruction of the ozone layer, if it were a real prospect, would be a threat to virtually everyone, yet it is at present uncertain whether human beings would even be responsible for it – the main cause appears to be volcanic eruption. If it should turn out that certain kinds of human activities cause this damage and if harm to human beings will be the result, once again, provided this is all demonstrated – i.e., due process is followed – those activities may be curtailed or even prohibited. After all, no one may place poison in the atmosphere with impunity, and the problem with the ozone layer is not unlike that –

the destruction of something that is not anyone's property and thus no one's to destroy at will, while it, nonetheless, serves to do harm to individuals.

Another type of problem to which it is difficult to construct a solution without specific relevant scientific evidence is illustrated by the destruction that is occurring in the Amazonian rain forest, in this case by persons or rather, governments who own it. (I leave it aside for now whether ownership was come by in a fashion consistent with individual rights!) Here, too, the only point that can be made is that if it is demonstrated that this destruction will produce a result that is injurious to others who have not consented to be so treated, the process must be legally stopped. The reason is, once again, that if one even unintentionally but knowingly violates the rights of others by depriving them of life, liberty or property – i.e., one does not set out to do this but one's actions can be known to result in that – the action can be a kind of negligent assault or even homicide. The more accessible model might be one's building a very tall but weak structure near another's home in the high wind region. Since the structure is very likely to invade the other's sphere of jurisdiction – private property – there is reason to forbid its building. The strong probability of causing such invasion is a justification for prohibition. If, then, cutting down the trees in the Amazonian rain forest can be shown to uniquely result in the destruction of the lives and properties of others, this can be just cause for legally prohibiting it.

Of course, when there are no proper institutional instruments – i.e., a constitution of natural human individual rights – to guard against such actions, it is difficult to suggest where one should turn. The most effective approach in these kinds of cases would be to tie various diplomatic negotiations – including military cooperation, bank credit, cultural exchanges – to terms that would effectively express the principles of private property rights. The quid pro quo approach might be utilized on numerous fronts – including in the drafting of treaties – and once the principles and terms have been firmly entrenched, even military action might be justified when environmental destruction occurs on a massive enough scale. Consider that if Brazil wishes to maintain friendly relations with the United States of America or some other neighboring country, and this other country's legal system firmly acknowledges the environmental implications of the private property rights system, such friendly relations would have to be manifest in part by Brazil's complying with the international implications of such a system. This would apply even if Brazil itself does not adhere to such legal measures within its borders.[15]

This is no different from other international agreements in which countries commit themselves to legal measures vis-à-vis citizens and organizations of other countries which they do not observe within their own borders. Trade agreements, contract laws, and numerous economic regulations bind foreign nationals in their interaction with a given country's population, even if within the foreign national's country these do not apply. The same kind of restrictions could be achieved on the environmental front.

We may now return to the more general implications of the private property rights approach to managing environmental problems. For one, we must acknowledge that in some cases protecting the rights of (of groups) of individuals in this strict manner may lead to their not enjoying certain benefits they might have regarded to be even greater than the benefit of not suffering the harm caused by, say, pollution.

But this is not relevant. The just treatment of individuals must respect their autonomy and their choice in judging what they think is best for themselves, even if and when they are mistaken, so long as this does not involve violating others' rights. Paternalism and consistent capitalism are incompatible political ideals! The system of rights which grounds the legal framework that supports consistent individualist-capitalism is sound, if it is, precisely because as a system of laws it is the one that is most respectful of individual rights – i.e., it rests on the acknowledgment of the sovereignty of individual human beings.

This general virtue shows equal respect for every person who embarks on social life, and it is this equal respect for all that justifies the establishment of government for all, even if such a system does not guarantee that everyone will in fact make the most of its provisions. Nor does it guarantee that all values sought by members of human communities would be best secured via such a system – for example, technological progress in outer space travel might be enhanced by not paying heed to the strict liability provisions of the natural rights individualist legal system.

In short, the ultimate objective of such a system is a form of justice – not welfare, not progress, not equality of condition, not artistic advancement. The justice at hand pertains to respecting every person's status as a being with dignity, that is, as a being with the freedom and the responsibility to achieve a morally excellent life in his or her own case.

UTOPIANISM MUST BE REJECTED

One must be careful not to expect something impossible of a certain field of inquiry. For too long demands placed on the fields of morality and politics have been unjustly severe: Final, irrefutable, timeless answers were sought, and in response to the inevitable failure to produce these a cynicism about the prospects of any workable answers has gained a foothold throughout the intellectual community, as well as among members of the general public. As a result, it is now part of the received opinion of the day that no solid intellectual solution to any of the value-oriented areas of human problems can be reached. The best we can expect is some kind of consensus which vaguely represents the tastes and preferences of a significant number of the concerned population. Yet this "consensus" is a house of cards. Tastes and preferences are unstable, flexible, and so indeterminable that the only thing to emerge is some kind of arbitrary public policy produced either by bureaucrats or by dictators, official or unofficial.

In morality and politics, and thus in public policy too, there can be some very general answers that are stable enough, ones that apply to human life, so long as there is such an identifiably stable phenomenon as human life. Human life and human community involve certain lasting considerations. And innumerable changing problems that emerge in them can be approached reasonably fruitfully by taking into account some of these considerations. Pollution is a relatively recent problem, one that proves to be an important, difficult test of political theories: of fascism, socialism, the welfare state, and individualist-capitalism. Collectivist systems, such as fascism, socialism and even the welfare state, would gauge the justice of the state by reference to considerations that are, in the last analysis, unnatural, namely, some idea of a common purpose to be served that may cancel out the rights of human individuals.

Individualism and its political economic system, capitalism, in contrast, stress the ultimate importance of the rights and value of the individual, gauging the acceptability of public policies by their success in protecting individual human rights, even where other values, such as progress in science and technology, might have to be set aside.

Yet, this discussion by no means exhausts the treatment of the pollution problem, nor does it enter into great technical detail concerning this quite essentially contemporary topic. These details could not be dealt with in relation to particular problems, ones which are encumbered by counter-charges, claims and counterclaims and in which harm or injury through pollution to specific persons would be at issue. Those particular problems are best dealt with in the judicial system where they can receive proper and full attention, just what is needed to settle such claims, once that system has been shaped by these broader considerations, via the political process.[16]

PASSING THE TEST OF A NOTABLY HARD CASE

What I have tried to show here is only that at least with one major issue the conflict between individual rights and human community values is only apparent. And this should not be surprising. In general, what is unique about human beings is that they are free, rational and creative living entities, But, just as many other living beings, they also flourish best in communities rather than in isolation. Indeed, because they are rational, the company of others will nearly always be potentially beneficial to human beings. Community life, then, is indeed natural for a human being. The individualism that stresses the need for choice and, thus, for individual rights must be seen not as an obstacle to but a necessary condition for healthy community living.

The choice-making aspect of human life, however, is more central than membership in communities. This is because it is by way of making choices that a human being can distinguish between good and bad communities. And that choice is certainly vital. The rejection of a communist, fascist, authoritarian, or other tyrannical community must be seen as a crucial capacity for a human being, indeed, one that each person ought to exercise. In such cases, where a conflict between community and the individual arises, clearly the rights of the individual are morally prior, even if in certain cases individuals will exercise these rights wrongly, badly. Even then, the fact that they have made a choice remains what is vital about their humanity. Other animals, too, flourish in communities, but only human beings must flourish by choice.

The example of environmental challenge to individualism is important because here we have what appears to be a clear demonstration of the need to reject individual rights in favor of community values. But, as it was argued above, that conflict is mythical. Given the nature of human life – its naturalism and individualism – the individual rights approach is indispensable in dealing with any of the problems surrounding human affairs. And the management of the problems of human community life, for example, the environmental crisis (to the extent that one exists), is no exception to this vital principle, one that has proven itself of great service to the creation of a reasonably decent life for human beings anywhere.

A final point: in this discussion I have considered the perhaps extremely different views of socialist and capitalist, collectivist and individualist, or libertarian and communitarian positions as the relevant contrasting views *vis-à-vis* the environment and, by implication, all problems of human community life. No doubt, there are watered down versions of each of these that we could examine, although that approach does not lend itself to systematic treatment. And when we are considering a political–economic system, we are dealing with the most general principles that ought to govern community life, even if for some perhaps even valid reasons the principles of the systems under inspection might need to be compromised in practice. I do not deny for a moment that actual community life is far more a matter of many shades of gray than simple black and white, to quote one early critic of this discussion. It is also true that without some clear enough idea of what the blacks and the whites come to, the various shades of gray could not be identified.

No sane political theorist holds that some system of political ideas and ideals will be adhered to perfectly, without exception, in a pure rendition, should the public become convinced of the worth of what he or she proposes. It is, for example, clear that Socrates creates his ideal polity "in speech" only, not as an actual community. Even the less idealistically oriented political theorists have usually realized that when optimal standards of justice are developed, it takes nearly impossible measures of human vigilance to sustain them in practice.

Nevertheless, it is vital that the standards be identified. It is to that end I have advanced my ideas here, testing them against what most people would recognize as a challenging case.

My thesis is, admittedly, radical, though it is quite out of line to compare it with views that motivate bombers and other terrorists. (We know that some of the more unstable people of any political persuasion embark on barbaric measures – e.g., those who oppose abortion, defend animal rights, support the emancipation of the poor, or wish to advance the overall quality of humanity.) Yet it is quite in line with the modern movement toward the strict defense of individual rights, one that has given rise to widely embraced public policies in criminal law and constitutional reform.

It is also a feature of my position that it envisions only human beings as owners, while leaving much of the rest of nature as subject to ownership. This should not be surprising, since it is human beings who are the only species in nature known to us to require moral space, a sphere of authority wherein they can interact with nature to the exclusion of others who would, were they to intrude, subvert the moral independence and responsibility of the victim. (Nature is divided in many other ways – things that swim versus those that do not, things that fly versus those that do not, things that are animals versus others that are not, etc. Thus the division between owners and non-owners is simply yet another of the many divisions and differences nature exhibits.)

Finally, there is something even more unusual about human beings, namely, their nature as creators, as causal agents who make things, including who are responsible for their own conduct, great or small. It is this capacity of human beings that accounts for their ability to go drastically wrong in life as well as be amazingly inventive. The system of private property that my thesis embraces is one that facilitates keeping track of individual moral and legal responsibility. It is my contention, that doing so will only enhance the quality of life, including the quality of the ecological environment that sustains and enriches human living.

In our age of so called "postmodernism" it may appear odd that someone proposes that a crucial element of modernity, the recognition of the essential individuality of human beings – not, however, to the exclusion of their sociality – be affirmed both philosophically and politically and that a rational, objective system of principles could be developed on its basis for both personal and public affairs. It seems that in our time there is much discouragement about some of the challenges this kind of a recommendation poses in ethics, law, and diplomacy. Some have become nihilists in the face of those challenges, embracing wholesale ambiguity, indeterminacy, subjectivity, and, ultimately, the rule of brute force (having found no criteria for judgments in any domain). It is part of my aim here to put forth a more optimistic approach and to apply it to environmental matters.

13

INDIVIDUALISM AND POLITICAL DIALOGUE

TOWARD AN INDIVIDUALIST DISCOURSE ETHICS AND POLITICS

In this chapter I will argue that a careful exploration of the nature of dialogue presupposes certain controversial and highly disputed individualist features of human life. I want to show that in terms of such explorations, the famous Marxian idea of specie-being – "The human essence is the true collectivity of man"[1] – must be rejected in favor of one in which human beings are essentially both individuals and social beings.

Some of what I will say is reminiscent of the theses advanced by discourse ethicists such as Jürgen Habermas, Bruce Ackerman, Frank van Dun, Hans-Herman Hoppe, and N. Stephan Kinsella, as well as some of the work done by neo-Kantians such as Ludwig von Mises and Alan Gewirth. Discourse ethics derives norms of personal and social conduct from a strict logical analysis of the assumptions that underlie meaningful dialogue. For example, in his recent book *A Theory of Socialism and Capitalism*, Hans-Herman Hoppe defends the right to private property on the basis of the presuppositions of discourse.[2]

Alan Gewirth's line of reasoning about political principles, in turn, derives both freedom and welfare rights from a logical exploration of human action. Earlier, Ludwig von Mises developed his system of praxeology based on what he deemed to be a logical – *a priori* – analysis of human action, from which he then proceeded to establish the conditions of a human economy. A similar approach is used by Jürgen Habermas and Bruce Ackerman. Their argument tends to support some form of socialist or welfare state, based on what they take to be the necessary presuppositions of democratic dialogue.

In all of these cases, there is a kind of *apriority* being employed for purposes of establishing substantive principles of human conduct. The distinctive aspect of the present discussion is the use to which it puts the kind of arguments employed by those mentioned above. I want to show, first, that discourse is not primary in how we should understand politics. Instead, it is human action itself that is primary, with discourse being only one form of human action. It is the presuppositions of human action that require certain political principles to be respected and protected. And human action needs to be understood by reference to human nature.

Based on this analysis, certain features of discourse help to ascertain not so much various norms of conduct but a normatively potent fact about human life, namely, its individualist character. Once this individualism is acknowledged, certain implications may be drawn for purposes of understanding political dialogue – for example, implications concerning its nature, its limits, and its scope. In particular I will argue that the scope of political dialogue should be limited to only those features of human social life that fall outside the authority of the individual, namely, interpersonal conflicts (rights violations). Political dialogue, within this individualist framework, could not include demands for actions pertaining to spheres over which only the individual has a final say.

HUMAN INDIVIDUALITY DENIED

In our time there is a clear resumption of the debate as to whether human beings are in some fundamental respect individuals or members of some collectivity. While, of course, the issue is ancient and has never departed from those being addressed in ethics and politics, there is today an epistemological tinge to the discussion. Thus, for example, in his defense of anti-individualist solidarity, Richard Rorty will bring in considerations derived from Ludwig Wittgenstein's argument against the possibility of a private language.[3] The general line of Rorty's argument is that since language is social (no one can have his or her own language) and since human life is intricately bound up with language, human life cannot be characterized as primarily individualist. Accordingly, since at the epistemic level individualism is inadequate, it cannot be sustained as an adequate ethical, social, or political outlook either. This, in turn, gives further support to the idea that the human individual is an invention. (Karl Marx was the most influential proponent of this idea, but it is also present in the thought of conservatives such as Edmund Burke.)

Marx went so far as to claim that individualism was invented as a historical necessity to provide capitalism with a needed ideology. Later Marxists, such as C. B. MacPherson, made a great deal out of this in an effort to place the individualist, classical–liberal view of politics at a philosophical disadvantage. And today it is communitarians who make use of this and related arguments, in an effort to give support to institutions that would overturn ones forged in response to classical–liberal influences – for example, basic individual rights to privacy and property. Since it is always possible to invoke individual rights in defense of practices generally deemed to be morally odious, such as the publishing of pornography, yellow journalism, ownership of firearms, greedy labor strikes, and misuse of lands, communitarians find in the doctrine of individualism – and the classical–liberal institutions it helps to spawn – serious obstacles toward improving the world around them. Thus Amitai Etzioni, whose book *The Spirit of Community* is something of a communitarian manifesto, regards the American Civil Liberties Union's opposition to sporadic police automobile searches for possible drug trafficking as a major obstacle to ridding communities of illicit drug use.

In any case, it is clear that a serious debate is afoot on whether the human individual is something of a whole being, not simply derivative of humanity or some branch thereof, such as the community, race, gender, family, tribe, clan, or ethnic group. And much hinges on the resolution of the dispute. As Rorty notes, if it goes his communitarian, or solidaritarian, way, a concept such as "the essential unity of the self" turns out to be no more than part of "a system of moral sentiments, habits, and internalized tradition that is typical of the politically aware citizen of a constitutional democracy. The self is, once again, a historical product."[4]

In a certain sense, there might be nothing deficient about something that is a historical product. After all, what is not a historical product? The world did not come into being with the human self intact. Like every other species, humans evolved from something else. But this is not what Rorty seems to have in mind. Rather, he sees the "self" as a sort of creation of some groups of human beings, to wit, Western classical liberals, as opposed to a notion of human community that has always been part and parcel of human life. In short, the self is a sort of fiction, one well entrenched but no more substantial, ontologically and metaphysically, than, say, the concept of "demon" or "housewife."

In consequence, any "ahistorical human 'rights'" need to be abandoned in any true political philosophy.[5] And in line with that idea, someone like Rorty could state that there is no moral difference between the system of the Soviets and that of Western classical liberalism – there is no "moral reality" that one captures better than the other.[6] If what is wrong with Stalinism is, in part, the abolition of individuality, and if individuality is just an accident in the histories of certain communities, the Stalinist era merely exhibited distinct historical characteristics; it did not foster something unnatural or antihuman.

HUMAN INDIVIDUALITY AFFIRMED

The trouble with all the arguments that aim to deny human individuality is that without such individuality, they fail to make room for what is actually going on in these arguments. Arguments are efforts by given human beings to establish the existence of something, unless they are mere exercises. In arguments an individual sets out to prove something. The individual gathers evidence and presents the evidence in an appropriate form, thus reaching some conclusion that is purportedly sound, thereby showing something to be the case.

Arguments are, accordingly, a type of creative activity. They require some organ or faculty by means of which they can be achieved. In other words, arguments are functions of a creative thinking organ, a human brain. Even in the most productive committee, say, in a scientific laboratory, it is individuals who take the first step toward making some discovery or producing an invention. They will, of course, draw on innumerable sources that are available in part because many other persons have built up knowledge in the field. But each step needed to be taken by someone.

Unless one were to give a purely mechanistic account of this process, the irreducible contribution of the individual participants is undeniable. This is most clearly attested to in the fact that even the most communitarian thinkers engage in criticism. Criticism presupposes that the critics adhere, of their own will, to certain criteria or standards that secure the value of their contributions. If one sociologist or historian or economist or philosopher criticizes another, there is an assumption that the target of this criticism is a responsible creative agent, accountable for what he or she did.

So the self is inescapably attested to whenever one begins to explore any intellectual or scientific topic. I am talking about the self as the human individual's essential being, what makes that person who he or she is – the "I" that thinks, recalls, creates, produces, invents, errs, is blameworthy, and so forth. The rationality of a person, the capacity by which discoveries can be made, is not a collective but an individual power. It needs to be started up and sustained by individuals, regardless of how much it draws upon resources supplied by others. One reason there has been so much trouble about accounting for human reasoning – why, for example, following a rule has occupied so much of Wittgenstein's attention and why throughout modern society the problem of criminal responsibility seems to be intractable – is this failure to appreciate the nature of thinking as a kind of self-propelled undertaking. In the words of J. F. M. Hunter:

> Our difficulty in understanding how people reason creatively may arise in part from an inclination to insist that this phenomenon must be reducible to some known model of explanation, and that if we could regard people . . . simply as a new kind of mechanism, there would either be no problem, or not that problem. It should not after all be so very surprising that people are unlike machines.[7]

It is true that in some cultures in some periods of human history, individuality has not been acknowledged or has even been actively denied, but that supports rather than alters the above point. The fact that human beings can vary so much as to how they characterize the world is itself testimony of the enormous influence of individuality in their form of life. Other animals differ markedly less from one another in how they view the world and act in it, whereas human beings are everywhere and anytime engaging in ironing out differences, variations, conflicts, and so forth. Even their most routine activities, such as eating or cleaning up, involve significant variations. If the group to which they belong has imposed upon itself an anti-individualist mode of life, the next group will stand as testimony against this effort.

If anything, the great variety of human groupings – the multicultural character of our human species – underscores just how much a part of human nature is our individuality and how it asserts itself even against the greatest odds. (The example of dissidents in all types of systems that have attempted to abolish individuality comes to mind here.) Even as children, human beings require a clear period of development within which they demarcate themselves from their parents, even when there seems little substantive reason for doing it other than to become fully human, to mature. The theme of individuality may not have been widely articulated in some eras of human existence, but in retrospect we can see evidence of it where human beings have left artistic or other creative marks for us to examine.

A prominent attack on this notion would have it that since conceptual knowledge grows only with language, and since language is innately social, human conceptual knowledge testifies to the impossibility of essential individuality. In his *Philosophical Investigations*, Ludwig Wittgenstein advances his famous argument against the privacy of even sensations such as pain. From that argument he seems to conclude: "Instinct comes first, reasoning second. Not until there is a language game are there reasons."[8] Accordingly, the reasoning process I have maintained testifies to individuality appears to be entirely dependent upon the social context.

Yet it is difficult, first of all, to imagine how language came about if we interpret Wittgenstein's account as a denial of the decisive role of the human individual in creative reasoning. Some full-blown language would have to have been around from the start. ("In the beginning was the Word," but this is not supposed to mean human language!) Furthermore, unlike other animals, human beings do not simply use some given set of signals or sounds by which to accomplish communication. Instead, although they draw heavily on what language already exists, they build on this constantly – via poetry, drama, song, and dialogue in general. (Joyce and Celine, for example, invented thousands of new and useful terms in their respective languages, English and French.) Also, human beings, unlike other animals, make errors and seem clearly to be at fault at times for having done so. There could be no sense to "being at fault" unless they have a decisive role in what they are doing *as individuals*.

As to the development of language, it seems more sensible to think that through a very gradual process of accretion, human beings made halting, barely articulate contributions to a language.[9] Perhaps regarding the first verbal expressions, pertaining to objects or even feelings, it would have been troublesome to try to correct anyone at that point. At this level of language usage, what human beings did was nearly identical to what other noise-making animals do, although with the latter it is instinctual. Human beings had to make a concerted effort, had to use their will, as it were. Gradually, in the company of others, individuals built their languages into elaborate conceptual systems. At this stage they had more opportunity for making mistakes, as well, through thoughtlessness or inattention to the degree of detail that may have been demanded for a given task of understanding and explaining. And in retrospect all this could easily be taken for some kind of mindless collective project.

Wittgenstein's own point about the impossibility of private languages may well apply to conceptual knowledge, where one needs to draw on elaborately developed concepts. Pointing and such, although seemingly simple when looked at from the point of view of a highly developed system of communication, could well amount to a highly developed mode of expression. But if we consider such tasks as learning of the existence of some object or a feeling we are experiencing, making note of this need not involve any, let alone any considerably developed, conceptual knowledge. Only upon reflecting on such matters does conceptual knowledge become necessary. After all, other animals know in this sense just as we do – the dog knows where its food can be found, knows that the ball thrown at it is not to be eaten, knows its owner's car. And while mistakes can be made here, even by dogs, there is not much of a problem about making a correction later, once one has a closer look at things. It is not necessary that there be others to offer criticism for one to make the discovery of error in one's ways, since error made at this level pretty much stares one in the face immediately after it has been committed.

The role of the individual self, then, is irreducible in a cogent account of human thinking and concept formation. It does not matter that human beings flourish far better in social settings than in isolation – nothing about the fundamental individuality of a human being precludes this from being the case. Just as in team sports the tasks are largely accomplished by means of the participation of several members, the individual, especially his or her initiative, is indispensable. (I like to illustrate the individualist form of social cooperation by the image of a very large sheet spread across a large territory, with individual steeples pressing upward and giving the enfolding of the entire canvas its decisive shape. Yet, of course, the individuals are linked among themselves, as the spans between them indicate, somewhat as mountain peaks are linked by the valleys and slopes that connect them.) In short, we are not talking about some caricature of individualism, such as the atomistic sort most often ascribed to the classical–liberal tradition of political philosophy. But it is a false alternative to propose that by rejecting such atomistic, neo-Hobbesian individualism, one must move to the collectivist alternatives of socialism or communitarianism.[10]

PREREQUISITES FOR INDIVIDUALIST DIALOGUE

It is notable that within the framework of collectivist discourse ethics, such as that of Jürgen Habermas, the socialist or communitarian features of politics are smuggled in at the outset, prior to any dialogue having actually taken place. This is to be explained by the absence of the individualist component of human life. If individuals are seen as powerless in and of themselves – if no potency can be justifiably ascribed to them, if they cannot do anything significant on their own initiative – then they must have various props provided for them prior to the discourse taking place, regardless of any outcome of the discourse itself. In short, basic needs *must* be satisfied, indeed, guaranteed, via the social system so as to get the discourse started. So Habermas and others postulate a substantially socialist economy so as to accommodate the requirement of dialogue.

If, however, we ascribe to individuals the power of creative reasoning, of beginning a process of thought and of discovering various ways in which their needs might be satisfied independently of welfare provisions by political means, the prerequisites for dialogue will change. What seems required is not the welfare aspects of the political community but its banning of crimes that inhibit liberty.

John Locke's way of thinking this matter through can offer a starting point here. Locke saw us as capable of a great deal of self-sustenance and progress outside of civil society. However, in such a state we would constantly be hampered by criminal intrusiveness. Because men and women can do the wrong thing, including invading one another when there is no just cause, the state of nature is unsafe or, at any rate, not as safe as civil society where, by common consent, special care is taken to restrain criminality. How can we know the limits of individual liberty so that we may correctly identify what criminal conduct consists of? This is where Locke's natural-rights perspective provides us with an individualist conception of the prerequisites of a functioning civil society.

Individual citizens must have their sovereignty guarded so that their participation in life, including politics, will not be subjected to coercion or forcible constraint. This applies even to democratic decision making. Indeed, it is one of the preconditions of effective democracy. The much debated issue of how democracy and capitalism are related cannot be resolved other than by affirming that without at least a substantial measure of effective protection of the right to private property, citizens cannot make political decisions without serious intimidation and, thus, the loss of their independence. Let me elaborate.

If the individual participants in the democratic process lacked such basic protection, they could not contribute their independent judgment, their true convictions, to the process, since they would have to be second-guessing which faction would win elections and might retaliate against those who opposed them. If one did not have the security of one's person and possessions *following a democratic decision-making process*, that process would not be assured of being genuinely democratic in the first place.[11] The threat of retaliation from the winners would corrupt democracy, especially if that threat could be disguised as a public policy outcome reached by democratic means.

While this may appear to be a mere quick and dirty way by which to dispose of this problem, its logic is not to be denied. Political participation that counts simply cannot be attained in a system where the majority has unlimited powers, because those powers are essentially threatening to those who may end up in the minority. To remedy this, it is necessary to give some rights a fundamental legal status. These would have to be the rights to life, liberty, and property, all essentially prohibitions on us to ever kill, restrain, or steal from people who have not themselves violated our equal rights. Unless this is achieved, by way of a fundamental legal document such as a constitution, democratic decision making itself becomes corrupted.

It seems, then, that a politics of dialogue, in order for it to do adequate justice to the human condition, must rest on individualist prerequisites, not collectivist ones. The familiar constitutional provisions of individual sovereignty – freedom of thought, speech, trade, religion, and so forth – would have to be included in order to facilitate democratic discourse.

LIMITS OF DISCOURSE POLITICS

Of course, we can see right away that the scope of authority of discourse politics in this framework would be limited from the outset. And why should this not be expected? Unless one were to expect discourse politics to amount merely to a substitute for totalitarian tyranny, whereby majorities rule everything and no realm of life outside of politics may be found, this is to be expected. Human beings have a political dimension to their lives, of course. In earlier times, when political communities were smaller, ideally a good deal of attention would have been paid to political matters, ergo, possibly to democratic discourse. However, as legal systems grew in their scope – for a great variety of reasons, not the least of which were desires for efficiency and power – it became less and less plausible to envision citizens devoting much of their time to political matters. This is what, in part, accounts for *representative* democracy in the first place – no one but a fanatic or specialist could be expected to be a full-time public servant. And in the bloated democracies of our time, it is probably impossible for anyone to be an effective, successful public servant; such a role is plainly a superhuman one, given its requirement of a multitude of tasks, obligations, restrictions, skills, commitments, aspirations, technical information, and so forth.

The individualist discourse politics I am defending restrains democracy, keeps it within a manageable scope of influence in society. Only bona fide public matters would be subjected to democratic dialogue and decision making. The rest of what human beings are concerned with would have to be dealt with outside politics. And there are innumerable communities outside politics. We are members of several of them at one and the same time, entering and exiting them in the ebb and flow of our lives. To even pretend that these might all be brought under the rubric of just one discussion, reigning throughout the political community, is unimaginable. Most of all, such a system would demean our human nature as individuals and members of innumerable and diverse social groups. It would do so no less than does a totalitarian regime, only with the mirage of participation to blunt its cruelty.

THE DISTINCTIVENESS OF INDIVIDUALIST
DISCOURSE POLITICS

As noted at the beginning of this chapter, there have been efforts at arriving at similar results via a method of analysis that may appear similar to the one used here. Thus Hans-Herman Hoppe, Frank van Dun, and N. Stephan Kinsella seem to have reached similar results by exploring the implications of human discourse.[12]

Yet this is a different approach altogether. First, no priority is given here to discourse *per se*. What is crucial is individual creativity. Human individuals do things on their own – they are rational agents, thinking beings whose actions are directed by ideas. But the relationship between ideas and actions is not one of cause and effect, so that there is first some spiritual thing called an idea, which then causes behavior. And when human beings use language, when they discuss various topics, this, too, is a creative process, a form of action. In short, they are acting as rational animals – biological entities that have highly developed brains and, thus, mentalities. That is what is central to this analysis.

Second, there is no contention involved here to the effect, spelled out by Kinsella, that the division between "coercive . . . and non-coercive" conduct is "purely descriptive."[13] Indeed, freely chosen human action is thoroughly normative, subject to moral evaluation. In particular, *coercive* conduct is identifiable only from the normative framework, as involving the violation of rights. (So what is involved in coercive conduct is not only force, but *rights-violating force*.)

Accordingly, when we look at the logic of discourse, we are simply looking at a species of human action. It is the general fact of the creative nature of such action, one requiring individual initiative, that requires the kind of basic provisions spelled out in a roughly Lockean form of government. It is because human beings do things of their own initiative, because they have the responsibility to do what they do correctly, that they must be treated as sovereign. That they do this also when they speak is, of course, true. But the logic, as it were, of their political order emerges not from their speech as such but from their nature as creative agents through and through.

14

INDIVIDUALISM VERSUS ITS CRITICS

WHY ANTI-INDIVIDUALISM NEEDS SCRUTINY

In the bulk of this work I have been spelling out various elements of a form of individualism I have called "classical." I have made the point in various places that this individualism may be traced to a view of human nature that emerges out of Aristotelian metaphysics and epistemology, one that respects the idea of "the nature of X" in a fashion that avoids the difficulties associated with the Platonic essentialism of the theory of forms or ideas.

What I wish to do here is address directly some of the criticisms of individualism that have been aired over the years, some ancient, others modern and most quite contemporary. This may involve some repetition of arguments and points but it will be useful to have before us these responses all under one roof, as it were. One reason is that anti-individualism is still very popular and despite the setbacks suffered by collectivists in the wake of the demise of the most prominent standard bearers, namely, centrally planned socialist political economy, there are renewed efforts to suggest that the individualist system of capitalism, of the regime of natural individual rights, is ill conceived and neglects what is supposed to be the essentially communitarian nature of human life.

Even by those who reject Marxism in all of its varieties, many versions of socialism, in particular democratic–socialist and market–socialist visions, are still widely championed. And all non-Marxian socialist views share this feature of the Marxian version, namely, that human beings are primarily if not exclusively social parts, with society, the class, or some other large collective as the significant entity to be considered as we organize our lives. Not that every communitarian champions the abolition of individualist type constitutional rights and liberties. Rather, many favor diluting those rights with measures that stress the solidarity or cohesive nature of various communities that we ought to consider of prior importance, of value over and above the individual's rights and liberties.

Communitarianism has been gaining prominence, particularly because its endorsement of the group is not linked explicitly to the term "socialism." The communities that stand above individuals in importance can be families, tribes, nations, races, or all of humanity. The main point here is only to note that in rejecting individualism of any kind, one is usually going to opt for one or another of these collective beings. (The term "collective" is, of course, problematic because it must refer back to the individuals who comprise it. At that point it becomes interesting just what the status of these individuals turns out to be.)

INDIVIDUALISM UNDER ASSAULT

Because individualism, as understood by a great many social-political theorists, has such a bad reputation (for example, Mary Midgley accused it of "willingly sacrificing all other human values so as to cultivate . . . a particular group of virtues – notably independence, courage and honesty"[1]), so does, as we have seen already, capitalism. This appears to give collectivist political systems and economies a clear moral advantage. As Susan Mendus puts it, the "liberal commitment to independence – to achieving things on one's own . . . is [factually] false . . . [and] morally impoverished."[2]

Individualism is, to repeat the point once again, taken to be an antisocial, atomistic, hedonistic, morally subjectivist account of human life, much of which is traceable to the philosophy of Thomas Hobbes. But the charges against individualism are open to serious criticism. To start with, often, the tone in which much of the criticism of individualism (as well as its broader social–political philosophy, classical liberalism) is articulated is reminiscent, in fact, more of political propaganda than of scholarly exchange. Some very harsh words roll off the lips of people who find fault with individualism and classical liberalism. Marx, for example, referred to it as an "insipid illusion"[3] – not exactly a kind term. Alasdair MacIntyre regards liberalism itself, in the broadest sense of that tradition, as vile, nasty, and very harmful:

> [T]he Marxist understanding of liberalism as ideological, as a deceiving and self-deceiving mask for certain social interests, remains compelling. . . . Liberalism in the name of freedom imposes a certain kind of unacknowledged domination, and one which in the long run tends to dissolve traditional human ties and to impoverish social and cultural relationships. Liberalism, while imposing through state power regimes that declare everyone free to pursue whatever they take to be their own good, deprives most people of the possibility of understanding their lives as a quest for the discovery and achievement of the good, especially by the way in which it attempts to discredit those traditional forms of human community within which this project has to be embodied.[4]

MacIntyre has argued[5] that individualism is an invention and that individual rights are artifacts based on it with no enduring, substantive moral significance.

This historicist approach – one that claims for ethical and political ideas no more than the temporary validity of being well received by certain social forces in certain historical epochs – consigns individualism and classical liberalism to the status of ideologies that arose at some point in history to serve some specific historical purpose – in the view of Marx, the purpose of facilitating social productivity.

To put it differently, what is wanted in moral and political philosophy is an identification of norms, principles of personal or community conduct, that can be established as sound, true, rather than arbitrary, a function of some people's preferences or otherwise arbitrary choices. MacIntyre and others have argued that individualism as a putative political theory rests on no more than such arbitrary preferences that happen to have been expressed in a given epoch of Western history. We have already seen Marx putting this point succinctly when he spoke of the fact that in earlier epochs

> the individual, and, therefore, the producing individual seems to depend on and belong to a larger whole: at first it is, quite naturally, the family and the clan, which is but an enlarged family; later on, it is the community growing up in its different forms.[6]

So prior to the seventeenth century, presumably, the individual as a choosing entity, one who is seen as having the right to choose his social relationships – via the principle of the "consent of the governed" – did not exist.

We might also recall, once again, John N. Gray's virulent frontal attacks on individualism. He attributes the following sentiments to J. A. Schumpeter, although they are clearly his own, given how he makes use of them: "[I]ndividualist cultures devour their own moral capital and slide into debt-ridden stagnation as individualism corrodes family life and long-term planning and investment."[7]

In less harsh but equally damaging terms, Richard Rorty maintains that individualism is a mistaken ideology that our age has come to accept. As Rorty puts it:

> [His own pragmatist-communitarian alternative] takes away two sorts of metaphysical comfort to which our intellectual tradition has become accustomed. One is the thought that membership in our biological species carries with it certain "rights," a notion which does not seem to make sense unless the biological similarities entail the possession of something non-biological, something which links our species to a nonhuman reality and thus gives the species moral dignity.[8]

Rorty's point is that if his especially radical pragmatic approach to politics is right, such that principles of social organization are a function of what a given community has chosen, collectively, to embrace, then rights, specifically those of the individual human being, are unfounded. They lack cognitive significance, so when one claims that one has such rights and no one should violate them, there is no basis for that claim. All such claims tell us is that the view is one that some groups of people have embraced, while other groups have decided to accept some other view.

Given these harsh or drastic conclusions, offered by some of the most prominent thinkers of our time, about how the polity of individual rights fares, let us first restate what individualism amounts to. Then, let us look at the views of some particular critics of individualism. Finally, we shall distinguish between two types of individualism, which I call "naughty" and "nice," and proceed to show that the nice version is, of course, superior to collectivist alternatives.

ESSENTIALS OF INDIVIDUALISM

Mary Midgley makes the point that "our own culture, in particular, has grossly exaggerated the degree of independence that individuals have, their separateness from other organisms, and also their degree of inner harmony."[9] However, she goes on to add:

> But these exaggerations do not affect the more modest facts that underlie them. Whenever people have to make decisions, the language of agency has to be used, and the reasons why it had to be invented constantly become obvious. The language of impersonal process, by contrast, can scarcely be used at all for many important aspects of human behavior and, when it is used there, it often serves only for fatalistic evasions.[10]

What are those modest facts that underlie an exaggerated individualism? They are few but vital for human existence. These facts may be distinguished, though not separated.

One such fact is a certain indispensable level of separateness of every person. A human being is an individual in part insofar as he or she experiences a measure of separateness – for example, that his or her death does not require the death of another human being. One dies by oneself. Insofar as that involves the extinction of one's identity in some important respect, one is an individual with some sort of separate identity.

Another component is an element of self-directedness. This lies in the social-psychological dimension of human life. Self-determination and free will are a part of individualism insofar as an individual is someone whose initiative – choices, decisions, and actions – is instrumental in who he or she is and will become. Individualism regards everyone as something of a self-made person, even if only in a minimal respect, culminating in no more than acquiescence. Individuals, according to the individualist tradition, do have a determining, decisive influence on their own lives, on who and what they will become over their lifetime of development. The idea is that how human beings develop is not reducible to the influence of other people, of history, or even of their parents.

Furthermore, the capacity for self-generated rationality is a part of the individualist conception of the human being. Every human being is capable of engaging – and, within different individual conceptions, more or less responsible to engage – in creative reasoning, figuring things out, learning of the world, understanding the world to some perhaps minimal but essential extent. Cognition, at least at the conceptual, idea-forming level, has to be generated by the person – it cannot be imposed. A person is not a container into which ideas are funneled or poured, or something that responds to various stimuli passively. There is an element of self-generated understanding, however minimal, on the part of the individual, according to the individualist social–philosophical tradition.

Individualism also upholds moral autonomy for human beings, in the sense that it identifies the individual as the source of moral choice. The point is not, as Steven Lukes argues, that individualism involves the sort of subjective autonomy that "will eventuate in ethical individualism, the doctrine that the final authority of ethical behavior, values, and principles is the individual alone."[11] What individualism requires is that the initiative to do what is right or wrong must come from persons and cannot be wholly explained by reference to external or structural causal forces (for example, cultural or genetic forces). It is neither others nor one's DNA or environment that is held responsible for what the individual does.

Thus, quite independently of whatever moral stance is applicable to guiding individual conduct – whether utilitarian, altruist, egoist, hedonist, Buddhist, Christian, or whatever – it is an essential point of individualism that it is the individual free agent who makes the moral choice, whose input is the most vital for whether that person takes the morally right or wrong action. Indeed, all bona fide moral blaming and praising are implicitly individualist. Those, for example, who are very concerned with recent legal developments whereby people are able to plead as an exonerating condition that they could not help themselves – where the defense of mental incapacitation comes in – are understandably associating this with the demise of individualism and the rise of "group thinking," where the notion reigns that "I" do not do anything; rather, "we" do things or things happen to us.

Also associated with individualism is the idea of the political sovereignty of the human being, the idea that in a polity, ultimately it is the individual members of that polity who are sovereign – not the polity itself, not the leaders of the polity, not some representative crook of the polity. It is you and I, as citizens, who are sovereign, who are not subjects of some other sovereign whose natural position or superiority or divine selection has come to entitle him or her to power over us. The political individualism that this sovereignty notion is associated with is, I think, very much a part of the American political tradition. Indeed, those of us who come to the United States from outside, from the very beginnings of our stirrings as Americaphiles, have kind of associated America with this individualism precisely for that reason; we always thought that when you come within the borders of the United States, you are not anyone else's master and neither is anyone else your master; you are sovereign. This is a form of individualism for which America is well known and also often criticized.

Finally, there is the idea that individual rights, negative rights to life, liberty, and property, are by nature to be ascribed to every adult human being.

I think individualism can be pretty much characterized by these six conditions (a certain level of separateness of every person, an element of self-directedness, the capacity for self-generated rationality, moral autonomy, individual political sovereignty, and individual rights to life, liberty, and property). I might have mentioned a seventh, but it takes us into the realm of metaphysics and is probably beyond the debate that I am participating in here. There was a hint of it in the first one – separateness. There is a metaphysical form of individualism that maintains that every being is a particular in an essential respect. There are no general or concrete universal beings. There is no such thing as society. There is no such thing as family as a concrete thing. There is no such thing as the team, or America, or blacks or whites, or women or men; there are beings and there are all beings; they can be of a specific kind, but in their actuality, they are individuals.[12] This form of individualism is slightly distinct from the one with which I am concerned here, although the two forms are often mixed up.

THE PLATONISTIC CRITICISM

We have seen a sketch of the nature of individualism. Let us now examine a few of the more severe criticisms of individualism. To begin with, here is another brief look at the most traditional, anti-individualist thesis, namely, a certain understanding of Platonism.

If one takes Plato's dialogues to actually spell out a philosophical viewpoint (which many authors and teachers do, although there is dispute about whether one should), then I think one comes to the conclusion that Plato favors the reality of *concrete universals* over concrete particulars or individual beings.

According to Plato, particular beings, you and I as we manifest ourselves in this actual, visible world, are in some sense inferior, imperfect versions of the perfect rendition of this being in a concrete universal. This can be taken on analogy to the way a perfect circle, as defined in geometry, is superior to any actual circular being. Thus it is human nature – the form of humanity – that has the elevated or noble status. We who imperfectly participate in this form are always inferior, and lamentably so. It is, accordingly, no accident that Western civilization has always had something of a disdain toward the body, whether it be in connection with work, sex, business, or material possessions. There is this legacy of the pure idea as superior to the actual approximation of it here in this world.

This is anti-individualist in that the individual is always an inferior part of reality. The truly elevated part of reality is the universal, the ideal. The criticism of individualism derivative of this Platonistic outlook is obviously embodied in a very comprehensive, philosophical point of view. In response, one would have to deal with at least some aspects of that point of view, which I will do below.

ARISTOTLE AS ANTI-INDIVIDUALIST

There is a more moderate view of ancient anti-individualism: the Aristotelian notion that the human being can be realized only as a part of the whole. We considered it briefly at the outset of this work and even indicated reasons why taking Aristotle to have embraced it might be seriously misguided.

The whole, as Aristotle's communitarianism is usually conveyed, does not have to be all of humanity, as is implicit in a certain reading of Plato, but something like the family, the *polis*, or some other group. Because Aristotle identifies human beings as essentially social, it is said to follow from his view that no individual can flourish apart from the realization of this communitarian good.

Aristotle himself seems to have been ambivalent on this matter, for the self-sufficiency he associates with living in the *polis* need not deny an essential individuality to every human being. One can be essentially both individual and social, given a certain understanding of these notions. But in histories of political theory, it is often claimed that Aristotle's much revered and highly influential position implies the rejection of individualism, mainly because everyone does best in life when belonging to a community.

There are many echoes of this view in our own time, what with the reemergence of communitarianism in the writings of MacIntyre, Rorty, Robert Bellah and colleagues, and Amitai Etzioni.[13] There are certain elements in Aristotle's position, as we have already seen, that stress individualism. He gives a prominent place to self-directedness, for one, something that does not square fully with an exclusively communitarian conception of human flourishing. The idea in Aristotle is that it is, in fact, the individual agent of conduct who is virtuous or vicious. It is in part, not wholly, through the individual's own effort that his or her character is achieved and thus the ethical (or unethical) life is lived. Still, certainly a lot of scholars who are critical of individualism draw on Aristotle in their criticism.

CHRISTIANITY *VIS-A-VIS* INDIVIDUALISM

Then there are some elements of Christianity that do not completely square with the individualist requirements that I have laid out, despite some that do. Crucial elements of individualism are suggested clearly enough by the idea that each human being is a distinct, unique child of God and that the saving of each individual's everlasting soul is the task of the ethical life. But there are also anti-individualist directions that one can find in Christian theology.

For example, Saint Augustine said that every part of the community belongs to the whole. Thus holism also seems to be present in Christianity, although there are aspects of Christianity that are individualist – such as that each individual has a separate soul and ought to seek salvation. Still, there appear to be certain ways in Christianity that the individual may be sacrificed to the whole, or at least the purposes of the whole. When Jesus said, "Compel them to come in," he was taken by some – for example, the more zealous missionaries – to suggest *coercing* people to join the faith; this is anti-individualist.

Debate as to whether Christianity is more individualist or more collectivist is certainly widespread in theological circles. Michael Novak and Robert Sirico seem to stress the individualist element in the American debate, while the Catholic bishops tend to stress the collectivist element, whereby compelling people to help the poor, thus denying their free choice in the matter of practicing the virtues of charity and generosity, seems to be favored.

RADICAL PRAGMATISM

Finally, I return to the radical pragmatist view of individualism. Pragmatism is most noted for its rejection of metaphysical foundations – of human knowledge, human morality, scientific understanding, indeed of everything.

The idea that there is something on which a belief system can rest, which can hold it firm, which gives it some sort of stability, is rejected by pragmatism. In some ways this is just another rejection of the mode of thinking encouraged by Descartes and his famous attempt to build all our beliefs on the one certainty that the individual thinker exists as a subjective, conscious self. That much all pragmatists have in common, including Charles Pierce, John Dewey, Willard Van Orman Quine, and Richard Rorty, just to mention the major ones.

Out of this position, Rorty advances the belief that when we do have some understanding, this rests on tenets of thought agreed to by members of different communities. In his famous essay "Solidarity or Objectivity?"[14] Rorty rejects the possibility of objective knowledge – the sort we imagine we might get of reality after hard work, research, and the clearing away of prejudices and preconceptions. It is a myth, he says, that we can know the world as it exists, unconditioned by the thinking that we do in coming to know it. We are able to keep a stable, apparently independent worldview intact only because our community supports us in this. We have our various communities, we belong to them, and in terms of what these communities give us, we formulate an understanding of the world.

Rorty goes so far as to indict much of our history of ideas, claiming:

> The tradition of Western culture which centers around the notion of the search for Truth, a tradition which runs from the Greek philosophers through the Enlightenment, is the clearest example of the attempt to find a sense in one's existence by turning away from solidarity to objectivity.[15]

This objectivity, if attainable, would make individuality possible – one could, at least now and then, take an independent view of reality and thus criticize even one's own community. But Rorty insists that no such objectivity is possible because, as he puts it, "we should have to climb out of our own minds" in order to attain such a stance. Indeed, he thinks, following Ludwig Wittgenstein, that any question that suggests that we need to do this is meaningless and "should not be asked."[16]

There is no role for the individual, with his independent consciousness, to ascertain reality or to stand apart and criticize the community's viewpoint. Rorty, as others have done, brings in Wittgenstein to give him support in this epistemological thesis. Wittgenstein has an argument, well known in contemporary philosophy, called the "private-language argument." In it he maintains that a certain type of empiricism is false, one according to which every individual gains sensory impressions of the world on which he then, individually, builds an understanding of reality by organizing, naming, and drawing inferences from these sense impressions.

Wittgenstein held that no individual could ever create a language, since such a language could never admit of being corrected. If I create my own language, every name that I give – such as a name I give to a person – is necessarily right, because it is an act of will or choice, not a matter of a publicly affirmable or correctable discovery. If I created a language all on my own, there would be no way anyone could correct what I say or do. No one could hold me responsible for having made a mistake.

Wittgenstein, no simple thinker to interpret, is taken to have argued that the only way that language can be understood as a medium within which errors and corrections can be made is if we look upon it as a social creation. Neither the subjective certainty of Descartes' individual mind nor that of the empiricists' subjective sensory impressions can provide us intelligible knowledge. Thus the argument is supposed to oppose individualism. Another statement of this view, which Rorty advances, was advanced by Auguste Comte:

> The man who dares to think himself independent of others, either in feelings, thoughts, or actions, cannot even put the blasphemous

conception into words without immediate self-contradiction, since the very language he uses is not his own. The profoundest thinker cannot by himself form the simplest language; it requires the co-operation of a community for several generations.[17]

So Rorty supplements his radical pragmatist view with Wittgenstein's private-language argument, thereby disposing of the notion that any individual could ever take a cognitive stand independent of his or her community. In effect, this means that true dissidents do not exist; there are only warring groups.

SOME ANSWERS TO CRITICS

There are other criticisms of individualism, such as social–psychological, socio-logical, historical, and related ones. But I will concentrate on those I discussed above, because the others tend to be derivative of them.

Was Plato's criticism a telling one? There are different ways of reading Plato, and one way to read it is to imagine that his dialogues present us with an image of how to keep some semblance of rationality *vis-à-vis* the hustle-bustle world facing us. One such way is to develop certain philosophical myths, useful suggestions embodying half-truths.

Thus it can be argued that the realm of perfect ideas is a philosophical myth, that it is not supposed to be some objective reality wherein actual ideals subsist as concrete universals, superior to individuals here in visible worlds. What Plato may have had in mind is that we should always have a set of standards to which we refer the actual and in terms of which the actual world might be improved. This reading of Plato does not exactly endorse individualism, but it certainly softens the blow against it. One has to become less of a Platonist and more of a supporter of Socrates, the more commonsensical teacher of Plato. Or, to put it another way, one should move in the direction of Aristotle's empiricism, remove the dualism entirely, and endorse a universe in which there really is just one kind of reality, within which the existence of the individual can be affirmed if we think about it carefully. And if we affirm the individual human being's existence within this one system of reality, I think the result will be that the individual is of paramount significance.

As to the claim that Aristotle was anti-individualist, here I would stress Aristotle's ethics, rather than the frequent interpretation of his politics. I would argue that to flourish, the individual has to be a member of a community, but it is not necessary for the individual to be a member of some particular community or to ignore one community over another. I think there are many different communities within which individuals can flourish. And if you retain the self-directedness portion of individualism, as you must with Aristotle, I think there is no conflict between Aristotle and individualism. As we have already noted Zeller's understanding of this,

Plato had demanded the abolition of all private possession and the suppression of all individual interests, because it is only in the Idea or Universal that he acknowledges any title to true reality. Aristotle refuses to follow him here. To him the Individual is the primary reality, and has the first claim to recognition. In his metaphysics individual things are regarded, not as the mere shadows of the idea, but as independent realities; universal conceptions not as independent substances but as the expression for the common peculiarity of a number of individuals. Similarly in his moral philosophy he transfers the ultimate end of human action and social institutions from the State to the individual, and looks for its attainment in his free self-development. The highest aim of the State consists in the happiness of its citizens. The good of the whole rests upon the good of the citizens who compose it. In like manner must the action by which it is to be attained proceed from the individual of his own free will. It is only from within through culture and education, and not by compulsory institutions, that the unity of the State can be secured. In politics as in metaphysics the central point with Plato is the Universal, with Aristotle the Individual. The former demands that the whole should realise its ends without regard to the interests of individuals; the latter that it should be reared upon the satisfaction of all individual interests that have a true title to be regarded.[18]

Zeller seems to me to make a convincing case, as do others who show Aristotle to be, as Miller puts it, a "moderate individualist" (rather than a radical individualist, such as that associated with Hobbes's nominalist ontology).[19]

As to the Christian criticism of individualism, it depends largely on how one is to appreciate the theological criticism of a philosophical position. Taking Christianity as a fairly straightforward doctrine, where it joins hands with philosophy, there appears to be no major conflict between certain crucial aspects of individualism and Christianity. Augustinian Christianity sees the individual as a moral agent with free will and the responsibility to live a virtuous life. Thomism draws on Aristotle and thus affirms the role of the individual ethical agent, since Aquinas takes seriously the place of the individual's moral choice or initiative, as did Aristotle. As such, there appears to be no major opposition between the main thrust of Western Christianity and individualism, especially if one adds to this the distinctive Christian doctrine that every individual person is a child of God and has the responsibility to achieve everlasting salvation by his or her own chosen beliefs and perhaps deeds.

There is one problem with this, though: because of the otherworldly aspects of Christianity, it is problematic just what exactly *is* the individual; that is, in light of this central otherworldly component, it may not be possible to get a clear idea of the nature of the human individual. So "Who is the 'I' from a Christian perspective?" is impossible to answer in a way that is accessible to non-Christians. There is also the often cited provision of the Bible that Christians may need to be forceful in bringing others to their faith. "Compel them to come in" can be rendered in such a way as to lead to policies that would rob the individual agent of his or her autonomy in making the decision to aspire to the kingdom of God.[20]

There is, then, some ambiguity in the individualism that is found within Christianity. That could, arguably, be a flaw in the Christian, as opposed to the secular, version of individualism, since if one is to appraise a theory of individualism, one has to know something about the nature of individuality – for example, the extent of the person's sovereignty and the implications of that sovereignty and self-directedness. One cannot answer such questions from a point of view that is heavily laden with supernatural references.

The Marxian view, examined earlier, is now somewhat out of favor, but many still embrace it. It even receives support from some scientists, such as the late Lewis Thomas, who endorsed the conception of humanity as an organic whole.[21] We have already addressed several of its tenets in an earlier chapter. It is worth noting here, however, that one of the flaws in Marxism is something wrong with all anti-individualist positions, namely, that it is contradicted by certain very evident facts that are demonstrated by every human being, especially someone like Marx – a creative intellectual.

All of us engage in original acts. We are not the kind of beings who can be entirely submerged as mere passive particles in some revolutionary progression of history. There is always the role individuals play in understanding human history, recasting and criticizing it, not to mention putting its lessons into practice. Marx is an especially renowned example of a critical human *individual* who has a personal, self-determined impact on events. That is one reason why the late Sidney Hook could not square the role of the individual in history with hard-line Marxism. Marx by implication excludes himself, as a powerful, potent member of the historical drama, from his understanding of human affairs. This is a powerful argument against the Marxian conception of humanity as a collective entity – because it cannot make room for people like Marx, there is a self-referential inconsistency in the system.

As to communitarians, including the radical feminists discussed in an earlier chapter and radical pragmatists, the following should make a telling critical point: First, as editors of *The Economist* noted in their 18 March 1995 issue, communitarians "caricature outrageously" the substance of Western or classical liberalism, "calling it a doctrine of economic atomism that pays no heed to man's social nature." This, as the editors noted, "is simply false." Second, the communitarians haven't a clue to which community we owe our loyalties. A little story will bring home this point: On a family trip in 1993, I put my three children through the agony of actually hearing a talk by Amitai Etzioni, broadcast on National Public Radio from the National Press Club. My children were then 14, 13, and 8. As I was listening to Etzioni, he went on and on about how "We ought to do this" and "We might do that." My oldest daughter was sitting in the back of the van, and at one point she cried out: "Papa, Papa. Who is this 'we' this man is talking about?"

Even a smart child can understand the problems in Etzioni's and many others' communitarianism. Which community is the decisive one? Is it my fellow ex-Hungarians, members of the professional community in which I work, my neighbors, fellow tennis players, fathers, drivers of minivans, lovers of travel or the blues or Fred Astaire's dancing, libertarians, divorced men, or what? What is the "we" into which the communitarian is grouping us so that we can be understood fully, as who we are, by reference to this group? From Etzioni's communitarianism no clue is forthcoming.

Nor is there anything better to be said for Rorty's solidaristic version of communitarianism. Rorty talks about solidarity replacing objectivity, but it is very difficult to figure out to which group we do or should proclaim this solidarity. Which one has this force of obligation upon us? Am I supposed to look at the world as a refugee? As a member of a particular faculty? Which is *our* point of view? That of an ex-Hungarian? An academic? A person with a given yearly income? It is entirely unclear, in terms of this position, where one refers to as a member of a community, concerning judgments one needs to make every moment of one's waking life.

Wittgenstein does not help here either. What the famous ordinary-language philosopher argued against was radical empiricism, the notion that any single mind, faced with nothing but groupings of bits of sensory impressions – sense data – could come to know the world, to attain *propositional* or *conceptual* knowledge. There is nothing in Wittgenstein to deny a human being the independent ability to perceive some parts of the world, just as other animals do, quite successfully, and use his or her perceptual information as a kind of anchoring point for checking what beliefs are urged upon us. The private-language argument does not tell against perceptual knowledge (knowledge based only on data collected through the senses).

As David Kelley argues (following Ayn Rand) in *The Evidence of the Senses* – written, incidentally, under Rorty's guidance when the latter was Kelley's dissertation guide at Princeton University[22] – the ground of knowledge is perceptual, not either sensory or conceptual. And as we would anticipate, it is from simple ordinary experience and reflection that human beings *begin* to know. They perceive the world and are not simply told about it. So even after they have mingled this knowledge with what they learn from others – including elaborate conceptual knowledge built on complex chains of concepts – they must take care, individually, to remain properly anchored, to keep their bearings. In the end, they must ground their understanding and thus their intellectual and moral independence on their intimate contact with the world, via their perceptual knowledge. This knowledge is something, incidentally, that they share with other higher animals, but unlike other animals, human beings must use this perceptual data in order to ground their much more developed form of conceptual knowledge. This is true even though once at the conceptual level, reliance on community is central.

Furthermore, the idea that knowledge *begins* with community runs aground when we consider just how this could happen. No community has a brain. It is the members who have brains. So even if after centuries of human history, the bulk of what any of us knows does come by way of what others teach us, *it could not have been like that from the start*. Nor is it always like that now – there are plenty of cases in which children stand their ground against their teachers, citizens against their leaders, ones who often try to indoctrinate or brainwash them and whose efforts often enough need to be and do get thwarted by individual resistance. (For Rorty and other communitarians, the heroic stance of the dissident is impossible – such folks are either deluded in thinking they are lone rebels or actually amount to lunatics.)

THE CASE FOR CLASSICAL INDIVIDUALISM

But of course, saying all this is not quite proving it. Does what I dub "classical individualism" have anything going for it? Just how difficult it is to answer this might be appreciated from the fact that the very idea of "the nature of something" – an idea vitally important to classical individualism as well as to most natural-law defenses of classical liberalism – has been under attack for several centuries. To this day, the dominant philosophical systems and positions have rejected the possibility of identifying the nature of human beings (or any other beings) as objectively real, a fact of independent reality. Indeed, one reason such doctrines as deconstructionism and relativism have fared well in our academic communities is that these simply extend the antinaturalist, skeptical viewpoint to special areas – to wit, literary interpretation and ethics.

INDIVIDUALISM HUMANIZED

Now, how does all this help us out of some of the problems and paradoxes that critics of individualism tend to focus upon? For one thing, since we now have a viable, sound, feasible conception of human nature – one that need not be timeless and yet has the stability one expects of what the nature of something is – we can identify some general principles that we could count on to guide our lives. These principles are going to be general enough to apply over time to succeeding generations, even if they will not be guaranteed to hold for eternity, as earlier naturalists had hoped.

Of course, as Aristotle already recognized, the precise application of the general principles that rest on our knowledge of human nature may not be exactly identical in different situations, at different times. Being honest in the twentieth century probably requires applying the principles to telephones, fax machines, and computers. Two hundred years ago, people did not have the responsibility to be honest in just this way. So honesty, although it may well be a very general human virtue that we all ought to practice, will have individual, regional, temporal, and cultural manifestations, as will other virtues, such as courage, prudence, and justice.

There can be very many general human traits of character that we ought to practice because they make for human excellence. That these must be applied in particular circumstances does not imply at all that they have to be subjective, mere preferences or choices that we invent at a given moment. These could well be human virtues, so that, for example, if we discover that a person four hundred years ago was a liar, we could say objectively that he did something morally wrong.

What is most unfortunate in the critiques of individualism is that no attempt is made by any of the critics to discover a more generous rendition of this social philosophy, one that sees the high regard individualism has for the human individual as somewhat meritorious, somewhat sensible, somewhat morally palatable. Instead, we find the critics stressing elements of individualism that seem obviously morally repugnant and often wholly unrealistic. Individualists are presented as isolated, atomistic creatures whose "independence" is not the virtuous motivation of someone who is set on ascertaining truth and justice objectively, without prejudice and free of group pressure, but the vice of fanta-sizing some kind of solitary existence, of denying moral connection and responsibilities to family, friends, and others. The fact that the individualist is mainly concerned with avoiding oppression and denying a natural subservience of the human being to some supposedly higher group – which is most often translated as subservience to some select other persons – does not appear to phase the critics very much (although some, such as Mary Midgley, make mention of this motivation).

A good example of this approach may be found in Charles Taylor's essay "Atomism."[23] Here Taylor claims that ascribing basic negative rights to individ-uals necessarily presupposes atomism, the view that human beings are self-sufficient apart from society. He links this view to Hobbes and Locke:

> Theories which assert the primacy of rights are those which take as the fundamental, or at least a fundamental, principle of their political theory the ascription of certain rights to individuals which deny the same status to a principle of belonging or obligation, that is a principle which states our obligation as men to belong to or sustain society, or a society of a certain type, or to obey authority or an authority of a certain type.[24]

Actually, there are theories of individual rights that begin if not with some obli-gation – that is, *enforceable* duty – to belong, then with the moral responsibility to find fulfillment in the company of other people, in society. Contrary to Taylor's claim, even Locke identifies such moral responsibilities:

179

> The state of nature has a law of nature to govern it, which obliges every one: and reason, which is that law, teaches all mankind, who will but consult it, that, being all equal and independent, no one ought to harm another in his life, health, liberty, or possessions.[25]

Locke unambiguously refers to "a law of Nature" that governs the "state of Nature" and "obliges every one." He does not claim that this is the *only* law of nature or moral principle. He does, however, state that this law obliges us all, so Taylor is wrong to think that Locke begins his understanding of politics with individual rights. Locke says that in the state of nature, there are obligations, and he calls attention to the obligation that "no one ought to harm another in his life, health, liberty or possessions." *This* obligation Locke treats as indeed enforceable. But it is too weak for those like Taylor, who want us to *belong* to society, to be society's possessions. (The East German socialists precisely implemented this belonging when they regarded everyone who tried to leave them as embarking on a kind of kidnapping of the self!)

Locke's obligation means that we ought to abstain from killing, assaulting, kidnapping, robbing, or otherwise harming others in their lives, health, liberty, or possessions, and that failure to abstain would justify forcible defensive response. But there may be other laws of nature – for example, "everyone is bound to preserve himself" – which may not be enforceable. Furthermore, "when his own preservation comes not in competition, [he] ought to as much as he can preserve the rest of mankind." But this is not enforceable. It is a moral, freely chosen obligation of generosity, even charity, toward others.

Locke also makes it clear, using a quotation from "the judicious Hooker," that human beings are by nature social: "[W]e are naturally induced to seek communion and fellowship with others."[26]

Taylor evidently thinks our choices are not always mature enough to guide us toward self-fulfillment. A moderate individualist would say: (a) assisting with the initial stages of self-development is the task of parents, not the state (that is, *strange* others who have come to govern society), and (b) ordinarily, each of us, except for the very unfortunate, will be able to set ourselves to the task of self-development, gaining any needed help from society, not the state. This fulfills every bit of the necessarily social component of human nature; there is no need to extend it to coercive impositions that arise from seeing each of us as belonging to society.

It is important to note that Taylor equates "belonging" and "obligation" when he uses the phrase "a principle of belonging or obligation." The two are very easy to differentiate. One may have the obligation to be generous or kind or helpful without belonging to those who would benefit from this. It is slaves who belong and do service not from their sense of morality but from the requirement to comply with the demands of those to whom they belong. Men and women who possess both free will and moral responsibilities do the right thing, including fulfilling their obligations, because they choose to do so. Taylor completely ignores this distinction between an enforceable and an ethical obligation. Because of this he never has to deal with whether the social nature of human beings is something they need to fulfill as a matter of their moral responsibilities or something they can be made to fulfill at the command of others.

Taylor might consider Francois Bondy's observations:

> [I]n a society where everything is nationalised and is the property of the state, anybody can be expropriated and subject to export. The East German Minister of Culture once announced in Leipzig that "Unsere Literatur gehört uns (Our literature belongs to us!) . . . ." What he meant was that it didn't belong to you, or to some "common national culture" of two separate states (which the DDR's constitution still mentions), most certainly not to the shared language or the outside world. In Germany the phrase for chattel slaves or indentured servants was Leibeigenen, for the bodies belonged to their owners; now we have the new concept of Geisteigene, for minds and spirits are also part of the new social property relations. When a bureaucracy considers itself to be the owner of literature, then it has the absolute personal right not only to cultivate its own garden but also to remove ruthlessly such weeds as it deems harmful.[27]

Taylor also claims that prior to Hobbes and Locke, there was no reference to rights, which is flatly contradicted by other scholars.[28] Furthermore, there is the occasional serious ambiguity in Taylor's use of the concept of "obligation." Are we to understand by that term a course of conduct that is mandatory and enforceable, or one that is a matter of moral requirement? If it is morally required, one needs to be free from the coercive interventions of others so as to fulfill the obligation. If it is mandatory, others may impose it upon one by force. But then no credit is due one who fulfills the obligation. A mark of a virtuous person is recognition that human nature requires, among others things, extensive social engagement, which is a part of one's self-development, fulfillment of one's nature. But human nature does not require that such engagement be unconditional.[29]

It does appear to be of importance for the critics of individualism to consider not only how wildly certain elements of our nature might be exaggerated, but also how exaggerating aspects of our nature one way may be far more harmful than exaggerating them another way. While it is true that individualism can be propounded in an arid fashion, such as the economists' approach to understanding human life, this has been far less harmful than the similarly exaggerated collectivist accounts. Surely one concern of a moral evaluation of alternative social systems ought to be to consider how corruptible respective systems can be. And collectivism certainly has fared badly in some of its renditions. Ethnic, religious, tribal, national, economic, and other human groupings have wreaked havoc aplenty upon humanity throughout history. The Nazi horrors, ethnic cleansings, lynch mobbings, the Inquisition, and the like all provide examples of collectivism having gone awry. Tatyana Tolstaya's observations on Soviet collectivism, related in Chapter 10, reinforce the point.

Tolstaya's choice of terms may suggest to some that the horrors of collectivism are often overstated. But are they? Marx himself refers to human society as "an organic body."[30] We have already seen that "belong" is Taylor's preferred term. And Saint Augustine states that "every part of the community belongs to the whole."[31] What else does this suggest but the idea that human beings are components of some larger body and are, thus, ultimately not self-directed? Indeed, it means that some folks – a majority, politburo, central committee, or dictator – will direct everyone's lives, not that the whole body will act in some kind of cohesive, integrated fashion!

In contrast, the worst that can be said about individualism is that when it is practiced apart from any consideration of human sociality – for example, in the context of highly calculative economic affairs – folks are not relating to one another in personable ways, kindly and compassionately. Indeed, they often objectify one another: the butcher, baker, and candlestick maker are mere instruments to one's purpose. Yet even here, such instrumentality is predicated on people's choices, on their willingness, under certain circumstances, to cooperate as instruments to each other's ends. Taken too far, this can be alienating indeed, but who says one has to take it too far? Who says one must even succumb to the pressure of the rat race?

Periodically, one may have to focus nearly exclusively on business, so parenting and friendship and generosity need to be set aside (for example, when there are upheavals in the marketplace or nature has dealt a blow to one's enterprise). But there is no necessity about remaining at that level of focus. One can recover one's more balanced approach to living. One is not herded into some helpless, subservient condition, as one surely is when the collectivist alternative goes astray!

In an attempt to understand human ideals, it is not enough to understand the best conceivable rendition of a given ideal. In Marx this would amount to thinking of a seamless whole that is humanity, living in total internal harmony with no part pitted against any other, akin to the way a high-caliber orchestra or a beehive functions at its best. There clearly are examples of human groups that behave in such a fashion, and there is something wonderful about that – as when an acrobatic or sports team shows itself to be fully coordinated. But it is also important to explore how readily such an image of human social life can disintegrate and become corrupted, how vulnerable the ideal is to instability and disharmony when it is implemented. Individualist conceptions of society, even in their radical, Hobbesian rendition, do not seem to yield the kind of corruption we find with collectivist ones, neither in what they logically allow or in their actual historical manifestation. The worst we find is that there is some measure of isolation among members of society, atomistic living, some preoccupation with "self" and lack of close knit community. Daniel Bell's *The Cultural*

Contradictions of Capitalism,[32] already mentioned in this work, spells out the liabilities of individualist capitalism and while some of those are clearly lamentable, none involve the kind of horrors evident in collectivist systems gone awry.

Furthermore, if, in fact, there is an irreducible individuality to every human being and if it is highly probable that a large enough segment of the population will act out its individuality rather than suppress it, then the ideal of collectivist life must be judged to be highly unstable and corruptible. So when societies are made to follow this ideal – as in the Third Reich or the USSR – there will very likely be recurring problems with keeping the collectives functioning in ways that come close to reflecting the ideal image.

With smaller collectives, such as kibbutzim or convents, especially where these are voluntarily entered by the individuals who comprise them, the probability of disharmony and instability will not be as great, because small groups can very well reflect the main attributes of the individuals who comprise them. Even if such groups are established and maintained coercively, stability is more likely because their configurations may well suit the individual purposes of their membership. But this is less and less likely as the collective becomes larger.

The individualist ideal can, of course, also be made to serve unsavory purposes, but never so readily and with such cataclysmic results as those of collectivism, small or large. Most important, individualism can be rendered in terms that are closer to the truth of the human situation, both actual human capacities and realizable human ideals. It seems, also, that many of the welcome features of collectivism, such as the emphasis on sociality, community, fellow feeling, generosity, and charity, can find a home within individualism *provided no violence is done to the element of free choice*. The only way one can take the criticism of individual freedom seriously, as some kind of telling point, is if one believes that an individual's freedom to choose means that what is right or wrong is something this choice determines. But there is no need for this subjectivist provision in individualism.

It is quite true that individuals ought to form social ties, that they often ought to be loyal to their groups, and that it is best for them to choose to be generous, compassionate, and kind toward others. It is also true that mere individual initiative will not lead to full human flourishing, which is the thrust of Aristotle's observation that human beings are by nature social–political animals. Even thinking cannot get much beyond mere familiarity with, as it were, the surface of the world, unless it is enhanced by the kind of education that only many generations' combined (individual) effort can produce. Just as the argument for individualism shows that the individual is indispensable, it also demonstrates that the company of other individuals is essential to the flourishing of human life.

But it does not follow from any of this that individuals ought to be coerced, by others, to comply with the tenets of any given social arrangement. All that can be demanded of anyone is that he or she respect everyone's personal moral jurisdiction – that is, respect the rights that make it possible for us to act on our own initiative. It is the hallmark of individualism that even what is dead right for someone to do must be a matter of choice. Without that, the very dignity of the human being – the capacity of a person to earn moral credit for doing what is right – is destroyed.

Of course, a good deal more needs to be taken care of to make the individualist position fly. Most important, it has to be possible for individuals to be agents of some of their central activities. In particular, human beings have to be the first causes of – or, to put it differently, initiate – their activity of understanding the world, of coming to know it and doing what they do about this knowledge. This is where the problem of free will, or causal agency, arises, and in an age dominated by mechanistic science, with the nearly exclusive reliance upon efficient causation for understanding everything, this is a difficult intellectual task, to say the least.

Free will is discussed at length in Chapter 2. Suffice it to note here that there is now a serious change of direction, at least in biology, concerning the adequacy of the mechanistic, scientistic model for understanding not just human behavior but also much of animal behavior. And in neurophysiology and psychophysics, some serious conclusions have been reached that give solid support to the idea that human brains are exactly the sort that enable human beings to function as causal, governing agents.[33]

Furthermore, it is evident enough that although there is a great deal of value in approaching much of the world along lines recommended by the methods of modern natural science, that method has been extrapolated too hastily to areas of inquiry where it fails to apply. The enthusiasm for combining social science and engineering, both spheres where individualism fares badly (excepting its radical version in economics), seems now to have abated. What may well be the missing element is the type of moderate, or classical, individualism that I have been defending in this book. Surely that much is suggested by the current concern that our society is abandoning individual responsibility and embracing the idea that we are all basically helpless in the face of our troubles.

In any case, the individualist stance is not by any means so unpalatable from the viewpoints of philosophy, ethics, science and common sense as some of its critics suggest. The main alternative placed before us in our time is a rather ambiguous kind of *we-ism*, a communitarianism in which the community is quite undefined. No answers are given to crucial questions: Which is the community to which we belong? Where is it? How long does it last? How do we come to belong to it? How do we leave one of them and go to the other? By what standard of assessment do we judge some communities to be barbaric or corrupt and make our way, if we can, to some others?

Despite what individualism's critics keep telling us, the story could indeed be exactly the opposite, at the end of the day. What the world needs most is a serious, thoughtful individualism, not a continued emphasis on groups.

15

REASON, INDIVIDUALISM, AND CAPITALISM

The moral vision of Ayn Rand

RAND'S PROJECT

This work on individualism would be incomplete without at least a cursory exploration of one thinker who gave its thesis a most forthright exposition throughout several decades of the twentieth century. If there is anyone who has come close to outlining – although not fully developing – the tenets of the clas-sical–individualist stance in moral and political thought, it is the novelist-philosopher Ayn Rand.

Why did Rand embark upon this task? And how should we assess the results of her work?

As to the first question, Rand herself provides a pretty good clue to the answer. She explains, in an essay that explicitly addresses her own career, that she wanted to make it possible for her to write about human beings as they ought to be, not as they usually are. In particular, the worldview she sought to express as an aspiring novelist was missing from the contemporary intellectual climate.[1] Instead, what reigned supreme during the early and middle portions of the twentieth century was either naturalism or some version of absurdism. So, as she explains, this required that she turn to the development of a philosophical system. She explains that she realized that only if she first developed a rational, reality-based philosophy would there exist a foundation and context for her romantic realistic fiction. Such a vision would have to be complex and nonu-topian, and inspire men and women to admire and defend the social and political system suitable for its realization, namely, capitalism.

How successful was Rand's project? The results of her undertaking are her literary artistry (as playwright and novelist) and objectivism (as philosopher). Together, I would argue – and have made the point in several places over the last three decades – these provide a philosophical foundation for a rational moral and political system and a vision of human life lived in accordance with such a system, superior – in the appropriately limited context of a general philosophy (as distinct from some concrete life plan) – to all other life options.

185

THE AMERICAN LEGACY OF POLITICAL ECONOMY

Within recent human history, the United States has approximated the system of capitalism. The political foundations of capitalism – by no means a mere economic system – were best expressed in the Declaration of Independence:

> We hold these truths to be self-evident, that all men are created equal, that they are endowed by their Creator with certain unalienable Rights, that among these are Life, Liberty and the pursuit of Happiness. – That to secure these rights, Governments are instituted among Men, deriving their just powers from the consent of the governed.

Despite the political substance of the Declaration, it is connected to a philosophical point of view and not simply to greedy motives, as alleged by capitalism's critics. Lincoln made this point eloquently in 1859:

> All this is not the result of accident. It has a philosophical cause. Without the *Constitution* and the *Union*, we could not have attained the result; but even these are not the primary cause of our great prosperity. There is something back of these, entwining itself more closely about the human heart. That something is the principle of "Liberty to all" – the principle that clears the *path* to all – gives *hope* to all – and, by consequence, *enterprise* and *industry* to all.[2]

The priority of commerce, or exchange, is not implied in the American system, even if we admit that it "clears the *path* to . . . *enterprise* and *industry* to all." Common sense plainly shows this, even in the face of widespread accusations about the necessary economic motivations of all human action and thought. The principle of liberty for all is not embraced within the American political tradition merely because this tradition rests on the view, shared by Hobbes and Locke, that life is the joyless quest for joy.[3]

THE CHALLENGE OF THE CRITICS

But more than common sense is required in order to uphold a good idea in any sphere of concern. Without a firm philosophical base, the free system *is* vulnerable, even if this base need not be at hand for every citizen.

The critics make the valid point that capitalism lacks moral fuel because it has yet to be widely and prominently associated with a comprehensive philosophical ethics. The problem with Western, classical–liberal capitalism is that the political liberty it cherishes (at least in the language of its political declarations) has not been adequately justified by the pursuit of human excellence. As

Solzhenitsyn has noted, "A society without any objective legal scale is a terrible one indeed. But a society with no other scale but the legal one is not worthy of man either."[4]

THE CHALLENGE CAN BE MET

The critics are wrong to claim, however, that because the bourgeois capitalist idea has not had a full moral–political case to back it up, it is a crass, callous, heartless, nihilistic, purely legalistic, and uninspired way of life. Capitalism, the socioeconomic system that has at its political foundation the principles announced in the Declaration of Independence, contains abundant normative elements. Even if understood merely as an economic system, capitalism is quite attentive to values, for it fosters personal responsibility and excludes force from human relationships. It requires the individual's initiative to achieve prosperity, however understood, with the clear implication that others' efforts must be respected. There is ample moral substance in this alone.

The problem has been that the political principles of capitalism, while in the main requiring every individual to lead the moral life, are neither sufficient as a moral code nor firmly linked philosophically with such a code. Two approaches to the problem have dominated the work of moral theoreticians – philosophers, theologians, and pedagogues.[5] The first has assumed a need for the religious ethical traditions of earlier times: loyalty to and faith in something superior to human life are supposed to sustain a culture. The second has denied that we can identify a moral foundation for any sort of political system; a culture rests only on human drives, vested interests, and economic, psychological, or social instincts.

PROBLEMS WITH THE RELIGIOUS AND AMORALIST ANSWERS

Looking first at the second alternative, we can see that the idea of a free society has come to be widely linked with amoralist tenets. This is due in part to the mistaken association of modern economics with scientific neutrality (especially regarding moral or political values). The point may be stated as follows: Modern economics both is scientific and gives support to the free market; introducing moral issues just weakens the scientific integrity of the case for liberty.

Those who have sought religious support for politics have, in turn, been willing to make compromises between liberty and slavery. They have denied Lincoln's premise that "no man is good enough to govern another man, *without that other's consent*,"[6] mainly on grounds of faith and tradition. For these individuals (mainly America's conservatives) liberty is a fine and productive thing, but in the end, various moral requirements call for its denial as a general principle of human relationships. Those taking this line find the very idea of rational morality socially destructive, since that would place human beings in a position of self-reliance – reliance upon their own reason.

The welfare-state alternative is but the secular version of the faith that there must be something outside the individual human being and his personal excellence to which each of us owes allegiance. Attempts to ground this supposed allegiance on a sound philosophy have ended in appeals to intuition, utopian visions, and theories of historical progress toward a glorious future all of us are obligated to usher in. None of these efforts are satisfactory for purposes of grounding a political system, because in none of these is it possible to establish the case for the system objectively so that everyone with normal conceptual and perceptual faculties might arrive at the same conclusions concerning the kind of system best suited for human beings.

Both economic and spiritual welfare statists have rejected any defense of capitalism based on a moral footing. Those who do try to defend capitalism have rejected the possibility of a rational normative approach completely. But in fact, capitalist society cannot be given sound support unless the rights of *all* individuals can be shown to be founded on sound, rational, objectively established moral theory demonstrating that altruistic considerations, while they have their place in human relations, do not play a primary, decisive role in human relations or justify depriving others of their liberty.

Adam Smith observed that modern moral philosophy is defective, and the defect to which he pointed suggests that a better philosophical approach to morality would be supportive of the free society:

> Ancient moral philosophy proposed to investigate wherein consisted the happiness and perfection of a man, considered not only as an individual, but as the member of a family, or a state, and of the great society of mankind. In that philosophy, the duties of human life were treated of as subservient to the happiness and perfection of human life. But, when moral as well as natural philosophy came to be taught only as subservient to theology, the duties of human life were treated of as chiefly subservient to the happiness of a life to come. In the ancient philosophy, the perfection of virtue was represented as necessarily productive to the person who possessed it, of the most perfect happiness in this life. In the modern philosophy, it was frequently represented as almost always inconsistent with any degree of happiness in this life, and heaven was to be earned by penance and mortification, not by the liberal, generous, and spirited conduct of a man. By far the most important of all the different branches of philosophy became in this manner by far the most corrupted.[7]

At this juncture, the work of Ayn Rand has to be considered, for it is this ancient perspective on the moral life of human beings that she has resurrected –

without the flaws contained in its renditions in ancient thought (for example, its metaphysical idealism and its reification of abstract, collective humanity).

RAND'S CONTRIBUTION

What Rand shows is that man has an objective need for morality, and that the morality appropriate to satisfy this need is one in which "the duties of human life [are] subservient to the happiness and perfection of human life."[8] The ethical theory of rational self-interest, articulated throughout Rand's philosophical works and displayed in her fiction, returns to a view advanced by Aristotle, among others, as to the place and function of morality in human life. But when applied within the sphere of human community life, Rand's ethics of rational self-interest implies a political system of capitalism in its purest form, not the semipaternalistic ideal of Aristotle's polity.

Also, Rand's idea of rational self-interest is entirely different from the Hobbesian and neo-Hobbesian versions of egoism. The reason why both Randian ethics and Hobbesian ethics are referred to as egoistic or individualistic is that, in each, the individual is placed at the pinnacle of the hierarchy of values in human existence, and in neither is any alternative arrangement seen. But the self for Rand is very different from what it is for Hobbes and his contemporaries, and the principles of morality that flow from these two forms of egoism are very different, which is clearly shown in the preceding chapters based on Rand's ethical theory.

The most important criticism of Rand's ethical teaching is hinted at by Michael Novak, who states that to ask humans to seek their own flourishing in life is insufficient inspiration and is, thus, socially and politically self-destructive. To guarantee the self-perpetuation of the social system, he says, we need a moral vision; to place the individual at the highest point of our value scale simply is not inspiring enough.[9] It is true that an individualist, or egoist, cannot construct some kind of collective moral vision. Rand's ethical theory, however, enables each of us to construct our own personal – but always human – ideal; and her philosophical inquiry demonstrates that that is everything there can and should be to a moral vision.

WHAT ABOUT THE VISION THING?

Ultimately, the capacity of a moral theory to provide a bona fide moral vision (as opposed to a fraudulent, utopian vision) confirms the truth of that theory. A valid moral vision is the highest realizable ideal, not an impossible dream. It will inspire good human beings to defend the conditions that make this ideal possible. But if what Novak and other newfound supporters of capitalism are asking for is a magic formula that can generate an inspired defense of the free society, then nothing will satisfy them. It is only human conviction that can supply such a defense, not some creed that purports to guarantee inspiration in us all.

Humans may not always be guided by truth, but when they are guided by falsehood, the likelihood of their becoming frustrated is so great that cynicism will result. What has prevented cynicism wherever corrupt moralities have taken root is an admixture of common sense. Thus the self-sacrifice that is part of most moralities is tempered with a requirement for honesty and integrity – virtues that promote anything but one's demise. But it is undeniable that cynicism has closed in upon us frequently enough in human history. If it is true today that the West has lost its will, it is true because we lack a sound moral code that nurtures realistic and robust moral visions.

In what sense does Rand's work enable one to create a moral vision? For Rand, as for Aristotle, the question "How should a human community be organized?" can be answered only after the question "How should I, a human being, live my life?" has been answered. Rand follows the Greek tradition of regarding politics as a subfield of ethics, although she envisions the actual substance of these two fields in ways that are significantly distinct enough to make it necessary to consider her views on their own. For Rand, the right way to live is the ground on which to establish the basic principles governing interpersonal behavior. These principles of community conduct establish the appropriate principles that govern political life.[10]

A moral vision is an image of the state of affairs that arises from living by a particular code of ethics. Virtually any moral point of view offers something akin to a moral vision for those who care to formulate it. Theologically based ethics have been accompanied by an other-worldly vision – a state of ultimate bliss – that would result from leading the moral life on earth. In secular altruistic moralities, images of the (loving) brotherhood of all men (such as that promised in the communist future) are envisioned. The function of such images is to remind one of the concrete implications of subscribing to the life of virtue. In practical terms, the images encourage loyalty to the principles being promoted.

A central feature of the persistent criticism of classical–liberal, democratic capitalism has been that it fails to project an inspiring moral vision. Within the tradition of capitalism, the value of liberty is socially paramount. However, liberty is by definition an absence of coercion, an absence of an evil. Liberty is not the presence of a concrete achievement, although, when possessed of liberty, a free individual can create a concrete good.

So classical liberalism admittedly lacks a complete moral vision, since it focuses on the political front alone. One of classical liberalism's greatest virtues, namely, its relegation of politics to a discrete realm of human life, is turned against it by a wide variety of collectivist demands. Indeed, it is a contradiction to demand that classical liberalism offer, in the context of a theory of limited politics, a total moral vision. Yet what classical liberalism has achieved is conceiving of a political order in conformity with human nature – a system requiring that each individual carry full responsibility for one's own moral achievements and failures. Only where others would obstruct this individual responsibility may the government – the instrument of our political concerns – make a move. Is this classical liberalism's shortcoming?

Irving Kristol puts it this way: "The enemy of liberal capitalism is not so much socialism as nihilism."[11] If by this, Kristol means that liberal capitalism can amount to a sound political system only if its political features alone can avoid nihilism – the abnegation of values – then he accepts the collectivist assumption that it is the function of politics to supply the full substance of morality. This assumption is in direct conflict with the individualist foundations of the capitalist system; and if these ethical foundations are sound, Kristol is simply asking for the impossible.

INDIVIDUALISM AND THE *SUMMUM BONUM*

A more complex objection to the individualist foundation of capitalism is advanced by Leo Strauss. In his characterization of Locke's view of human nature, Strauss remarks:

> Through the shift of emphasis from natural duties or obligations to natural rights, the individual, the ego, had become the center and origin of the moral world, since man – as distinguished from man's end – had become the center or origin.[12]

Strauss sees the base of morality in the classical–liberal ethos not as an ideal to be reached, but as a need to be satisfied. For Strauss, the individual denies the idea of a *summum bonum* – some highest good toward which to aspire, or the supreme good from which all others are derived – and "in the absence of *summum bonum*, man would lack completely a star and compass for his life if there were no *summum malum*"[13] – a worst evil from which to escape (for example, the death of oneself). However, Rand's view is that man is an end in himself qua man, that is, that the realization of the rational capacity in one's particular life is a *summum bonum*. She thereby rejects the possibility of separating human life and human good.[14]

From analyses such as Strauss's, many have concluded that classical–liberal capitalism, the free society, lacks normative backing and cannot be morally justified. If it is true that only by reference to the idea that human beings are driven (by genes, history, evolutionary forces, or instinct) can the free society be defended, the foregoing conclusions follow. But the conclusion is ill founded: it is possible, clearly, that the type of society defended on neo-Hobbesian grounds can also be defended on the basis of a quite different understanding of human existence. It may be true that if the Hobbesian viewpoint is correct, then capitalism suits us well. But it is false that if the Hobbesian view is wrong, then capitalism does not suit us well.

Ayn Rand set on course a train of philosophical-ethical reflections that enables us to construct for ourselves a moral vision that is not so deceptively simple as the theocratic and collectivist alternatives. The payoff is that each individual can achieve a credible, realizable moral vision that incorporates private and public (that is, distinctively political) components.

Such a vision is not simple, because it takes into account the individuality of everyone, as well as everyone's essential humanity. Since individuality thus conceived does not occupy some inferior metaphysical and moral position – as with Plato and Marx – it has to be regarded seriously. However, it does not boil down to mere quantitative significance, as individualism does within a nominalist/atomistic framework. Liberalism based on atomistic individualism could not withstand attacks such as Marx's, since, as Marx observed, "the freedom in question is that of a man treated as an isolated monad and withdrawn into himself."[15]

In the metaphysical position that Rand briefly intimates, the particular and the universal are inseparable. Accordingly, her principles of moral conduct support a moral vision of both aspects of each individual's life – humanity and individuality – equally and inseparably. Each person's excellence involves the process of achieving and sustaining the human life that is one's own, requiring that there be upheld both a unity of persons and a distinctiveness, even separateness, of each person from the other.

From an individualist perspective, basic virtues would still guide the life of a good person. But the results of the implementation of these virtues cannot be assimilated into a uniformly applicable concrete picture. Each person can have a moral vision, but there can be no collective moral vision. In lieu of a collectivist vision, Rand establishes a vision of the moral life as it applies to basic human relationships in a political context:

> I am neither foe nor friend to my brothers, but such as each of them shall deserve of me. And to earn my love, my brothers must do more than to have been born. I do not grant my love without reason, nor to any chance passerby who may wish to claim it. I honor men with my love. But honor is a thing to be earned.
>
> I shall choose friends among men, but neither slaves nor masters. And I shall choose only such as please me, and them I shall love and respect, but neither command nor obey. And we shall join our hands when we wish or walk alone when we so desire. For in the temple of his spirit, each man is alone. Let each man keep his temple untouched and undefiled. Then let him join hands with others if he wishes, but only beyond his holy threshold.[16]

The political vision here suggested – and further developed throughout this book – makes considerable demands upon us, for it must be filled in by each of us with concrete content. It postulates the individual's aspiration to excellence, but precludes any guarantee that this social moral vision will be achieved. To give this personal moral vision of individualism public expression is a difficult artistic task indeed. Certain forms of art serve as the medium for this purpose. The novel, play, ballet, and painting all are media for such expression of more or less widely applicable moral visions that exalt and inspire. Unfortunately, this domain of feeling associated with the arts has been almost the exclusive province of religion. Rand explains:

> Religion's monopoly in the field of ethics has made it extremely diffi-
> cult to communicate the emotional meaning and connotation of a
> rational view of life. Just as religion has preempted the field of ethics,
> turning morality against man, so it has usurped the highest moral
> concepts of our language, placing them outside this earth and beyond
> man's reach.[17]

THE SPIRITUALITY OF RAND'S ETHICS VERSUS NIHILISM

Given the long history of religion's dominance in the arts and the only recent tolerance of secular artistic expression, it is to Rand's artistic credit that despite her unambiguous atheism, some have proclaimed her a profoundly religious writer. The meaning of E. Merrill Root's praise of her, for example, is none other than that she has been able to inspire and produce exaltation with her artistry and that many people have no way of explaining this other than by linking it with something mystical, despite the rational philosophical foundations of all of Ayn Rand's ideas and imagery.

It is imperative that those who are concerned with the spiritual revitalization of the West stress the need for a rational morality and an individualist moral vision. But will these be adequate to counter nihilism? Once again, consider Irving Kristol:

> In every society, the overwhelming majority of the people lead lives of
> considerable frustration, and if society is to endure, it needs to be able
> to rely on a goodly measure of stoical resignation. In theory, this could
> be philosophical rather than religious; in fact, philosophical stoicism
> has always been an aristocratic prerogative; it has never been able to
> give an acceptable rationale of "one's station and one's duties" to those
> whose stations are low and duties are onerous.[18]

With certain widely, though implicitly, accepted assumptions embedded in these observations, what Kristol is saying seems almost commonplace. No one is always satisfied, and we all know of some who are entirely desperate, even in the best of times. Does it follow that for such people to have hope, something of a fancy story – a Platonistic "noble lie" – must sustain them?

It does not, once the assumptions are made explicit. First, Kristol flatly accepts the view that at root, morality consists of duties. So conceived, a morally excellent life comes down to a life dominated by chores. This makes it plausible that to live a moral life, one would need some incentive beyond life itself, such as rewards in heaven or avoidance of hell.

Second, in Kristol's detached framework, the issue of the truth of religion seems to be set entirely aside. From his god's-eye point of view, religion has, in fact, no basis; yet he, unlike the rest of us, is in possession of the aristocratic prerogative and sees that we need religion. If "in theory," morality could be defended philosophically, then religion is not indispensable unless human beings are somehow naturally divided into those who can live with truth and those who require deception. That Kristol finds this the proper attitude toward his fellow humans is indicative of why he believes that life for most must be accepted stoically.

Despite the evidence that supports some of what Kristol says, we would be fooled by what is blatantly apparent – for example, via newspapers, television, magazines, and the rhetoric of politics – to think that human life is as dismal as he reports. He fails to mention, for example, the private lives of millions who totally escape news reporting and sociological inquiry. I am here focusing mostly on the quality of life linked to a so-called bourgeois society. In contrast, one need but examine reports from totalitarian states and consider the fate of millions who have lived through the epochs of feudalism, Caesarism, theocracy, and tribalism.

When one also recalls what one these days is prominently said to have a natural right to (explained, for example, in the United Nations Universal Declaration of Human Rights adopted in December 1948 and held up as a model of the just social system ever since), it is not difficult to see that despite appearances to the contrary, stoicism is not what is required. It is true that even in the United States, the state has rigged circumstances so that the lives of many people are legally stymied (or kept artificially at a point of parasitic prosperity), and some people lead lives of considerable deprivation and genuine frustration. But there is no reason why this needs to remain so for these persons individually.

There is, then, no reason to accept the pessimism Kristol projects. Neoconservatives such as Kristol and William Bennett, just as communitarians such as Michael Sandel and Charles Taylor, are correct to be concerned with morality, but they mislead us about the nature of morality and what is required to explain it and give it force within our culture. The former are playing into the hands of irrationalism by seriously advocating religion as the opiate of the masses, while the latter encourage group thinking, the sort of morality that produces reliance on an elite that will speak for the community as a whole and whose consequent exercise of power will violate the worth of individual human beings.

ALTRUISTIC LEGACIES

Throughout history in most countries, religion, with virtually absolute links to the state, has monopolized reflection – theorizing, teaching, and criticizing – about morality. Even in the United States, public education evolved very early, usually as a secular substitute for reliance on religious schooling. In both theocratic and democratic traditions, morality has retained its altruistic emphasis (at least as officially taught), in the first instance stressing the primacy of one's duty to God or to gods, in the second one's duty to the state or one's fellows. Since the message in both instances bodes ill for all those who are being addressed, it is not surprising that either a heaven or a role in making a future heaven-on-earth has been promised to achieve compliance.

Aside from other problems, the idea that hope lies in the revitalization of a supernaturalist religious moral perspective is a will-o'-the-wisp. The only type of moral perspective left is secular, which is why Marxism – the most extreme secular altruistic/collectivist perspective on human life – has fared so well in the absence of alternative secular normative positions. In the end, we need to keep in mind that pessimism about the capacity of a philosophical secular ethics rests mainly on the prior acceptance of the view that ethics requires self-denial. This realization reaffirms the enormous influence of the modern outlook on ethics referred to by Adam Smith: "heaven [is] to be earned by penance and mortification, not by the liberal, generous, and spirited conduct of a man."

But abandoning the pessimistic stance is justified, especially in light of Ayn Rand's work. Its paramount significance is that it has paved the way for us to realize that from an ethical viewpoint, the rational conceptualization and pursuit of one's own happiness are clearly possible and noble – everyone's life can be inspired akin to how an artist's work often is, leading to exaltation of a naturalist kind instead of getting lost in the hopelessly incoherent aspirations that are set before us by altruism.

Rand's ethical–egoist, or classical–individualist, ethics is not the promise of making mankind perfect, but it is the promise of the possibility of self-perfection, of being the best person one can be in the context of one's existence. This requires, however, that humans undertake the supreme moral effort to think conscientiously and to live by the judgment of such conscientious thought.

A FINAL WORD ON THE MARXIAN CHALLENGE

Among the numerous concerns, genuine or otherwise, that have stood in the way of accepting the possibility of a moral vision of rational egoism – individualism within the moral/political framework of capitalism – a final one demands rebuttal. This is the Marxian and theocratically inspired lament that in social terms, the ethics of self-interest means mere "egoistic calculation." The question is: "Does ethical egoism really resolve personal worth into exchange value? Is commerce satanic?"

Rand may on first sight appear to be simply classified among those who reduce all human relationships to exchange value. In John Galt's famous speech in *Atlas Shrugged*, we are told, for example, "We, who live by values, not by loot, are traders, both in matter and in spirit. A trader is a man who earns what he gets and does not give or take the unearned."[19]

A close look should make clear that this understanding of trade has little to do with the *Homo economicus* conceptions of human relationships. There is nothing purely materialistic or involving economic cost–benefit analysis in the trader image of man in Rand's viewpoint. For Rand, emphasis is on the *terms* of human relationships, not on their motivation or the alleged economic impetus for all human conduct. A rational egoist is not a utility maximizer, a calculating hedonist, but an individual who acts on principle, by reference to a code of values that is not reducible to, but merely subsumes (within a certain social domain), market values.

Rand anticipates the attempt to dismiss her position by those who assimilate it within the materialist, reductionist tradition. She distinguishes between the sort of subjective value (or revealed preference) stressed by economists and some other defenders of the free society as the only meaningful value and the value various anticapitalist critics find to be in need of emphasis. Rand notes that:

> the market value of a product does not reflect its philosophically objective value, but only its socially objective value. . . . [The former is] estimated from the standpoint of the best possible for man, i.e., by the criterion of the most rational mind possessing the greatest knowledge, in a given category, in a given period, and in a defined context. . . . [The latter is] the sum of the individual judgments of all the men involved in trade at a given time, the sum of what *they* valued, each in the context of his own life.[20]

So, unlike the economic advocates of the free market, Rand does not equate all types of value – for example, artistic, economic, moral, and scientific. In the marketplace where people know very little of each other, exchange value may indeed be as close a measure of personal worth (between those involved in trade) as can reasonably be expected of the traders. A good chef will gain esteem as such; a bad taxi driver will fail to do so. It is probable that outside of economic engagements, individuals reach levels of nobility or dishonor not evident in the marketplace, yet indifference about this in commercial relationships is nothing to lament. One does not require the total recognition of one's worth or worthlessness from others one knows but slightly.

The market does not prevent a rational communication of value between those who trade with each other, but it does not fancy itself the court of last resort in these matters, contrary to what collectivists imagine to be required for human self-esteem. As Nathaniel Branden explains:

> Under capitalism, men are free to *choose* their "social bonds" – meaning, to choose whom they will associate with. Men are not trapped within the prison of their family, tribe, caste, class, or neighborhood. They choose whom they will value, whom they will be-friend, whom they will deal with, what kind of relationships they will enter. This implies and entails man's responsibility to form independent judgments. It implies and entails, also, that a man must *earn* the social relationships he desires.[21]

Replying to Erich Fromm, one of capitalism's long-time severest neo-Marxian critics, Branden shows just how misconceived is the view that "the principle underlying capitalist society and the principle of love are incompatible."[22] Fromm, following the early Marx (who followed Ludwig Feuerbach), advocates in effect that the intimacy of love between persons can be grafted onto the human race at large. Capitalism is unacceptable to him since it does not adjust itself to this fantasy and instead makes "the fairness ethic . . . the particular ethical contribution of capitalist society."[23]

But Fromm's idea and corresponding program are an illusion and a horror chamber, as recent history has shown so vividly. Contrary to what some stubborn apologists for Marx still cling to – namely, the view that the Marxist-inspired (though not *caused*) Soviet Union, Stalinism, gulags, and other totalitarian evils throughout the world are merely perversions of an essentially human philosophy – Marxism, as Leszek Kolakowski has observed, may not have been "predestined to become the ideology of the self-glorifying Russian Bureaucracy . . . [but] it contained essential features, as opposed to accidental and secondary ones, that made it adaptable for this purpose."[24] To try to make mankind conform to an ideal suited to how two people might, if very good and very lucky, relate to each other in personal intimacy is to bring forth barbarism and inner death.

Subsuming some human relationships within the economic exchange framework is not only inoffensive, but morally commendable, even inspiring. Trading with the grocery clerk or plumber, we can only feign close friendship unless we come to know each other very well by spending a great deal of time together. Close relations require knowledge and appreciation of a person's history, aspirations, character, dreams, foibles, tastes, and so forth. Unless we come to know a person as an individual, we deal with him more justly by rewarding him for the little he has in fact done for us in engaging in a particular transaction. We each can leave the market and find ourselves being appreciated by others for different reasons, and we always have as a last – and perhaps best – resort our own self-esteem. To fantasize about a closer relationship is to build utopian dreams that are the stuff of fairy tales, not of political philosophy.

What we can and should do is pay persons the respect due them for having done admirable work. Via the money we exchange, provided it represents value (honest earnings, not officially inflated "notes"), both can assume the work is done well enough that others might enter the same transaction. In a free market, it is this basic trust we can ask of our relations with one another. We can even begin to become friends. All over the world, every hour of the day, humans befriend each other. But it is false that they are duty-bound to do so and intolerable that they should be forcibly organized accordingly.

One lamented consequence of our market dealings – as well as some nonmarket ones – is the possibility of benefiting persons of whom, if one knew them, one would disapprove. One might, indeed, be exchanging value with a serious enemy: for example, a Jew might inadvertently trade with an anti-Semite, neither knowing that the other is an antagonist. But at least it is possible to avoid such exchanges in a free marketplace, where boycotts and other voluntary economic inducements are possible. In socialist and other planned economies, one cannot choose whom one will benefit. In general, the beneficial consequences of market impartiality – the concrete result of the "fairness ethic" – are considerable. Most of this is evident from common sense and is obscured only when we view the world with ideological blinders.

IDEALISM WITHOUT UTOPIANISM

Those who dream of a society that will guarantee for everyone a collective utopian vision will always find the free society objectionable. Those who discuss the moral foundations of capitalism and its capacity to sustain a moral vision are usually theoreticians who assess the issues with the aid of elaborate theories. Or they are unaware of the theoretical support for *laissez-faire* capitalism, so they tend to accept the distorted history, handed down under ideological influences, that is hostile to capitalism.

Commerce can appear to be satanic to such individuals, especially if they have accepted impossible ideals by which to evaluate political systems and have not questioned the belief that capitalist societies are to be viewed in the mode of a boxing ring. In the tradition of Aristotelian[25] (not Hobbesian) ethical theories, personal economic well-being is one aspect of a larger concern for all human life. Thus capitalist human relations need not be crass.

Ayn Rand's ethical conception of human life, personal and social, enables one to sustain a moral vision that is both realistic and exalting – capable of inspiring humans to heights never before attempted. To date, however, Ayn Rand has not received her due from the intellectual community as an advocate of the philosophical and ethical base of free society. Although her novels have been bestsellers since their original publication, most intellectuals have merely alluded to her ideas in asides. Rand's observation on this topic is instructive:

> It is only the American people – not the intellectuals – who have given signs of rebellion against altruism. It is a blind, groping, ideologically helpless rebellion. But it would be a terrible crime of history if that rebellion is allowed to be defeated by silent default.[26]

Unfortunately, such default appears to be in the making today. Those intellectuals who would speak of the need for spiritual fuel must recognize the supreme social importance of liberty; and those who value liberty must value morality, the fuel of the spirit. The likes of Peter Unger and Peter Singer, for example, who are repeatedly advocating altruism (the placing of others, even animals, ahead of the individual human being's rational self-interest), are a testimony to the justifiability of Rand's concern.

Yet matters can change, and to any who would seriously consider a change for the better, Rand's words could be of considerable value:

> Now is the time to assert, to proclaim and to uphold the ideas that created America – and thus save this country and, incidentally, to offer guidance to a perishing world. But, this cannot be done without rejecting the morality of altruism.[27]

While this may appear hyperbolic to many, it is what I have been developing throughout this work: a serious warning. The human species is best guided by an ethical system in terms of which every individual ought to place his or her own human flourishing as a rational animal in first place on one's list of priorities. That is what classical individualism proposes, and it seems to be the ethics that is most conducive to human living.

EPILOGUE

The idea of this book is really rather straightforward: human beings are the most important aspects of nature, and each individual human being ought to treat himself or herself accordingly. Affirming this point appears to be dangerous to many because of the risk of irrational self-aggrandizement associated with it. Yet there is a far greater risk of utter confusion from the thesis that for each of us, it is others who are most important. This cannot make clear sense to anyone: Why are those others so important when oneself is not? Why be obliged to take care of those who don't deserve it? Why are we to accept what so many preachers and moralists advocate, put most succinctly, perhaps, by a Graham Greene character, who says, "None of us has a right to forget anyone. Except ourselves"?[1]

More likely, each one of us ought to regard his or her life as supremely important and appreciate, through this, that this is equally true of everyone else. The politics that will emerge is no less clear-cut: The free society in which everyone is a sovereign citizen, not subject to the will of others unless this is consented to. That the truth of such a clear-cut idea is in need of some showing is not in question – that explains this book. Yet the truth of the idea is also something that is or ought to be plain common sense. Indeed, it is probably shown through the actual conduct of many, many people, even if when they articulate their ethics, they speak confusedly. But that, I think, is well explained by W. D. Falk, who ascribes it to the fact that in public discourse, we tend to focus mainly on what people ought, morally, to do for one another, even though this is not the whole story by any means as to how each person ought to carry on in life. In the last analysis, as Falk indicates, "the social virtues derive joint support from our natural concern for our own good and for that of society."[2]

What the classical–individualist position comes to, then, is a view that guides one to be virtuous in the sense that will enhance one's life as a human being. Since what it is to be human is to have the basic capacity to think and act rationally, doing so will be the broadest imperative of this ethical position.

Of course, ideas can go only so far in serving us with guidance. Personal resolve is equally necessary – indeed, without such resolve, we will never think the ideas we need to guide our living. Thus a discussion of morality is only that, a discussion. The task is to live ethically, to do the right thing, and that is some-thing for which much more information is needed than that provided by any ethical system.

NOTES

PREFACE

1 Ayn Rand, *Atlas Shrugged* (New York: Random House, 1957), p. 1012. This idea is developed considerably in Nathaniel Branden, "Free Will, Moral Responsibility, and the Law," in T. R. Machan, ed., *The Libertarian Alternative* (Chicago: Nelson-Hall, 1974), pp. 419–44. Aristotle's idea that human beings are by nature rational animals expresses the point less elaborately, and Thomas Aquinas, as well as Immanuel Kant (but in a significantly different sense), follows suit. In each case the fact that is central, essential, about being human is that one is a biological organism whose survival and flourishing are best secured by the choice and initiative to think, to be rationally conscious on the conceptual level.

2 To clarify, it should be noted that although Rand's works taught me a good deal of the broad outline of what follows, that itself was due, in some measure, to my own early sensibilities and reflections, albeit not well developed and articulated at that time – that is, during my childhood and adolescence. The evolution of my thinking is recounted in some of my unpublished autobiographical writings and do not belong in the present work.

3 Tibor R. Machan, *Capitalism and Individualism: Reframing the Argument for the Free Society* (New York: St. Martin's Press, 1990).

4 Thomas Hobbes, "Good," Chapter 6 of *Leviathan* (New York: Collier Books, 1962), p. 48.

5 Quoted in Paul Zweig, *The Heresy of Self-Love* (Princeton, N.J.: Princeton University Press, 1968), p. 26.

6 Zweig, *The Heresy of Self-Love*, p. 27.

7 For the individualist elements of Islam, among other religions of the world, see Marshall G. S. Hodgson, *The Venture of Islam: Conscience and History in a World Civilization*, 3 vols (Chicago: University of Chicago Press, 1974). Hodgson takes account of certain radical individualist aspects of Islamic thought, whereby the faithful are taken to be wholly unique in their relationship with God.

8 Eduard Zeller, *Aristotle and the Earlier Peripatetics*, trans. B. F. C. Costelloe and J. H. Muirhead (London: Oxford University Press, 1897), pp. 224–6 (quoted in Fred D. Miller, Jr., *Nature, Justice, and Rights in Aristotle's* Politics [Oxford: Clarendon Press, 1995], pp. 200–1). For an individualist understanding of Aristotle's metaphysics, see Emerson Buchanan, *Aristotle's Theory of Being* (Cambridge, Mass.: Greek, Roman, and Byzantine Monographs, 1962). As he puts it, "in identifying *ousia* (Being) with [what it is for each thing to exist], Aristotle is asserting that the fundamental reality on which everything else depends is the existence of the individual" (p. 2).

9 Shirley Robin Letwin, "Romantic Love and Christianity," *Philosophy* 52 (April 1977): 134–5.
10 See, for example, Fred D. Miller, Jr., *Nature, Justice, and Rights in Aristotle's* Politics (Oxford: Clarendon Press, 1995), and Zeller, *Aristotle and the Earlier Peripatetics.* Miller does a superb job of demonstrating Aristotle's moderate individualism, as distinct from what is usually attributed to him, a moderate or even full-fledged collectivism.
11 John Locke, *Two Treatises of Government* (London: Everyman, 1993), p. 117.
12 So designating the position would, however, be extremely risky in light of the very close affinity the term "egoism" has to neo-Hobbesian radical individualism.
13 Karl Marx, "On the Jewish Question," in *Selected Writings*, ed. David McLellan (London: Oxford University Press, 1977), p. 126.

1 INDIVIDUALISM AND CLASSICAL LIBERALISM

1 Karl Marx, "On the Jewish Question," in *Selected Writings*, ed. David McLellan (Oxford: Oxford University Press, 1977).
2 Irving Kristol, *Two Cheers for Capitalism* (New York: Basic Books, 1973). This book includes the text of Kristol's Mt. Pelerin Society talk mentioned above.
3 Bernard Mandeville's motto "private vice, public benefit" captures this idea best. It has been the impetus for a good deal of economic thinking since the publication of Adam Smith's *The Wealth of Nations* in 1776. When we consider the details of economic theory itself, we find that it is not self-interested behavior but so-called utility-maximizing behavior that we are all driven to engage in, and the content of the utility is entirely subjective – thus the thesis ultimately comes to be tautological, since, of course, we all do what we do because we do it. By this "explanation" of human behavior, no wonder everything is fully explained, from suicide and marriage to bank robbery and multibillion-dollar corporate mergers. In all these cases, people do what they do because they want to do it, and the way we can test the truth of this claim is by noticing that they are indeed doing it. For a discussion of why this is no explanation at all, see my *Capitalism and Individualism: Reframing the Argument for the Free Society* (New York: St. Martin's Press, 1990).
4 Among those who have approached ethics along such sociological lines are David Hume, Adam Smith, Adam Ferguson, and Bernard Mandeville.
5 The most ambitious effort to debunk individualism on a regular basis consists in the launching of the journal *The Responsive Community*, edited by Amitai Etzioni of George Washington University. See, also, his book *The Spirit of Community* (New York: Crown, 1993). Some more subtle efforts in this direction have been made by such philosophical luminaries as Richard Rorty. See, for example, his *Objectivity, Relativism, and Truth* (Cambridge: Cambridge University Press, 1991), especially Chapter 1, "Objectivity versus Solidarity," in which the result of a pragmatic theory of knowledge abolishes objectivity in all disciplines of human knowledge and replaces it with the communitarian ideal of solidarity.
6 See Rorty, *Objectivity, Relativism, and Truth*, p. 31 ff, where he flatly rejects the theory of individual rights, basing his argument on his communitarian, or solidaristic, outlook, as well as on a pretty blatant mischaracterization of the idea of individual rights.
7 George Stigler, "Economics or Ethics?," in Sterling M. McMurrin, ed., *Tanner Lectures on Human Values, 1980* (Cambridge: Cambridge University Press, 1981).
8 This radical subjectivist position on ethics developed after and in contrast to Hobbes's thesis, in which there was at least one objective value to be pursued by all, namely, survival.

9 Daniel Bell, *The Cultural Contradictions of Capitalism* (New York: Basic Books, 1972).
10 Thomas Hobbes, "Good," Chapter 6 of *Leviathan* (New York: Collier Books, 1962), p. 48.
11 See Ludwig Wittgenstein, *Philosophical Investigations* (Oxford: Basil Blackwell & Mott, 1953), as well as extensions of his argument as presented by others, e.g., Richard Rorty, Susan Mendus – claiming that his objection to the possibility of a private language is, in fact, a blanket rejection of the possibility of any individual human act.

2 ETHICS AND FREE WILL

1 I have explored a number of crucial works in this area and found either no mention or barely a hint concerning whether human beings are beings that possess free will. See, for example, Alan Goldman, *The Moral Foundations of Professional Ethics* (Totowa, N.J.: Rowman & Littlefield, 1980); Albert Flores, ed., *Professional Ideals* (Belmont, Calif.: Wadsworth, 1988); Nicholas Fotion and Gerard Elfstrom, *Military Ethics* (London: Routledge & Kegan Paul, 1986); Lloyd J. Matthews and Dale E. Brown, eds, *The Parameters of Military Ethics* (New York: Pergamon-Brassey's, 1989); and Darrell Reeck, *Ethics for the Professions: A Christian Perspective* (Minneapolis: Augsburg, 1982). The same holds in both the general and the specialized applied-ethics works, as well as journal papers.
2 See, for more on this, Walter Olson, *The Excuse Factory* (New York: The Free Press, 1997).
3 The injustice would arise only if the confusion were a result of culpable negligence. Yet, of course, the problem we are exploring is itself whether the very idea of injustice can be made sense of within the widespread confusion that abounds.
4 It is interesting to observe that already at this point of our discussion, what has been termed "the determinist's dilemma" confronts us, namely, whether such lamentations could even make sense concerning human behavior, including forming a belief in certain propositions, unless individuals had the capacity and power to undertake changing their conduct of their own accord. See James N. Jordan, "Determinism's Dilemma," *Review of Metaphysics*, 23 (September 1969): 48–66.
5 B. F. Skinner, *Beyond Freedom and Dignity* (New York: Bantam Books, 1971). I have discussed Skinner's views in Tibor R. Machan, *The Pseudo-Science of B. F. Skinner* (New Rochelle, N.Y.: Arlington House, 1974).
6 Arguably, philosophers express their praise and blame somewhat subtly, not always using the most direct terms to signify blaming or praising. (Consider when philosophers criticize one another on grounds of logic alone – that kind of comment, too, invokes certain norms that presumably the target of criticism ought to heed!) Moreover, we may, without any distortion, include within our class of beliefs and utterances various proclamations concerning what people should or should not do, what sort of conduct and practices by persons and human organizations should or should not be carried out.
7 Not just journals proliferate, but also textbooks, conferences, and university courses, featuring claims as to what various professionals should or should not do. And of course, philosophers are active in the various controversies about multiculturalism, feminism, freedom of expression, and so forth, which abound on university campuses, so here, too, they immerse themselves in ethics and need to be clear about whether they are addressing themselves to human beings who can make free choices or to beings who are being moved about by forces over which they cannot exert any independent, original control.

8 Some, such as John Kekes, argue that there can be exceptions to this idea. See John Kekes, "'Ought Implies Can' and Kinds of Morality," *Philosophical Quarterly*, 34 (October 1984): 460–7. See, also, his *Facing Evil* (Princeton, N.J.: Princeton University Press, 1991), which includes the bulk of the discussion from the aforementioned paper as well as others, such as "Freedom," *Pacific Philosophical Quarterly*, 61 (October 1980): 368–85.

Even Kekes does not deny that it holds in most cases when we claim that someone should or should not do something. Also, when Kekes argues that there are exceptions to "ought implies can" in such cases as when someone regrets (not) having done something even if there is no way he or she could (not) have done it, a problem arises. The point rests too much weight on a given understanding of what could be at issue. Instead of denying "ought implies can" on the basis of such rare cases, we might explain them as cases of confused thinking, of which there surely is ample evidence. False guilt is clearly the material of a great deal of psychoanalysis. Indeed, there would be no point in identifying such false guilt if there were not instances of genuine guilt. Kekes attempts, of course, to develop an alternative analysis, based on his contrast between choice and character morality, claiming the latter makes better sense of our moral experiences. I would dispute this, but this is not the place for that.

One may view Kekes's analysis as making more of ordinary-language materials than may be warranted. A bit of philosophy may help those caught in such confusions; indeed, philosophy may well be provided by psychotherapists, in their somewhat indirect ways, to those who may need it but may have to be approached somewhat gingerly.

It is also to be noted that in Kekes's discussion, "choice" is ambiguous: it could mean "selection" as well as "initiation," yet the free-will thesis requires the latter sense; the former is fully compatible with determinism – animals, as well as anything else in motion, may be said to be involved in making selections. Indeed, Kekes, in his paper "Freedom," as well as in discussions at the 1981 Summer Liberty Fund Seminar, in Santa Barbara, California, argues for a conception of freedom as involving not being made to do what one does by others, that is, doing things on one's own. In other words, when one makes one's selections oneself, one is free. But self-initiation of one's actions, including the mental processes that selection presupposes, is denied by Kekes, who thinks modern science renders this incongruous. I argue in this book that science does not preclude self-initiation of our behavior. See, also, my books *Individuals and Their Rights* (La Salle, Ill.: Open Court, 1989) and *The Pseudo-Science of B. F. Skinner*.

Others, such as Michael Slote, deny that free will is necessary for ethics. See Michael Slote, "Ethics Without Free Will," *Social Theory and Practice*, 16 (Fall 1990): 369–83. See, also, Michael Slote, *From Morality to Virtue* (London: Oxford University Press, 1992). Slote holds that virtue ethics, as well as utilitarianism, can make good sense of blaming and praising, as devices by which to habituate people to behave well. Still, there is always going to remain some requirement for the role of initiation in human action, for if we deny it, ethics will vanish, just as the credibility of witchcraft vanished once certain other powers were denied. (Aristotle's virtue ethics made choice a prerequisite of moral virtue.) Of course, that may be simply true, and so much the worse for ethics.

9 John Rawls, *A Theory of Justice* (Cambridge, Mass.: Harvard University Press, 1971).

10 Robert Nozick, *Anarchy, State, and Utopia* (New York: Basic Books, 1974).

11 Brian Barry, *Political Arguments* (London: Routledge & Kegan Paul, 1965); Nicholas Rescher, *Distributive Justice* (New York: Bobbs-Merrill, 1966).

12 John Rawls, "The Independence of Moral Theory," in *Proceedings and Addresses of the American Philosophical Association*, vol. XLVII (Newark, Del.: American Philosophical Association, 1975), pp. 5–22.

13 Rawls, "The Independence of Moral Theory," p. 21.

14 David Hume, A *Treatise of Human Nature* (Garden City, N.Y.: Dolphin Books, 1961).

15 Of course, these general schools divide into many subsections based on innumerable refinements on the main features of these broadly characterized schools. Some of them may not agree with the position I ascribe to them above. Yet there need be little argument about this here, for in their central claims, these schools do find it unlikely, if not outright impossible, that philosophy will properly handle normative, especially ethical and political, problems.

16 One may suppose that this provision is part of the process so as to avoid total arbitrariness, which intuitionism *per se* would entail. Yet there is reason to think that introducing the proviso robs the method of its independence. See Tibor R. Machan, "A Note on Independence," *Philosophical Studies*, 30 (1976): 419–21.

17 These are only the most prestigious of the ethics and public affairs journals. We can also include *The Journal of Value Inquiry, Business and Professional Ethics Journal, The Journal of Business Ethics*, and *Environmental Ethics*, where this practice still prevails. Obviously, there have also been exceptions. But the connection between substantive ethical claims and the topic of free will is rarely explored.

18 I did, in fact, so argue in Machan, "A Note on Independence."

19 Rawls, *A Theory of Justice*, p. 104. Incidentally, if this view is not a kind of metaethical position, not much else would qualify. In light of Rawls's "independence" thesis, it is difficult to see why he can rest any beliefs on it. Furthermore, once the topic is broached, it would be instructive to see what exactly Rawls's view on this topic is – to wit, if character depends only "in large part" upon fortunate circumstances, what little bit of self-responsibility can we expect human beings to have? And how is such self-responsibility to be accounted for in understanding ethics and public policy matters?

20 I discuss some of this in greater detail in Tibor R. Machan, "Rescuing Victims – from Social Theory," in Diane Sank and David I. Caplan, eds, *To Be a Victim, Encounters with Crime and Injustice* (New York: Plenum Press, 1991), pp. 101–16. See, also, Tibor R. Machan, *Capitalism and Individualism: Reframing the Argument for the Free Society* (New York: St. Martin's Press, 1990), for a discussion of economists' explorations of which of the competing political–economic options has the greatest merit as a system of human community life.

21 This has been accepted in the phenomenal portion of Kantian reality and has not been challenged widely except by Kant, who did this by postulating noumenal reality that made freedom possible.

22 The mechanistic model allows for nuanced differences based on highly technical amendments to the broad framework, contributed by, say, quantum physics. Yet that will not change the basic result, namely, that self-responsibility is disallowed and, thus, ethics is rendered impossible.

Of course, challenges exist – for example, those advanced by Karl Popper and John C. Eccles in *The Self and Its Brain* (New York: Springer International, 1977) and by John C. Eccles in *Evolution of the Brain: Creation of the Self* (London: Routledge, 1989). Popper and Eccles argue that quantum mechanics makes room for free will in some fashion, although they seem to adopt a new dualism, reminiscent of Kant's project. The effort has not resonated with much approval within the community of philosophers, let alone moral and public policy theorists. Part of the problem is that quantum mechanics, especially the Heisenberg uncertainty principle, does not provide ethics with a metaphysical grounding. It provides only a pseudo-epistemological grounding, leading to the possible result that randomness is part of the universe. This is not at all the same as self-responsibility.

In social-science circles, too, there have been dissenters – for example, Isidor Chein, in *The Science of Behavior and the Image of Man* (New York: Basic Books, 1972), and Nathaniel Branden, in *The Psychology of Self-Esteem* (New York: Bantam Books, 1969). It is fair to note, however, that these did not make an impact in applied ethics.

23 One may argue that all the determinist is saying is that it would be better to believe in determinism than not to, not that one ought to. Yet the "ought" is implicit in our addressing ourselves with the idea, since that makes sense only with the expectation that we may change our minds. Some of this is discussed in Joseph Boyle, G. Grisez, and O. Tollefsen, *Free Choice* (Notre Dame, Ind.: University of Notre Dame Press, 1976). See, also, Jordan, "Determinism's Dilemma."

24 See Roger W. Sperry, *Science and Moral Priority* (New York: Columbia University Press, 1983), and his numerous technical papers in such journals as *Perspectives in Biology and Medicine*.

25 Aristotle, *Nicomachean Ethics*, book 2, chap. 5, 1106a2, 1113b13. It is interesting that Kekes, in *Facing Evil*, classifies his own views as akin to those of Aristotle, in virtue of their being on the side of character as distinct from (Kantian) choice moralities. Yet Aristotle connects moral virtue with choice and ties being vicious or virtuous to our power to be one or the other. These features of Aristotle's ethics – or, rather, metaethics – appear to place Aristotle's version of character morality within the class of choice moralities.

Indeed, it is arguable that Kekes's "ethics" is only a theory of value, with little to say about morality as such, which is a very special category of value, namely, value that moral agents can gain or lose on their own (within, of course, the requisite setting in the world). When Kekes explains morality, he in fact describes only a theory of values based on the enhancement of human life. Yet many factors enhance or damage human life; some of them are brought about by persons, and some of them are not, so it is important for the cogency of any bona fide theory of morality that personal initiative be explained.

26 To pick just one topic, what is "lack of fairness" if not a lack of integrity as applied in a certain domain of one's conduct?

27 John Kenneth Galbraith, "The Dependence Effect," reprinted in numerous business ethics texts and collections. See, for example, Thomas L. Beauchamp and Norman E. Bowie, *Ethical Theory and Business* (Englewood Cliffs, N.J.: Prentice Hall, 1983). For a critical discussion of this issue, see Douglas J. Den Uyl's essay on advertising in Tibor R. Machan, ed., *Commerce and Morality* (Totowa, N.J.: Rowman & Littlefield, 1988). See, also, F. A. Hayek's essay "The Non Sequitur of 'The Dependence Effect,'" in a few business ethics collections, including Beauchamp and Bowie, *Ethical Theory and Business*.

3 HUMAN ACTION AND THE NATURE OF MORAL EVIL

1 Laurie Calhoun, "Moral Blindness and Moral Responsibility: What Can We Learn from Rhoda Penmark?" *Journal of Applied Philosophy*, vol. 13 (1996): 41. In this chapter I develop my understanding of Ayn Rand's conception of moral evil as most fundamentally a policy of mental *evasion*. See Ayn Rand, *The Virtue of Selfishness, a New Concept of Egoism* (New York: New American Library, 1964), especially "The Objectivist Ethics."

2 Rudolph H. Weingartner, *The Unity of the Platonic Dialogue* (Indianapolis: Bobbs-Merrill, 1973), p. 30.

3 Quoted in F. A. Hayek, "Dr. Bernard Mandeville," in *New Studies in Philosophy, Politics, Economics, and the History of Ideas* (Chicago: University of Chicago Press, 1978), p. 264. Ferguson, who believed that human actions are motivated by "sub-rational drives," advanced his views in *An Essay on the History of Civil Society* (Edinburgh: Printer for A. Millar, 1767).

4 J. L. Austin, *Philosophical Papers* (Oxford: Clarendon Press, 1961), p. 150.

5 Hayek, of course, wanted somehow to distinguish between the kind of behavior that is acceptable, genuine, authentic to human beings, and the kind that causes trouble, without entering the murky waters of ethics or moral theory. He may have thought that this distinction between what is natural and what is not, by way of the categories of spontaneous and intentional action, could perhaps accomplish that goal.

6 As this suggests, it is impossible to reasonably conceive of human action without assuming some version of the doctrine of free will in its compatibilist version, wherein the agent is a kind of cause. For a discussion of free will, see Chapter 2.

7 David L. Norton, "Individual Initiative," in Konstantin Kulenka, ed., *Organization and Ethical Individualism* (New York: Praeger, 1988).

8 Gary Becker, "Q & A: Nobel Laureate Gary Becker: How Economics Meets Social Issues," *Hoover Institution Newsletter* (Winter 1993) 8–9.

9 Gary Becker, "When the Wake-Up Call Is from the Nobel Committee," *Business Week*, 20 (2 November 1992).

10 Ludwig von Mises, *Human Action* (New Haven, Conn.: Yale University Press, 1949), p. 19.

11 For more on this, see Tibor R. Machan, "Reason in Economics versus Ethics," *International Journal of Social Economics* 22, no. 7 (1995): 19–37.

12 Gary Becker, *The Economic Approach to Human Behavior* (Chicago: University of Chicago Press, 1976).

13 For a discussion of "ought implies can," see Chapter 2.

14 George Stigler, "The Adam Smith Lecture: The Effects of Government on Economic Efficiency," *Business Economics*, 23 (January 1988): 7–13.

15 B. F. Skinner, *Beyond Freedom and Dignity* (New York: Bantam Books, 1971).

16 B. F. Skinner, *Science and Human Behavior* (New York: Macmillan, 1953).

17 Milton Friedman, *Capitalism and Freedom* (Chicago: University of Chicago Press, 1962), p. 12.

18 Quoted in Michael A. Walker, ed., *Freedom, Democracy, and Economic Welfare* (Vancouver, Canada: Fraser Institute, 1988), p. 367. (This volume reproduces papers presented at a conference chaired by Milton Friedman in October 1985, in Napa Valley, California.)

19 Such full development pertains to capacities, not their realization, which is precisely what the individual person has, unless severely incapacitated by others or nature's interference, either achieved or failed to achieve in an ongoing process, more or less consistently, in the living his or her life.

20 It is important to understand the "must" here in a non-Platonistic way. See Tibor R. Machan, "Epistemology and Moral Knowledge," *Review of Metaphysics*, 36 (September 1982): 23–49.

21 This is a point stressed in both the fictional and non-fictional works of Ayn Rand, although it is made by others, as well, who have noted that fundamental role of right reason or judgment in human life – Socrates, Aristotle, William of Ockham, Spinoza, Locke, Kant, Wittgenstein, *et al.*

22 For more on this, see Tibor R. Machan, "A Revision of the Doctrine of Disability of Mind," *Persona y Derecho*, vol. 33 (May 1995): 213–22.

4 WHY OBJECTIVE ETHICAL CLAIMS APPEAR SUBJECTIVE

1 Principles of conduct are problematic because they are supposed to pertain to the achievement of a goal. If the goal is objectively good, then the principle is true if following it achieves the goal. But if the goodness of the goal is subjective, then the principle cannot be shown to be true or false. It will merely be an expression of what one prefers.

2 Even those who object to the claim that norms can be objective make purportedly objective claims when they say that others, too, ought to reject this claim. The "ought" may be only a very mild moral rebuke in this instance, yet judging by the intensity and seriousness with which it is advanced, it is hardly to be taken as an expression of a mere preference.

3 Milton Friedman, *Capitalism and Freedom* (Chicago: University of Chicago Press, 1962), p. 12.

4 Richard Rorty, "The Seer of Prague," *The New Republic*, 1 July 1991, p. 37. By "we," Rorty means "non-metaphysicians," that is, those who understand that words and ideas do not represent some reality "out there."

5 Just how prominent it is can be gleaned from the proclamation offered by Richard Posner, judge of the Ninth Circuit Court of Appeals and professor at the University of Chicago School of Law, that he subscribes to pragmatism "in approximately the sense in which pragmatism is expounded and defended by the philosopher Richard Rorty" (Richard Posner, "Pragmatism and the Rule of Law," lecture given at the American Enterprise Institute, Washington, D.C., 7 July 1991).

6 "Objective" is used, in ordinary discourse, as a way to distinguish claims that are unbiased from those that are not. But in the philosophical sense, to call claims "objective" is to focus on the possibility of knowing what they assert, since these claims supposedly rest on what is "out there," that is, features of objective reality – the properties, relationships, attributes, aspects, and so forth of what exists in the world, as distinct from what we feel about them, prefer them to be, desire from them or of them, and so forth.

7 It might be objected here that what I have listed are at most "good policies" and that a policy cannot be true. Yet arguably, the claim that these are good policies could be either true or false, and the objectivist would try to show that it is true that they are good.

8 Those who deny the objectivity of moral principles usually contrast this with their view that other claims, pertaining to what science discovers or what we observe in the world around us, are capable of being true or false, that what is being asserted in these areas, in contrast to ethics, politics, or aesthetics, is knowable, or cognitively significant. Yet in these areas there is rarely universal agreement about the truths that can be ascertained, nor do all those who address the issues involved make identical knowledge claims. But those who uphold this thesis would tend to account for the lack of universal agreement not in terms of the impossibility of reaching it but, rather, in terms of certain impediments some people face as they attempt to figure out what is true or come to know what is the case. Of course, there are those, including Rorty, who would extend their skepticism not just to value judgments and moral claims but also to claims advanced in the sciences and other non-normative areas. They would hold that even in these the possibility of objective truth is an illusion. See, for example, Rorty's essays "Solidarity or Objectivity?" and "Science and Solidarity," in Richard Rorty, *Objectivity, Relativism, and Truth* (Cambridge: Cambridge University Press, 1991), pp. 21–45.

9 I mean here that as we discuss what we should or should not do in personal, social, political, international, and other contexts, we do adduce reasons and sometimes

even reach agreements because of these reasons, despite what such thinkers as Posner tell us, namely: "I am denying the priority of reason in human [moral] judgment. I am suggesting that we can, because we do, have confident beliefs without reasoning to them from unimpeachable truths, unimpeachable or non-unimpeachable, because I haven't suggested and don't mean to suggest that our strong moral intuitions are true. They are merely undislodgeable at the time, an undislodgeable part of our grounds for action, and that is good enough for me, because I don't think we can do better" (Rorty, *Objectivity, Relativism, and Truth,* p. 8). Of course, these intuitions are dislodged aplenty, for example, by people who do horrible things, for which Posner and those who agree with him give no explanation. One reason many think moral judgments do not lend themselves to being established as true is that they mistakenly assume that truths in non-normative disciplines can be established with timeless, unchanging, infallible certainty. Yet truth everywhere is different from this. When we know something, or when we have shown some claim to be true, we have the best possible cognitive grasp of it. Although this is difficult to explain by analogy since such a feat is unique – not surprisingly, since the human capacity for conceptually knowing the world is, so far as we know, unique – one might get some assistance for grasping the idea by thinking of how some object can be (literally) covered up. To cover up an object does not require having done so totally, fully, perfectly, completely, only adequately for the purposes at hand. Covering something up *absolutely* may be impossible, in the sense that no conceivable improvement on the task is possible, whereas covering it up is possible. Thus knowing something absolutely is impossible, but knowing it is possible. (We can also fail to cover something up, just as we can fail to know something.)

10 Don Bellante, "Subjective Value Theory and Government Intervention in the Labor Market," *Austrian Economics Newsletter,* Spring/Summer 1989, pp. 1–2. This is not, incidentally, a comment about the supposed impossibility of completely knowing an agent's values or motives. Bellante and other economists would not claim that what the agent values or what the agent's motives are cannot be known – indeed, for many economists, just that is revealed in the course of market transactions (referred to, in the literature of economists, as "revealed preferences" insofar as an agent's behavior is observable and thus gives evidence of why he or she has taken a job or made a purchase, namely, because he or she prefers to).

11 Quoted in A. J. Ayer and Jane O'Grady, eds, *A Dictionary of Philosophical Quotations* (Oxford: Blackwell, 1994), p. 60. In the history of discussing this topic, sometimes it is values, sometimes norms, and yet other times moral standards that are being referred to. A value, such as the goodness of some act or state of affairs, is taken to be a property. This property might be intrinsic, relational, subjective, objective, or some combination. When it comes to moral values, however, the idea refers to some action or policy that serves to produce a valued state of affairs. Honest conduct is a moral value, for example, because it produces beliefs that are likely to be true, which is supposed to be something that is good. Prudent conduct is supposed to be something that is good because it produces benefit to the agent.

12 Richard Tuck, *Hobbes* (London: Oxford University Press, 1989), p. 116.

13 For a very well worked out application of this model, see Martha Nussbaum, *The Therapy of Desire* (Princeton, N.J.: Princeton University Press, 1994). See, also, Ayn Rand, "The Objectivist Ethics," in *The Virtue of Selfishness: A New Concept of Egoism* (New York: New American Library, 1964).

14 I do not want to suggest that "norms" and "ethics" mean the same thing. The former term is used to mean standards of evaluation, of judging something a good, mediocre, or bad instance of its kind, as when some gardener uses certain norms by which to evaluate the flowers in the garden. The latter is a narrower category of standards,

pertaining to judging human conduct or institutions, so the phrase "ethical norm" is used to mean some standard by which we judge how we ought to act.

15 Thomas Nagel, "The Limits of Objectivity," in Sterling M. McMurrin, ed., *The Tanner Lectures on Human Values, 1980* (Cambridge: Cambridge University Press, 1980), p. 100.

16 At this point let me briefly sketch a typology of ontological domains corresponding to different truth claims. Reality at large includes a very large domain wherein only nonevaluative claims can be true or false, a much smaller domain (of living beings) wherein evaluative claims can be true or false, and a far smaller domain wherein moral-political evaluative claims can be true or false. (I leave aside for now a consideration of where room may be found for aesthetic claims.)

17 Nagel, "The Limits of Objectivity," p. 68. In reference to these charges, see Julius Kovesi, *Moral Notions* (London: Routledge & Kegan Paul, 1978). Kovesi shows why such criteria for what ought to suffice as moral support are confused and *ad hoc*. Indeed, if these criteria were to hold for every rational discipline, there would be none – certainly biology and medicine would not qualify. The remarks recall Aristotle's point about the different standards of precision that apply in different fields.

18 Raimond Gaita, "The Personal in Ethics," in P. Winch and D. Z. Phillips, eds, *Wittgenstein: Attention to Particulars* (New York: St. Martin's Press, 1989), p. 127.

19 I will not embark on some exact classification of these facts in terms such as "contingent" and "necessary," because such classifications are themselves replete with philosophical difficulties. What is a contingent fact contingent upon? God's will? Our awareness of the fact? The actual world? I will, instead, depend on common-sense distinctions that we invoke normally, in our daily lives, such that "contingent" means dependent on something variable, while "necessary" means firm, not alterable at will.

20 See David Hume, *A Treatise of Human Nature* (Garden City, N.Y.: Dolphin Books, 1961), p. 423.

21 For some efforts to place the ethical dimension of human life into a nonreductionist naturalist framework, see Roger W. Sperry, *Science and Moral Priority* (New York: Columbia University Press, 1983); and Mary Midgley, *The Ethical Primate* (London: Routledge, 1994). See, also, Tibor R. Machan, *The Pseudo-Science of B. F. Skinner* (New Rochelle, N.Y.: Arlington House, 1974).

22 True claims of this sort are often probabilistic. There is always chance to contend with, and that is by definition something unforeseeable.

23 For an illuminating discussion of this point, see Douglas J. Den Uyl, "Teleology and Agent-Centeredness," *Monist*, 75 (January 1992): 14–33. See, also, Henry B. Veatch, "Ethical Egoism, New Style: Is Its Proper Trade Mark Libertarian or Aristotelian?" in *Swimming Against the Current in Contemporary Philosophy* (Washington, D.C.: Catholic University of America Press, 1990), pp. 27–8.

24 See Tibor R. Machan, "Some Reflections on Richard Rorty's Philosophy," *Metaphilosophy*, 24 (January/April 1993): 123–35.

25 Barry Stroud, "Wittgenstein and Logical Necessity," in G. Pitcher, ed., *Wittgenstein* (Garden City, N.Y.: Anchor Books, 1969), p. 496.

5 A DEFENSE OF PROPERTY RIGHTS AND CAPITALISM

1 I discuss the different kinds of freedom that are of concern to us in "Two Senses of Human Freedom," *The Freeman* 39 (January 1989): 33–7. It needs to be noted, however, that freedom, or liberty, in the sense discussed here concerns respect for the sovereignty of persons, their realm of authority, not their material or spiritual facility

to make headway in life. This latter, rather special, sense of "freedom" is what is focused upon by those like Karl Marx, who stress what they call "human freedom" as distinct from mere "bourgeois freedom." But achieving such "freedom" by subjecting others to involuntary servitude requires the sacrifice of liberty; it is, thus, opposed to human morality.

2 I develop a substantial case for these ideas in Tibor R. Machan, *Human Rights and Human Liberties* (Chicago: Nelson-Hall, 1975), and *Individuals and Their Rights* (La Salle, Ill.: Open Court, 1989).

3 Karl Marx, *Selected Writings*, ed. David McLellan (Oxford: Oxford University Press, 1977), p. 53.

4 I have in mind such eminent economists as Milton Friedman, James Buchanan, Gary Becker, and the late George Stigler, F. A. Hayek, and Ludwig von Mises, all of whom stress those aspects of the free market that pertain to its efficiency and generally eschew concern with whether the system is in accord with, for example, prudence and justice.

5 Some argue that rights should be thought of as metanormative principles in that they bear directly not on how one ought to conduct oneself, but on the conditions required by everyone in a community for making the choice about how to live. For more on this, see Douglas B. Rasmussen and Douglas J. Den Uyl, *Liberty and Nature: An Aristotelian Defense of Liberal Order* (La Salle, Ill.: Open Court, 1991). The point is not crucial here, however.

6 Something along these lines applies to any applied science, for example, engineering. They assume that what is to be done is morally justifiable, though dwelling on that issue is not in their province.

7 Robert Nozick, *Anarchy, State, and Utopia* (New York: Basic Books, 1974), p. 57.

8 James Sadowsky, "Private Property and Collective Ownership," in T. R. Machan, ed., *The Libertarian Alternative* (Chicago: Nelson-Hall, 1974), p. 123. It might be noted, though, that judgments could well qualify as work. Intellectual labors are certainly part of human productive work.

9 I explain this further in *Individuals and Their Rights*. I draw there on ideas advanced originally in Ayn Rand, "The Objectivist Ethics," in *The Virtue of Selfishness: A New Concept of Egoism* (New York: New American Library, 1964), although the point has been lurking around in the ethics of numerous philosophers who have stressed the role of reason and choice in the moral life of a human being.

10 Democritus of Abdera wrote: "The same thing is good and true for all men, but the pleasant differs from one and another." Quoted in Barry Gordon, *Economic Analysis before Adam Smith* (New York: Barnes & Noble, 1976), p. 15.

11 *King Lear*, act 4, scene 2.

12 The doctrine of moral intuitionism has gained considerable support at the hands of John Rawls. See his *A Theory of Justice* (Cambridge, Mass.: Harvard University Press, 1971), in which the role of moral intuitions as the central feature of the foundation of political justice is vigorously endorsed.

13 Some of this is implicit in the Austrian economists' famous discovery of the calculation problem under socialism. See Trygve J. B. Hoff, *Economic Calculation in the Socialist Society* (Indianapolis, Ind.: Liberty Press, 1981). For additional discussion of the right to private property versus collectivism, see Chapter 11.

Perhaps there is yet another expression of this same difficulty, in connection with the various impossibility theorems showing that rational public choice is not possible in a fully democratic society, one in which citizens may demand the satisfaction of their desires from the government. See Kenneth J. Arrow, *Social Choice and Individual Values*, 2nd ed. (New York: Wiley, 1963). See my "Rational Choice and Public Affairs," *Theory and Decision* 12 (September 1980): 229–58, for an attempt to spell out the criteria by which we should determine whether something falls within the public domain and is, thus, subject to public policy decision making. I develop this line of thinking further in Tibor R. Machan, *Private Rights and Public Illusions* (New Brunswick, N.J.: Transaction, 1995).

14 Walter Block, *Defending the Undefendable* (New York: Fleet Press, 1976).

15 This may be doubted by some, but consider that when private property rights are protected, boycotts and ostracism are viable options in an effort to influence others' behavior and character. Those who exhibit greed and envy can be discouraged via the withdrawal of association and support.

16 Without private property, generosity, for example, is not possible. For more on this, see Chapter 10.

17 See Sadowsky, "Private Property," p. 124.

18 For a more detailed treatment of this issue, see Machan, *Private Rights and Public Illusions*, chap. 8.

19 Herbert Spencer, "State Tampering with Money Banks," in *Essays* (New York: D. Appleton, 1891).

6 AMERICA'S FOUNDING PRINCIPLES AND MULTICULTURALISM

1 Colin Morris, *The Discovery of the Individual, 1050–1200* (New York: Harper & Row, 1972), p. 2. A very interesting response to this view is advanced by Amartya Sen, "Human Rights and Asian Values," *The New Republic*, July 14–21, 1997, pp. 33–40. As Sen puts it, "In the most general form, the notion of human rights builds on our shared humanity. These rights are not derived from citizenship in any country, or membership in any nation. They are taken as entitlements of every human beings." (p. 39).

2 Karl Marx, *Grundrisse*, trans. Martin Nicolaus (New York: Vintage Books, 1973), p. 100; Karl Marx, *Grundrisse*, ed. and trans. David McLellan (New York: Harper Torchbooks, 1971), p. 39. Marx's term was translated as "organic whole" by Nicolaus, but McLellan used "organic body" to convey Marx's meaning in English.

3 Auguste Comte, *A General View of Positivism* (New York: Robert Speller & Sons, 1957), pp. 401–3.

4 Marx, *Grundrisse*, ed. and trans. David McLellan, p. 17.

5 Michael J. Sandel, "America's Search for a New Public Philosophy," *Atlantic Monthly*, March 1996, p. 58. Exactly what "self-government" means is not made clear by Sandel. Presumably, it has to do with a community being governed so as to make itself behave in progressive ways. For related critiques of individualism, see Shlomo Avineri and Avner de-Shalit, eds, *Communitarianism and Individualism* (New York: Oxford University Press, 1992).

6 Robert Bellah *et al.*, *Habits of the Heart: Individualism and Commitment in American Life* (Berkeley: University of California Press, 1985).

7 Amitai Etzioni, *The Spirit of Community* (New York: Crown, 1993).

8 Despite the fact that books defending the free, capitalist economic system, which is implied by individualism, are few and far between and tend to be published by other than the most prestigious houses, authors who write the very prominently published and discussed books that criticize the system are avid when they discuss it. In its review of two scathing attacks on capitalism, Robert Kuttner's *Everything for Sale* (New York: Alfred A. Knopf, 1997) and William Greider's *One World, Ready or Not* (New York: Simon & Schuster, 1997), the popular and widely read American weekly *Newsweek* began as follows: "Free-market capitalism is the secular religion of our time. It is a creed triumphant . . . . Today . . . the central precept of laissez-faire

capitalism . . . underpins most economic-policy decisions" (10 February 1997, p. 67). Yet this is blatantly false. There is no system of *laissez-faire* anywhere on the globe. At most, what we have are mixed economies, including the economy of the United States, where the state owns massive amounts of land and other property; runs hundreds of services and facilities, such as the Postal Service, water and electric utilities, and the only passenger railroad; imposes domestic and international barriers to trading goods and services; and determines what will be produced to the extent that it taxes, spends and manages a great deal of property (such as the National Forests and Parks).

One might assume that when critics need some blatant falsehoods for one of their premises, so that they can then proceed to attribute all social ills to this fictitious system, they are somewhat insecure in the merits of their case. Why not simply say, "There is this idea circulating in some circles that *laissez-faire* ought to be expanded much more broadly than it is, and we dispute its wisdom for these reasons"?

9 John Gray, "From Post-Modernism to Civil Society," *Social Philosophy and Policy*, 10 (Summer 1993): 44.

10 Ibid.

11 Howard W. French, "The Ritual Slaves of Ghana: Young and Female," *New York Times*, 20 January 1997, p. 4. One Ghanaian priest who supports the practice reportedly stated, "To you this may seem like a miscarriage of justice, but the girl will have to atone. It is the spirit, our fetish, who has made things work this way, and only he can explain." What usually happens is that the priest keeps the girl as a sexual servant until she becomes middle-aged, after which the family has to replace her with a new virgin, on and on until the atonement has been completed. It is difficult to see how this differs from some ritual adopted by the Mafia to satisfy its criminal practices, except that in Ghana the practice is only now beginning to be outlawed. But communitarians could regard that effort to outlaw it as a form of "corrosive" individualist imperialism, not progress toward justice.

12 Quoted in "Endpaper," *New York Times Book Review*, 5 November 1995, p. 46.

13 David L. Norton, *Personal Destinies: A Philosophy of Ethical Individualism* (Princeton, N.J.: Princeton University Press, 1976), p. x.

14 Robert Nozick, *Anarchy, State, and Utopia* (New York: Basic Books, 1974), "Utopia", pp. 297–334.

15 Tatyana Tolstaya, "The Grand Inquisitor," *The New Republic*, 29 June 1992, p. 33.

16 Michael Walzer, "Are There Limits to Liberalism?" review of *Isaiah Berlin*, by John Gray, *New York Review of Books*, 19 October 1995, p. 28.

17 Harry F. Rosenthal, "Teacher's firing may symbolize a cultural trend," *USA Today*, 3 April 1996, p. A4.

18 Douglas B. Rasmussen and Douglas J. Den Uyl, *Liberalism Defended: The Challenge of Post-Modernity* (Cheltenham: Edward Elgar, 1998).

19 See, for example, John Rawls, *A Theory of Justice* (Cambridge, Mass.: Harvard University Press, 1971), p.488, where Rawls claims that "[a]mong persons who never acted in accordance with their duty of justice except as reasons of self-interest and expediency dictate there would be no bonds of friendship and mutual trust" (p. 488). Note how this loads the issue, by equivocating between self-interest – ethical individualism – and expediency. But it is clear that it could well be against one's self-interest to be expedient. Indeed, as Socrates says in the *Phaedo*, "Just what I am always telling you. If you look after yourselves, whatever you do will please me and mine and you too, even if you don't agree with me now." (E. Hamilton and H. Cairns, eds, *The Collected Dialogues of Plato* [New York: Pantheon Books, 1961], p.95 [115b3].) Furthermore, political individualism does not legally require someone to

act as an ethical egoist or individualist, although it certainly makes such conduct possible.

20 For more on this, see Chapter 10 of this book; Tibor R. Machan, *Capitalism and Individualism* (New York: St. Martin's Press, 1990), p. 8 and chap. 4; Tibor R. Machan, *Generosity, Private and Public* (Washington, D.C.: Cato Institute, 1998); and David Kelley, *Unrugged Individualism* (Poughkeepsie, N.Y.: Institute for Objectivist Studies, 1996). It is, in any case, quite sensible to believe that in treating others with generosity or benevolence, one is, in the overall scheme of things, enhancing one's life as well, not necessarily by securing various goods and services in return but, rather, by cultivating a gregarious and sociable way of life that cannot but, as a rule, be of benefit to oneself.

7 RADICAL FEMINISM AS UNIFORMITARIANISM

1 Catherine A. MacKinnon, *Feminism Unmodified* (Cambridge, Mass.: Harvard University Press, 1987), p. 93.

2 MacKinnon, *Feminism Unmodified*, p. 93.

3 MacKinnon, *Feminism Unmodified*, p. 94. Of course, a fetus is a form of life – but that is not the issue. Bacteria are also forms of life, but no pro-life partisan worries about killing these life-forms. What matters is whether a fetus is a (young) human being, an unborn *child*. That would make it a full-fledged rightsholder, as all children are (with appropriate modifications accorded them due to lack of full human development). Pro-choice partisans hold that in the early months of pregnancy, when most abortions are wanted, only a potential child exists. They argue that although in numerous cases, abortions are immoral – frivolous, a terrible waste of what could have been, and so forth – they are not violations of individual rights.

4 MacKinnon, *Feminism Unmodified*, p. 96.

5 Karl Marx, *Selected Writings*, ed. David McLellan (Oxford: Oxford University Press, 1977), p. 126.

6 A very good exposition of this point may be found in David L. Norton, *Personal Destinies: A Philosophy of Ethical Individualism* (Princeton, N.J.: Princeton University Press, 1976).

7 John Rawls, *A Theory of Justice* (Cambridge, Mass.: Harvard University Press, 1971), p. 104.

8 Robert Nozick, *Anarchy, State, and Utopia* (New York: Basic Books, 1974), p. 163.

9 MacKinnon, *Feminism Unmodified*, p. 100.

10 MacKinnon, *Feminism Unmodified*, p. 101.

8 HUMAN RIGHTS REAFFIRMED

1 See Tibor R. Machan, *Human Rights and Human Liberties* (Chicago: Nelson-Hall, 1975), and *Individuals and Their Rights* (La Salle, Ill.: Open Court, 1989).

2 For surveys of such efforts between the 1940s and the 1980s, see Tibor R. Machan, "Some Recent Work in Human Rights Theory," and Rex Martin and James W. Nickel, "Recent Work on the Concept of Rights," in Kenneth G. Lucey, ed., *Recent Work in Philosophy* (Totowa, N.J.: Rowman & Allanheld, 1983). Human rights are defended by neo-Kantians (e.g., Alan Gewirth), utilitarians (e.g., Russell Hardin), and natural-rights theorists (e.g., Douglas Rasmussen, Douglas Den Uyl, Eric Mack, and myself). The latter see human rights only for preserving "moral space" (Nozick's term) for each in society. See Robert Nozick, *Anarchy, State, and Utopia* (New York: Basic Books, 1974), p. 57.

3 See Leo Strauss, *Natural Right and History*, 2nd ed. (Chicago: University of Chicago Press, 1970).

4 Some even seem to believe that it is morally objectionable to call "any specific right . . . [a] . . . human right." See John O. Nelson, "Against Human Rights," *Philosophy* 65 (Summer, 1990): 341–8. Nelson adds that "such a designation is not only fraudulent but, in case anyone might want to say that there can be noble lies, grossly wicked, amounting indeed to genocide" (p. 341). Nelson quotes Ruth Benedict, *Patterns of Culture* (Cambridge, Mass.: Riverside Press, 1934): "The good man [qua Domuan] is the one who has . . . thieved, killed children, cheated whenever he dared" (p. 172). Yet Nelson also calls the idea of human rights "grossly wicked." Contra Ruth Benedict, see Jane Jacobs, *Systems of Survival: A Dialogue on the Moral Foundations of Commerce and Politics* (New York: Random House, 1992), chap. 5, pp. 57–92. See, also, Amartya Sen, "Human Rights and Asian Values," *The New Republic*, July 14–21, 1997, pp. 33–40.

5 See Richard Rorty, *Objectivity, Relativism, and Truth* (Cambridge: Cambridge University Press, 1991), pp. 31 and 177; and John Gray, *Post Liberalism* (London: Routledge, 1993).

6 See Ernest van den Haag, "Against Natural Rights," *Policy Review*, no. 23 (Winter 1983): 143–75.

7 See Nelson, "Against Human Rights."

8 See David Hume, *A Treatise of Human Nature* (Garden City, N.Y.: Dolphin Books, 1961), p. 423. Hume laments efforts to *deduce* normative (ought) conclusions from positive (is) ones. Hume himself *argues for* such conclusions, however, in his ethical and political writings. For more on such efforts, see Tibor R. Machan, "Epistemology and Moral Knowledge," *Review of Metaphysics* 36 (September 1982): 23–49.

9 John Gray, *Liberalism* (Minneapolis: University of Minneapolis Press, 1986), p. 43.

10 John Gray, *Liberalisms* (London: Routledge, 1989), p. 258. This claim is akin to that offered by Nelson, to be examined shortly.

11 Gray, *Liberalisms*, p. 258.

12 See, for example, Rorty, *Objectivity, Relativism, and Truth*.

13 See, for example, Frank M. Coleman, *Hobbes and America* (Toronto: University of Toronto Press, 1977). See, also, Edward Andrew, *Shylock's Rights* (Toronto: University of Toronto Press, 1988).

14 See C. B. MacPherson, *Possessive Individualism* (London: Oxford University Press, 1962); Andrew C. MacLaughlin, *The Foundations of American Constitutionalism* (Greenwich, Conn.: Fawcet, 1961); and Harry V. Jaffa, *How to Think About the American Revolution* (Durham, N.C.: Carolina Academic Press, 1978). A less explicitly Marxian rendition of this argument is to be found in Alasdair MacIntyre, *After Virtue* (Notre Dame, Ind.: University of Notre Dame Press, 1981).

15 Nelson, "Against Human Rights," p. 344.

16 According to Nelson, "human nature is not in fact simple or regular or even consistent in its components. It is much more like a crazy quilt than a triangle." He reiterates: "Human nature itself is the most wild and certainly woolly crazy quilt. . . . But not only wild and woolly but, conflating temporalities into timelessness, as indicated by the notion of essence, even 'contradictory'" (Nelson, "Against Human Rights," p. 344).

17 See, for example, Ayn Rand, "Man's Rights," in *Capitalism: The Unknown Ideal* (New York: New American Library, 1967); Machan, *Human Rights and Human Liberties* and *Individuals and Their Rights*; and Douglas B. Rasmussen and Douglas J. Den Uyl, *Liberty and Nature: An Aristotelian Defense of Liberal Order* (La Salle, Ill.: Open Court, 1991).

18 Many, for example, Richard Rorty, have bitten the bullet and taken ethical skepticism all the way to wholesale skepticism. But see Tibor R. Machan, "Some Reflections on Richard Rorty's Philosophy," *Metaphilosophy* 24 (January/April 1993): 123–35.

19 For a good discussion of this, see Douglas J. Den Uyl, "Teleology and Agent-Centeredness," *Monist* 75 (January 1992): 14–33.

20 See Douglas J. Den Uyl, *The Virtue of Prudence* (New York: Peter Lang, 1991).

21 This is H. L. A. Hart's phrase, attributed to Locke without reference in "Are There Any Natural Rights?" *Philosophical Review*, 64 (October 1955): 175–91.

22 For a discussion of how human rights theories become deficient, see Tibor R. Machan, "Wronging Rights," *Policy Review*, no. 17 (Summer 1981): 37–58.

23 Voluntary affirmative action is not at issue here. If individuals choose to allocate their wealth – including jobs they may have to offer – on the basis of certain convictions about others' special needs, they are acting within their rights.

24 See, for example, Roger W. Sperry, "Changing Concepts of Consciousness and Free Will," *Perspectives in Biology and Medicine* 9 (Autumn 1976): 9–19. (See, also, the discussion of free will in Chapter 2 of this book.)

25 Werner Jaeger, *Aristotle* (London: Oxford University Press, 1934), p. 152.

26 David Ross, *Aristotle* (The Hague, Netherlands: Methuen, 1964), p. 201.

27 Gray's and Rorty's treatments of rights theories are awfully thin, albeit their skepticism cuts very deep.

28 Laszlo Versenyi, "Virtue as a Self-Directed Art," *Personalist*, 53 (Summer 1972): 282.

29 Nelson, "Against Human Rights," p. 344.

30 See Machan, *Individuals and Their Rights*, p. 110 ff., and "Epistemology and Moral Knowledge."

31 For a good discussion of this, see Hanna F. Pitkin, *Wittgenstein and Justice* (Berkeley: University of California Press, 1970).

32 It is difficult to comprehend how Nelson could see this position as "grossly wicked, amounting indeed to genocide" (Nelson, "Against Human Rights," p. 341).

33 Some of the material in this chapter was drawn from my paper "Justice, Self, and Natural Rights," in James Sterba, ed., *Morality and Social Injustice: Alternative Views* (Lanham, Md.: Rowman & Littlefield, 1994).

9 DO ANIMALS HAVE RIGHTS?

1 Tom Regan, *The Case for Animal Rights* (Berkeley: University of California Press, 1983).

2 Henry S. Salt, *Animals' Rights* (London: George Bell & Sons, 1892; Clark Summit, Pa.: Society for Animal Rights, 1980). This is perhaps the major philosophical effort to defend animals' rights prior to Tom Regan's treatise on the same topic.

3 See Charles Darwin, *The Descent of Man*, chaps 3 and 4, reprinted in Tom Regan and Peter Singer, eds., *Animal Rights and Human Obligations* (Englewood Cliffs, N.J.: Prentice Hall, 1976), pp. 72–81.

4 On these points, both the deontologically oriented Regan and the utilitarian-leaning Peter Singer tend to agree, although they differ considerably in their arguments.

5 Peter Singer holds that "we would be on shaky grounds if we were to demand equality for blacks, women, and other groups of oppressed humans while denying equal consideration to nonhumans" ("All Animals are Equal," in Regan and Singer, *Animal Rights*, p. 150).

6 Tom Regan contends that "[it] is not to say that practices that involve taking the lives of animals cannot possibly be justified. . . . [I]n order to seriously consider approving such a practice [it] would [have to] prevent, reduce, or eliminate a much

greater amount of evil" ("Do Animals Have a Right to Life?" in Regan and Singer, *Animal Rights*, pp. 203–4).

7 This is the gist of Singer's thesis.

8 Bernard E. Rollin, *Animal Rights and Human Morality* (Buffalo, N.Y.: Prometheus Books, 1981), p. 4.

9 Stephen R. L. Clark, *The Moral Status of Animals* (Oxford: Clarendon Press, 1977), p. 13.

10 Rollin, *Animal Rights*, p. 14.

11 Rollin, *Animal Rights*, p. 14.

12 See a discussion of this in Mortimer Adler, *The Difference of Man and the Difference It Makes* (New York: World Publishing, 1968), p. 73 ff.

13 Adler, *The Difference of Man*, p. 73.

14 Adler, *The Difference of Man*, p. 73.

15 Adler, *The Difference of Man*, p. 75.

16 John Hospers, review of *The Case for Animals Rights*, by Tom Regan, *Reason Papers*, no. 10 (Fall 1985), p. 123.

17 This does not deny that animals can be legal rightsholders in the sense that they could be judged, for example, to have a right to an inheritance upon being made the beneficiaries of a will. It is this line of reasoning that allows Christopher Stone to defend the claim that they might have "standing" in *Should Trees Have Standing? Toward Legal Rights for Natural Objects* (Los Altos, Calif.: William Kaufmann, 1974).

10 POLITICS AND GENEROSITY

1 See Robert Nozick, *The Examined Life* (New York: Simon & Schuster, 1989), pp. 286–7. Oddly, Nozick does not defend his claim to this effect, he merely asserts it and leaves the matter at that.

2 For a very illuminating approach to this issue, see J. L. Austin, "Other Minds," in *Philosophical Papers* (Oxford: Clarendon Press, 1961).

3 See Tibor R. Machan, "Justice and the Welfare State," in T. R. Machan, ed., *The Libertarian Alternative* (Chicago: Nelson-Hall, 1974).

4 Tibor R. Machan, *Human Rights and Human Liberties* (Chicago: Nelson-Hall, 1975) and *Individuals and Their Rights* (LaSalle, Ill.: Open Court Publishing Company, 1989).

5 Karl Marx, *Selected Writings*, ed. David McLellan (Oxford: Oxford University Press, 1977), p. 56.

6 Some confuse this with the idea that everyone is justified in deciding what is right or wrong. In fact, however, it means that everyone is justified in being the author of conduct that is either right or wrong.

7 Karl Marx, *Grundrisse*, ed. and trans. David McLellan (New York: Harper Torchbooks, 1971), p. 39.

8 For a discussion of the place of personal property in Marx, see Thomas Keyes, "The Marxian Concept of Property: Individual/Social," in Tibor R. Machan, ed., *The Main Debate, Communism versus Capitalism* (New York: Random House, 1987), pp. 311–30.

9 There is a case to be made that Marx does admit of human individuality. However, the nature of such individuality turns out to be one that is fully emerged into society, the individuality of a specie-being – that is, one who is whole only when completely coordinated with or belonging to the membership of his species.

10 For a more elaborate examination of generosity, see Tibor R. Machan, *Generosity, Private and Public* (Washington, D.C.: Cato Institute, 1998).

11 UNDERSTANDING EASTERN EUROPEAN
DEVELOPMENTS

1 Karl Marx, *Grundrisse*, trans. Martin Nicolaus (New York: Vintage Books, 1973), p. 100.

2 Karl Marx, *Selected Writings*, ed. David McLellan (Oxford: Oxford University Press, 1977), p. 456.

3 In a letter published in *Encounter* (May 1986), Hook discounts the significance of this passage from Marx. He claims that by "complement each other," Marx "obviously refer[red] to their coordination in a world socialist economy" but without resort to a "forceful expansion." In my view, the problem lies with the term "coordination"; as I noted in response to Hook, "Such a thing does not happen anywhere without force. People by their own volition do not accommodate such a coordination but tend, rather, to upset the scheme (just as Marx was aware when he lamented the existence of business cycles in an exchange economy). Every socialist system requires someone's labor, or other belongings, being expropriated by another – the coordinator" (*Encounter*, December 1986, p. 80). To this Hook answered: "It is obvious that in the democratic welfare states of the West, even under Socialist Party regimes, 'coordination' and 'complementary' functioning of the private and public sectors of the economy go on without necessarily involving 'forceful expansion.'" To this I can answer only that if one may include under the concept "forceful" any process that is legally mandated rather than entered into voluntarily, then Hook's counter-example from democratic societies fails.

4 Karl Marx, "Critique of the Gotha Program," in Robert C. Tucker, ed., *The Marx–Engels Reader* (New York: W. W. Norton, 1978), p. 535.

5 Quoted in Steven Greenhouse, "Soviet Economists Say Shift to Free Market Is Inevitable," *New York Times*, 18 February 1991, p. 21.

6 Karl Marx, "Teh German Ideology," in Tucker, *The Marx–Engels Reader*, p. 163.

7 Ibid.

8 Karl Marx, "The Possibility of Non-Violent Revolution," in Tucker, *The Marx–Engels Reader*, p. 523.

9 Marx, *Selected Writings*, p. 126.

10 Quoted in Lloyd Easton and Kurt H. Guddat, eds and trans., *Writings of the Young Marx on Philosophy and Society* (Garden City, N.Y.: Anchor Books, 1967), p. 39.

11 Karl Marx, *Grundrisse*, ed. and trans. David McLellan (New York: Harper Torchbooks, 1971), p. 131.

12 See Tibor R. Machan, *Marxism: A Bourgeois Critique* (Bradford: MCB University Press, 1988).

13 For a detailed criticism of Marxism from the viewpoint of classical–liberal (economic) theory, see David Conway, *A Farewell to Marx* (Middlesex: Penguin Books, 1987). For a detailed critique of neo-Marxism, especially the "analytical Marxists," see N. Scott Arnold, *Marx's Radical Critique of Capitalist Society: A Reconstruction and Critical Evaluation* (New York: Oxford University Press, 1990).

14 See Karl Popper, *The Poverty of Historicism* (London: Routledge & Kegan Paul, 1961).

15 Janos Kornai, *The Road to a Free Market* (New York: W. W. Norton, 1989). Kornai has pointed out the inherent problems of planned economies since the 1950s. See his *Contradictions and Dilemmas: Studies on the Socialist Economy and Society*, trans. Ilona Lukacs *et al.* (Cambridge, Mass.: MIT Press, 1986). The pioneer of theorists arguing that socialism is inherently unworkable as an economic system is Ludwig von Mises. See his *Socialism, an Economic and Sociological Analysis*, trans. J. Kahane (New Haven, Conn.: Yale University Press, 1951), originally published in German

in 1922. Von Mises' student F. A. Hayek carried on the discussion. See F. A. Hayek, ed., *Collectivist Economic Planning: Critical Studies on the Possibilities of Socialism* (London: Routledge & Sons, 1935).

16 Some critics of what they dub "capitalist" developments in the former Soviet colonies – for example, George Soros, in his "The Capitalist Threat" (*Atlantic Monthly*, February 1997) – fail to appreciate that to transform a society into a free system, it is not sufficient merely to abandon central planning. The legal infrastructure of private property rights, contract law, and a wide array of other features of modern capitalism is needed for the system to have a fighting chance of becoming functional.

17 Robert Heilbroner, "After Communism," *New Yorker*, 10 September 1990, p. 92.

18 Heilbroner, "After Communism," p. 92.

19 Heilbroner, "After Communism," p. 92.

20 Aristotle, *Politics* 1262a30–37; Garrett Hardin, "The Tragedy of the Commons," *Science*, 13 December 1968, pp. 1243–8.

21 For more on this, see Tibor R. Machan, *Private Rights and Public Illusions* (New Brunswick, N.J.: Transaction, 1995).

22 See Robert Kuttner, *Everything for Sale* (New York: Alfred A. Knopf, 1997).

23 See William Greider, *One World, Ready or Not* (New York: Simon & Schuster, 1997). Among many issues one could dispute in the above two books by Kuttner and Greider, one stands out: both assert that what prevails in our time is unbridled capitalism. One very favorable review of these books, by Michael Hirsch of *Newsweek* (10 February 1997), asserts: "Free-market capitalism is the secular religion of our time. It is a creed triumphant." See my observations about this matter in Chapter 6, note 8.

24 Interestingly enough, though not very surprisingly to those who do not embrace the Marxist idea of class consciousness, the billionaire financier George Soros holds a view similar to that of the socialist economist Robert Heilbroner: markets need to be tamed, lest market agents get out of hand. (See Soros's essay in the February 1997 issue of *Atlantic Monthly*.) Soros, however, confuses capitalism with the criminal anarchies of many post-Soviet Eastern countries, wherein none of the constitutional and other legal prerequisites of a free-market system – private property rights, contract law, and so forth – are in evidence. He also embraces Karl Popper's confusing idea of an "open society," in which there are no stable principles of human interaction; instead, a kind of piecemeal, trial-by-error interventionist welfare statism reigns.

25 Karl Marx, "Preface to the First German Edition [of *Capital* Volume One], in Tucker, *The Marx–Engels Reader*, p. 297.

12 INDIVIDUAL RIGHTS AND THE COMMON GOOD

1 There are some, rather prominently featured environmentalists, such as David M. Garaber, a scientist with the National Park Service, who, in reviewing Bill McKibben's *The End of Nature* (New York: Random House, 1989), said "Until such time as Homo sapiens should decide to rejoin nature, some of us can only hope for the right virus to come along" (*The Los Angeles Times Book Review*, October 22, 1989, p. 9). McKibben, in turn, quotes with approval John Muir, the founder of the Sierra Club, who said "Honorable representatives of the great saurians of older creation, may you long enjoy your lilies and rushes, and be blessed now and then with a mouthful of terror-stricken man by way of a dainty" (McKibben, p. 176). I would actually include some of the more mainstream advocates of environmental reform among those who advocate rather frightening policies concerning how human beings should understand their relationship to their environment. These

include such well known people as Jeremy Rifkind and Albert Gore, the vice-president of the United States of America. Their position is well generalized, beyond environmentalism, by D. W. Ehrenfeld, in *The Arrogance of Humanism* (New York: Oxford University Press, 1978), a book that mostly regrets the capacity of human beings to manage parts of nature for their own ends (as if other animals didn't already do this to some extent, as a matter of their life requirements). The idea seems to be that human beings ought to resign from life, just because they have the capacity for making mistakes, for doing what is wrong. This view is excessively negative and indeed underestimates the sturdiness of the rest of nature.

In this essay I shall ignore the dispute about whether human beings are part of nature and whether nature has value in itself. For more on this, see Tibor R. Machan, "Environmentalism Humanized," *Public Affairs Quarterly*, vol. 7 (April 1993), pp. 131–47, and George Reisman, "The Toxicity of Environmentalism," in Hans Sennholz, ed., *Man and Nature* (Irvington-on-Hudson, NY: Foundation for Economic Education, 1993) pp. 118–39.

2 Actually, one should note that such evil will hurt them and those who have voluntarily chosen to associated with them, for better and for worse – corporate partners, spouses, etc.

3 Richard McKeon, ed., *The Basic Works of Aristotle* (*Politics* 1262a30–37), (New York: Random House, 1941), p. 1148. We should note that Aristotle's argument is more of what is often called a *practical* rather than a *moral* one, although it clearly hints at certain moral matters by its reference to the harm that collective ownership does to personal moral responsibility.

4 A distinction needs to be noted here between a common goal or end and some common principle(s) of conduct of organization. The distinction is made well in Robert Nozick, *Anarchy, State, and Utopia* (New York: Basic Books, Inc., 1974), as between common end states and equally applicable procedures.

5 Ludwig von Mises, *Socialism*, 2nd edition (New Haven: Yale University Press, 1951 [originally published in German in 1922]).

6 Robert Heilbroner, "After Communism," *The New Yorker* (September 10, 1990), p. 92.

7 It is noteworthy that some analysts of the Soviet socialist era have argued that even the welfare state is liable to produce consequences that undermine the prosperity of a country. Janos Kornai notes, in his *The Road to the Free Market Economy* (New York: W. W. Norton, 1990) that any welfare statist aspirations cannot be attempted in Eastern Europe until after the free market has been fully implemented. Critics of the welfare state might observe, that, of course, until wealth has been produced by free entrepreneurs, there will be a problem about transferring or, better, confiscating and redistributing it. Any piecemeal social objective governments impose upon citizens will have to be funded from wealth created most effectively in a free market system. This does not, however, address the matter of whether any government has the rightful authority to embark upon such wealth transference.

8 Heilbroner, "After Communism," p. 99.

9 Heilbroner, "After Communism," p.100.

10 Few, if any, dispute that the command economies of Eastern Europe have left many more environmental problems to be dealt with than have mixed economies.

11 For the explication of this idea, see Garrett Hardin, "The Tragedy of the Commons," *Science*, vol. 162, (December 13, 1968), pp. 1243–8. We saw already that Aristotle advanced the idea several centuries before Hardin developed it in some detail. The thrust of it is that when resources or valued items are owned in common, they will be used up much more rapidly and with far less care about conserving them than if they are owned individually. And, contrary to what so many moralizers and

purveyors of guilt feelings would claim, the tragedy does not consist of people's acting greedily but of their inability to know just what is going wrong while they are taking care of their perfectly morally legitimate tasks.

12 It is evident, here, that I am treating human beings as natural entities, even if in certain respects unique and different from other natural living beings. Yet, just as the unique capacity of fish to swim or birds to fly does not place them outside of the rest of nature, so the unique capacity of human beings to think and initiate their own actions does not make them unnatural, either.

13 I draw this term, judicial inefficiency, from Kenneth J. Arrow, who used it in his "Two Cheers for Government Regulation," *Harper's* vol. 276 (March 1981), pp. 17–21.

14 The point is that the only sensible conception of the common good, one that most people who respond sympathetically to that concept, turns out to be one that makes no sacrifice of any individual member of the community. Indeed, how could something be for the common good if some member of the community is normally illegitimately harmed by it?

15 This approach is actually being taken, here and there, by the U. S. State Department, the World Bank and the International Monetary Fund *vis-à-vis* countries asking for financial support for various projects. Conditions, such as extensive selling off of state property and privatization, are laid down which need to be met prior to the granting of support. The same might be the approach, indeed, more in line with justice, in negotiations about ecological behavior.

16 Actually, we would optimally have a system where the particular informs the general and vice versa.

13 INDIVIDUALISM AND POLITICAL DIALOGUE

1 Karl Marx, *Selected Writings*, ed. David McLellan (Oxford: Oxford University Press, 1977), p.126.

2 Hans-Herman Hoppe, *A Theory of Socialism and Capitalism* (Boston: Kluwer Academic Publishers, 1989).

3 See Richard Rorty, *Objectivity, Relativism, and Truth* (Cambridge: Cambridge University Press, 1991), p. 31. Unfortunately, Rorty characterizes the human rights thesis in a way that nearly makes it nonsense. For him the thesis is "the thought that membership in our biological species carries with it certain 'rights,' a notion which does not seem to make sense unless the biological similarities entail the possession of something non biological, something which links our species to a non human reality and thus gives the species moral dignity. This picture of rights as biologically transmitted is so basic to the political discourse of the Western democracies that we are troubled by any suggestion that 'human nature' is not a useful moral concept." See, however, Roger Trigg, "Wittgenstein and Social Science," in A. Phillips Griffiths, ed., *Wittgenstein Centenary Essays* (Cambridge: Cambridge University Press, 1991), pp. 209–22.

4 Rorty, *Objectivity, Relativism, and Truth*, p. 189 n.

5 Rorty, *Objectivity, Relativism, and Truth*, p. 177.

6 Richard Rorty, "The Seer of Prague," *The New Republic*, 1 July 1991, pp. 35–40. Here is how Rorty put it in his review of Jan Patock's philosophical works: "Non-metaphysicians [of whom Rorty and, by his account, all other wise men are members] cannot say that democratic institutions reflect a moral reality and that tyrannical regimes do not reflect one, that tyrannies get something wrong that democratic societies get right." (p. 37)

7 J. F. M. Hunter, "Logical Compulsion," in *Essays After Wittgenstein* (Toronto: University of Toronto Press, 1973), p. 189.

8 Ludwig Wittgenstein, *Philosophical Investigations* (Oxford: Basil Blackwell and Mott, 1953), no. 689.

9 See Vitaly Shevoroshkin, "The Mother Tongue," *The Sciences*, May/June 1990, pp. 20–7.

10 Tibor R. Machan, *The Virtue of Liberty* (Irvington-on-Hudson, N.Y.: Foundation for Economic Education, 1994), Chapter 7. Perhaps such caricaturing is, if not unavoidable, at least unlikely to be avoided, given that a great many people do not choose to consider matters thoroughly but accept the lazy road of dichotomies: either we are specie-beings – "The human essence is the true collectivity of man," as Marx said – or we are separate, atomistic individuals (like Robinson Crusoe), as the Hobbesian legacy would have it. The present work opts for a moderate individualism, which by no means precludes the essential sociality of human beings.

11 Tibor R. Machan, *Private Rights and Public Illusions* (New Brunswick, N.J.: Transaction Publishers, 1995), chapter 2.

12 See Hoppe, *A Theory of Socialism and Capitalism*; Frank van Dun, "The Philosophy of Argument and the Logic of Common Morality," in E. M. Barth and J. L. Martens, eds, *Argumentation: Approaches to Theory Formation* (Amsterdam: John Benjamins, 1982), pp. 281–6; and N. Stephan Kinsella, "Estoppel: A New Justification for Individual Rights," *Reason Papers*, no. 17 (Fall 1992), pp. 61–74.

13 Kinsella, "Estoppel," p. 64.

14 INDIVIDUALISM VERSUS ITS CRITICS

1 Mary Midgley, *The Ethical Primate* (London: Routledge, 1994), p. 123.

2 Susan Mendus, "Liberal Man," in G. M. K. Hunt, ed., *Philosophy and Politics* (London: Cambridge University Press, 1991), p. 47.

3 Karl Marx, *Grundrisse*, ed. and trans. David McLellan (New York: Harper Torchbooks, 1971), p. 16.

4 Alasdair MacIntyre, "Nietzsche or Aristotle?," in Giovanna Borradori, ed., *The American Philosopher* (Chicago: University of Chicago Press, 1994), p. 143.

5 See Alasdair MacIntyre, *After Virtue* (Notre Dame, Ind.: University of Notre Dame Press, 1981).

6 Karl Marx, *Grundrisse*, p. 17.

7 John Gray, "From Post-Modernism to Civil Society," *Social Philosophy and Policy* 10 (Summer 1993), p. 44. Gray, as others, has made mention of, for example, Singapore's supposed economic success without the benefit of liberal political institutions, mainly to dispute by this the often heard claim of classical liberals that economic and political liberty are closely linked. See, however, Amartya Sen, "Human Rights and Asian Values," *The New Republic*, July 14–21, 1997, pp. 33–40. Sen notes that "There is little general evidence, in fact, that authoritarian governance and the suppression of political and civil rights are really beneficial in encouraging economic development. The statistical picture is much more complicated." He adds, after indicating how the evidence lines up, that "On balance, the hypothesis that there is no relation between freedom and prosperity in either direction is hard to reject. Since political liberty has a significance of its own, the case for it remains untarnished." (Admittedly, Sen's construes "political liberty" in more democratic than individualist terms.)

8 Richard Rorty, *Objectivity, Relativism, and Truth* (Cambridge: Cambridge University Press, 1991), p. 31.

9 Midgley, *The Ethical Primate*, p. 103.

10 Midgley, *The Ethical Primate*, p. 103.

11 Steven Lukes, *Individualism* (London: Oxford University Press, 1973), p. 101.

12 For some interesting and powerful defenses of individuality, see Brian John Marine, *Individuals and Individuality* (Albany, NY: SUNY Press, 1984), Jose Gracia, *Individuality* (Albany, NY: SUNY Press, 1988) and, especially, David L. Norton, *Personal Destinies: A Philosophy of Ethical Individualism* (Princeton, NJ: Princeton University Press, 1976).

13 See, for example, Amitai Etzioni, *The Spirit of Community* (New York: Crown, 1993), and Robert Bellah *et al.*, *Habits of the Heart: Individualism and Commitment in American Life* (Berkeley: University of California Press, 1985).

14 Richard Rorty, *Objectivity, Relativism, and Truth*.

15 Rorty, *Objectivity, Relativism, and Truth*, p. 21.

16 Rorty, *Objectivity, Relativism, and Truth*, p. 7.

17 Auguste Comte, *A General View of Positivism* (New York: Robert Speller & Sons, 1957), p. 246.

18 Eduard Zeller, *Aristotle and the Earlier Peripatetics*, trans. B. F. C. Costelloe and J. H. Muirhead (London: Oxford University Press, 1897), pp. 224–6 (quoted in Fred D. Miller, Jr., *Nature, Justice, and Rights in Aristotle's* Politics [Oxford: Clarendon Press, 1995], pp. 200–1). For an individualist understanding of Aristotle's metaphysics, see Emerson Buchanan, *Aristotle's Theory of Being* (Cambridge, Mass.: Greek, Roman, and Byzantine Monographs, 1962). As he puts it, "in identifying *ousia* (Being) with [what it is for each thing to exist], Aristotle is asserting that the fundamental reality on which everything else depends is the existence of the individual" (p. 2).

19 For more on the measure of individualism and the natural rights of individuals in Aristotle's philosophy, see Miller, *Nature, Justice, and Rights*.

20 For more on this, see J. D. P. Bolton, *Glory, Jest, and Riddle: A Study of the Growth of Individualism from Homer to Christianity* (New York: Barnes and Noble, 1973).

21 Lewis Thomas, *Lives of a Cell* (New York: Viking, 1971).

22 David Kelley, *The Evidence of the Senses* (Baton Rouge: Louisiana State University Press, 1986).

23 In Charles Taylor, *Philosophy and the Human Sciences* (Cambridge: Cambridge University Press, 1985).

24 Taylor, *Philosophy and the Human Sciences*, p. 188.

25 John Locke, *Two Treatises of Government* (London: Everyman, 1993), p. 117.

26 Locke, *Two Treatises of Government*, p. 122.

27 Francois Bondy, "European Diary, Exist This Way," *Encounter*, February 1981, pp. 42–3.

28 See, for example, Brian Tierney, "Origins of Natural Rights Language: Text and Contexts, 1150–1250," *History of Political Thought* 10 (Winter 1989): 615–46, and "Conciliarism, Corporatism, and Individualism: The Doctrine of Individual Rights in Gerson," *Christianesimo hella Storia* 9 (1988): 81–111; and Cary J. Nederman, "Property and Protest: Political Theory and Subjective Rights in Fourteenth-Century England," *Review of Politics* 58 (Spring 1996): 323–44. See, also, Miller, *Nature, Justice, and Rights*. There is little doubt that prior to any talk of atomistic individualism, individual rights had been invoked in political discussion. We should not be prejudiced against such rights by the fact that when they were finally incorporated in a robust theory and thus needed to be reconciled with prevailing views about science, knowledge, ontology, and so forth, they did not receive the treatment and support we can give them today, apart from such an intellectual background. In other words, the first theoretical defense of a concept that may very well be sound and useful might not be the only one it could receive. A better one could arise in the light of the subsequent reconsideration of the problems the concept was addressed to solve.

29 In his *Philosophy and the Human Sciences*, Taylor allows that there are "certain theories of belonging ... which hold that our obligation to obey, or to belong to a particular society, may in certain circumstances be inoperative" (p. 188). But he discounts this exception and says that "in theories of belonging it is clear that men qua men have an obligation to belong to and sustain society" (p. 188). Taylor makes too little of what is, after all, a rather important qualification on so-called theories of belonging. For if a person has the authority to withdraw from a perverse society, he or she will have the authority, also, to determine what criteria to use for this purpose. This is not an epistemological carte blanche, of course, but a serious moral responsibility to find out what kind of society is suitable to human flourishing.

30 Marx, *Grundrisse*, p. 33.

31 Saint Augustine, quoted in Thomas Beauchamp, ed., *Ethical Issues in Death and Dying* (Englewood Cliffs, N.J.: Prentice Hall, 1984), p. 103.

32 Daniel Bell, *The Cultural Contradictions of Capitalism* (New York: Basic Books, 1972).

33 See the work of Roger W. Sperry, for example, his *Science and Moral Priority* (New York: Columbia University Press, 1983), as well as Midgley, *The Ethical Primate*.

15 REASON, INDIVIDUALISM, AND CAPITALISM

1 Ayn Rand, "The Goal of My Writing," *Objectivist Newsletter*, October 1963, pp. 37–42.

2 Quoted in Harry V. Jaffa, *How to Think about the American Revolution* (Durham, N.C.: Carolina Academic Press, 1978), p. 1.

3 That Hobbes and Locke shared this view is alleged by Leo Strauss, in *Natural Right and History*, 2nd ed. (Chicago: University of Chicago Press, 1970), p. 251. I address this issue further in Tibor R. Machan, "Libertarianism and Conservatives," *Modern Age*, vol. 24 (Winter 1980). For a different view, see John P. East, "The American Conservative Movement of the 1980's," *Modern Age*, vol. 24 (Winter 1980).

4 Aleksandr Solzhenitsyn, "A World Slit Apart," *Imprimis*, 7 (1978): 4.

5 There are other approaches to take, but all are so hostile to liberty as not to bear discussion. There are extremes of the left and the right where liberty is not even regarded as a value, so the suggestion of a compromise between liberty and some version of slavery does not arise. Certain theocratic political doctrines on the right and totalitarian views on the left would fit this characterization.

6 Quoted in Jaffa, *How to Think about the American Revolution*, pp. 1–2 (emphasis in original).

7 Adam Smith, *The Wealth of Nations* (New York: Random House, 1937), p. 726.

8 Ayn Rand, "The Objectivist Ethics," in *The Virtue of Selfishness: A New Concept of Egoism* (New York: New American Library, 1964), pp. 13–35.

9 See Michael Novak, *The American Vision* (Washington, D.C.: American Enterprise Institute, 1978). Novak seems to argue this point with the support of, among others, Bernard-Henri Levi. More recently, George Gilder, in *Wealth and Poverty* (New York: Basic Books, 1981), which is regarded as a brilliant Christian, antirationalist defense of capitalism, stresses the view that only an ethics of altruism can defend the free market, by reference to the notion that as an act of faith, each person should seek to create, to engage in entrepreneurship and trade, with the motivation of helping others, not of furthering his own proper ends.

10 Ayn Rand, *For the New Intellectual* (New York: New American Library, 1961), p. 182.

11 Irving Kristol, "Capitalism, Socialism, and Nihilism," *The Public Interest*, no. 31 (Spring 1973): 8.

12 Strauss, *Natural Right and History*, p. 251.

13 Strauss, *Natural Right and History*, p. 251.

14 See Rand, *For the New Intellectual* and *The Virtue of Selfishness*.

15 Karl Marx, *Selected Writings*, ed. David McLellan (Oxford: Oxford University Press, 1977), p. 53.

16 Ayn Rand, *Anthem* (New York: Signet Books, 1946), p. 111.

17 Ayn Rand, *The Fountainhead* (New York: New American Library, 1968), p. ix. See, in this connection, E. Merrill Root, "What about Ayn Rand?" *National Review*, 30 January 1960, pp. 76–8.

18 Kristol, "Capitalism, Socialism, and Nihilism," p. 12.

19 Ayn Rand, *Atlas Shrugged* (New York: Random House, 1957), p. 1022.

20 Ayn Rand, "What Is Capitalism?," in *Capitalism: The Unknown Ideal* (New York: New American Library, 1967), pp. 24–5.

21 Nathaniel Branden, "Alienation," in Tibor R. Machan, ed., *The Main Debate, Communism versus Capitalism* (New York: Random House, 1988), pp. 72–3.

22 Erich Fromm, quoted in Branden, "Alienation," p. 36.

23 Erich Fromm, quoted in Branden, "Alienation," p. 36. It is interesting that Fromm, in his *Man for Himself* (New York: Henry Holt and Company, 1947), advances a kind of egoistic ethic that is very close to the classical individualism defended in the present book. Fromm states, for example, that a human being "is an individual with his peculiarities and in this sense unique, and at the same time he is representative of all characteristics of the human race." But then he adds, "while every human being is the bearer of all human potentialities, the short span of his life does permit their full realization . . . " (p.51). As Douglas Rasmussen notes, "The issue here is of course whether the universal 'all' is taken abstractly (some form can be any) or concretely. If the latter, then our individuality and mortality cut us off from our nature, and we are necessarily alienated. If no God, then we can find fulfillment only in and through others. Yet, not just some others, it must be all of humanity, the whole, the collective." (Personal correspondence, May 1997.) In addition, Fromm also sees this as a kind of aberration in nature – "self-awareness, reason, and imagination – made man into an anomaly, into a freak of the universe."(pp. 39–40) But why does a serious difference exhibited by a species *vis-à-vis* others constitute being a freak? Are birds freaks, as compared to land-bound animals, fish when compared to those that cannot live under water?

24 Leszek Kolakowski, quoted in Michael Harrington, review of *Main Currents of Marxism*, by Leszek Kolakowski, *The New Republic*, 2 February 1979, p. 32.

25 For a discussion of the egoistic aspects of Aristotle's ethics, see W. F. Hardie, "The Final Good in Aristotle's Ethics," *Philosophy*, 40 (October 1965): 277–95. But this should not be taken as a claim that Rand's case for egoism is the same as Aristotle's. For a discussion of various recent versions of egoism, including Rand's, see Tibor R. Machan, "Recent Work in Ethical Egoism," *American Philosophical Quarterly*, 16 (January 1979): 1–15. For our purposes, "egoism" and "individualism" are interchangeable; both concern normative positions in terms of which the highest priority in life is to secure what is best for the individual human being one is – in short, oneself.

26 Ayn Rand, *The Moral Factor* (Palo Alto, Calif.: Palo Alto Book Service, 1976), p. 12.

27 Rand, *The Moral Factor*, p. 12.

NOTES

EPILOGUE

1 Graham Greene, *Loser Takes All* (Baltimore: Penguin, 1993), p. 51.
2 W. D. Falk, "Morality, Self, and Others." In Falk, *Ought, Reasons, and Morality* (Ithaca, N.Y.: Cornell University Press, 1986), p. 209.

BIBLIOGRAPHY

Adler, Mortimer. *The Difference of Man and the Difference It Makes*. New York: World Publishing, 1968.

Andrew, Edward. *Shylock's Rights*. Toronto: University of Toronto Press, 1988.

Aristotle. *Nicomachean Ethics*. Buffalo, NY: Prometheus Books, 1987.

——. *Politics*. Trans. by Carnes Lord. Chicago: University of Chicago Press, 1984.

Arnold, N. Scott. *Marx's Radical Critique of Capitalist Society: A Reconstruction and Critical Evaluation*. New York: Oxford University Press, 1990.

Arrow, Kenneth J. *Social Choice and Individual Values*. 2nd ed. New York: Wiley, 1963.

——. "Two Cheers for Government Regulations," *Harper's* vol. 276 (March 1981).

Austin, J. L. *Philosophical Papers*. Oxford: Clarendon Press, 1961.

Avineri, Shlomo, and Avner de-Shalit, eds. *Communitarianism and Individualism*. New York: Oxford University Press, 1992.

Ayer, A. J., and Jane O'Grady, eds. *A Dictionary of Philosophical Quotations*. Oxford: Blackwell, 1994.

Barry, Brian. *Political Arguments*. London: Routledge & Kegan Paul, 1965.

Beauchamp, Thomas, ed. *Ethical Issues in Death and Dying*. Englewood Cliffs, N.J.: Prentice Hall, 1984.

Beauchamp, Thomas L., and Norman E. Bowie. *Ethical Theory and Business*. Englewood Cliffs, N.J.: Prentice Hall, 1983.

Becker, Gary. *The Economic Approach to Human Behavior*. Chicago: University of Chicago Press, 1976.

——. "Q & A: Nobel Laureate Gary Becker: How Economics Meets Social Issues." *Hoover Institution Newsletter*, Winter 1993.

——. "When the Wake-Up Call Is from the Nobel Committee." *Business Week*, 2 November 1992.

Bell, Daniel. *The Cultural Contradictions of Capitalism*. New York: Basic Books, 1972.

Bellah, Robert, *et al*. *Habits of the Heart: Individualism and Commitment in American Life*. Berkeley: University of California Press, 1985.

Bellante, Don. "Subjective Value Theory and Government Intervention in the Labor Market." *Austrian Economics Newsletter*, Spring/Summer 1989.

Benedict, Ruth. *Patterns of Culture*. Cambridge, Mass.: Riverside Press, 1934.

Block, Walter. *Defending the Undefendable*. New York: Fleet Press, 1976.

Bolton, J. D. P. *Glory, Jest, and Riddle: A Study of the Growth of Individualism from Homer to Christianity*. New York: Barnes & Noble, 1973.

Bondy, Francois. "European Diary, Exist This Way." *Encounter*, February 1981.

Boyle, Joseph, G. Grisez, and O. Tollefsen. *Free Choice*. Notre Dame, Ind.: University of Notre Dame Press, 1976.

Branden, Nathaniel. "Alienation." In Tibor R. Machan, ed., *The Main Debate*. New York: Random House, 1988.

———. "Free Will, Moral Responsibility, and the Law." In T. R. Machan, ed., *The Libertarian Alternative*. Chicago: Nelson-Hall, 1974.

———. *The Psychology of Self-Esteem*. New York: Bantam Books, 1969.

Buchanan, Emerson. *Aristotle's Theory of Being*. Cambridge, Mass.: Greek, Roman and Byzantine Monographs, 1962.

Calhoun, Laurie. "Moral Blindness and Moral Responsibility: What Can We Learn from Rhoda Penmark?" *Journal of Applied Philosophy*, vol. 31, no. 1 (1996).

Chein, Isidor. *The Science of Behavior and the Image of Man*. New York: Basic Books, 1972.

Clark, Stephen R. L. *The Moral Status of Animals*. Oxford: Clarendon Press, 1977.

Coleman, Frank M. *Hobbes and America*. Toronto: University of Toronto Press, 1977.

Comte, Auguste. *Catéchisme positiviste*. Paris: Temple de l'humanité, 1957.

———. *A General View of Positivism*. New York: Robert Speller & Sons, 1957.

Conway, David. *A Farewell to Marx*. Middlesex: Penguin Books, 1987.

Den Uyl, Douglas J. "Teleology and Agent-Centeredness." *Monist*, vol. 75 (January 1992).

———. *The Virtue of Prudence*. New York: Peter Lang, 1991.

East, John P. "The American Conservative Movement of the 1980's." *Modern Age*, vol. 24 (Winter 1980).

Easton, Lloyd, and Kurt H. Guddat, eds and trans. *Writings of the Young Marx on Philosophy and Society*. Garden City, N.Y.: Anchor Books, 1967.

Eccles, John C. *Evolution of the Brain: Creation of the Self*. London: Routledge, 1989.

Ehrenfeld, D. W. *The Arrogance of Humanism*. New York: Oxford University Press, 1978.

Etzioni, Amitai. *The Spirit of Community*. New York: Crown, 1993.

Falk, W. D. "Morality, Self, and Others." In *Ought, Reasons, and Morality*. Ithaca, N.Y.: Cornell University Press, 1986.

Ferguson, Adam. *An Essay on the History of Civil Society*. Edinburgh, 1767.

Flores, Albert, ed. *Professional Ideals*. Belmont, Calif.: Wadsworth, 1988.

Fotion, Nicholas, and Gerard Elfstrom. *Military Ethics*. London: Routledge & Kegan Paul, 1986.

French, Howard W. "The Ritual Slaves of Ghana: Young and Female." *New York Times*, 20 January 1997.

Friedman, Milton. *Capitalism and Freedom*. Chicago: University of Chicago Press, 1962.

Fromm, Erich. *Man for Himself*. New York: Henry Holt and Company, 1947.

Gaita, Raimond. "The Personal in Ethics." In P. Winch and D. Z. Phillips, eds, *Wittgenstein: Attention to Particulars*. New York: St. Martin's Press, 1989.

Gilder, George. *Wealth and Poverty*. New York: Basic Books, 1981.

Golding, Martin P. "The Concept of Rights: A Historical Sketch." In E. B. Bandman, ed., *Bioethics and Human Rights*. Boston: Little, Brown & Co., 1978.

Goldman, Alan. *The Moral Foundations of Professional Ethics*. Totowa, N.J.: Rowman & Littlefield, 1980.

Gordon, Barry. *Economic Analysis before Adam Smith*. New York: Barnes & Noble, 1976.

Gracia, Jose. *Individuality*. Albany, N.Y.: SUNY Press, 1988.

Gray, John. "From Post-Modernism to Civil Society." *Social Philosophy and Policy*, vol. 10 (1993).

——. *Liberalism*. Minneapolis: University of Minneapolis Press, 1986.

——. *Liberalisms*. London: Routledge, 1989.

——. *Post Liberalism*. London: Routledge, 1993.

Greene, Graham. *Loser Takes All*. Baltimore: Penguin, 1993.

Greenhouse, Steven. "Soviet Economists Say Shift to Free Market Is Inevitable." *New York Times*, 18 February 1991.

Greider, William. *One World, Ready or Not*. New York: Simon & Schuster, 1997.

Hardie, W. F. "The Final Good in Aristotle's Ethics." *Philosophy*, vol. 40 (1965).

Hardin, Garrett. "The Tragedy of the Commons." *Science*, 13 December 1968.

Harrington, Michael. Review of *Main Currents of Marxism*, by Leszek Kolakowski. *New Republic*, 2 February 1979.

Hart, H. L. A. "Are There Any Natural Rights?" *Philosophical Review*, vol. 64 (October 1955).

Hayek, F. A., ed. *Collectivist Economic Planning: Critical Studies on the Possibilities of Socialism*. London: Routledge & Sons, 1935.

——. "Dr. Bernard Mandeville." In *New Studies in Philosophy, Politics, Economics, and the History of Ideas*. Chicago: University of Chicago Press, 1978.

Heilbroner, Robert. "After Communism." *New Yorker*, 10 September 1990.

Hobbes, Thomas. *Leviathan*. New York: Collier Books, 1962.

Hodgson, Marshall. G. S. *The Venture of Islam: Conscience and History in a World Civilization*. 3 vols. Chicago: University of Chicago Press, 1974.

Hoff, Trygve J. B. *Economic Calculation in the Socialist Society*. Indianapolis: Liberty Press, 1981.

Hoppe, Hans-Herman. *A Theory of Socialism and Capitalism*. Boston: Kluwer Academic Publishers, 1989.

Hospers, John. Review of *The Case for Animals Rights*, by Tom Regan. *Reason Papers*, no. 10 (Fall 1985).

Hume, David. *A Treatise of Human Nature*. Garden City, N.Y.: Dolphin Books, 1961.

Hunter, J. F. M. "Logical Compulsion." In *Essays After Wittgenstein*. Toronto: University of Toronto Press, 1973.

Jacobs, Jane. *Systems of Survival: A Dialogue on the Moral Foundations of Commerce and Politics*. New York: Random House, 1992.

Jaffa, Harry V. *How to Think about the American Revolution*. Durham, N.C.: Carolina Academic Press, 1978.

Jeager, Werner. *Aristotle*. London: Oxford University Press, 1934.

Jordan, James N. "Determinism's Dilemma." *Review of Metaphysics*, vol. 23 (September 1969).

Kekes, John. *Facing Evil*. Princeton, N.J.: Princeton University Press, 1991.

——. "Freedom" *Pacific Philosophical Quarterly*, vol. 61 (October 1980).

——. "'Ought Implies Can' and Two Kinds of Morality." *Philosophical Quarterly*, vol. 34 (October 1984).

Kelley, David. *The Evidence of the Senses*. Baton Rouge: Louisiana State University Press, 1986.

——. *Unrugged Individualism*. Poughkeepsie, N.Y.: Institute for Objectivist Studies, 1996.

Keyes, Thomas. "The Marxian Concept of Property: Individual/Social." In Tibor R. Machan, ed., *The Main Debate*. New York: Random House, 1987.

Kinsella, N. Stephan. "Estoppel: A New Justification for Individual Rights." *Reason Papers*, no. 17 (Fall 1992).

Kornai, Janos. *Contradictions and Dilemmas: Studies on the Socialist Economy and Society.* Translated by Ilona Lukacs *et al.* Cambridge, Mass.: MIT Press, 1986.

——. *The Road to a Free Market.* New York: W. W. Norton, 1990.

Kovesi, Julius. *Moral Notions.* London: Routledge & Kegan Paul, 1978.

Kristol, Irving. "Capitalism, Socialism, and Nihilism." *Public Interest*, Spring 1973.

——. *Two Cheers for Capitalism.* New York: Basic Books, 1973.

Kuttner, Robert. *Everything for Sale.* New York: Alfred A. Knopf, 1997.

Letwin, Shirley Robin. "Romantic Love and Christianity." *Philosophy*, vol. 52 (April 1977).

Locke, John. *Two Treatises of Government.* London: Everyman, 1993.

Lucey, Kenneth G., ed. *Recent Work in Philosophy.* Totowa, N.J.: Rowman & Allanheld, 1983.

Lukes, Steven. *Individualism.* London: Oxford University Press, 1973.

Machan, Tibor R. *Capitalism and Individualism: Reframing the Argument for the Free Society.* New York: St. Martin's Press, 1990.

——. ed., *Commerce and Morality.* Totowa, N.J.: Rowman & Littlefield, 1988.

——. "Environmentalism Humanized". *Public Affairs Quarterly*, vol. 7 (April 1993).

——. "Epistemology and Moral Knowledge." *Review of Metaphysics*, vol. 36 (September 1982).

——. *Generosity, Private and Public.* Washington, D.C.: Cato Institute, 1998.

——. *Human Rights and Human Liberties.* Chicago: Nelson-Hall, 1975.

——. *Individuals and Their Rights.* La Salle, Ill.: Open Court, 1989.

——. "Justice and the Welfare State." In T. R. Machan, ed., *The Libertarian Alternative.* Chicago: Nelson-Hall, 1974.

——. "Justice, Self, and Natural Rights." In James Sterba, ed., *Morality and Social Injustice: Alternative Views.* Lanham, Md.: Rowman & Littlefield, 1994.

——. "Libertarianism and Conservatives." *Modern Age*, vol. 24 (Winter 1980).

——. *Marxism: A Bourgeois Critique.* Bradford: MCB University Press, 1988.

—— "A Note on Independence." *Philosophical Studies*, vol. 30 (December 1976).

——. *Private Rights and Public Illusions.* New Brunswick, N.J.: Transaction, 1995.

——. *The Pseudo-Science of B. F. Skinner.* New Rochelle, N.Y.: Arlington House, 1974.

——. "Rational Choice and Public Affairs." *Theory and Decision*, vol. 12 (September 1980).

——. "Reason in Economics versus Ethics." *International Journal of Social Economics*, vol. 22, no. 7 (1995).

——. "Recent Work in Ethical Egoism." *American Philosophical Quarterly*, vol. 16 (January 1979).

——. "Rescuing Victims – from Social Theory." In Diane Sank and David I. Caplan, eds, *To Be a Victim: Encounters with Crime and Injustice.* New York: Plenum Press, 1991.

——. "A Revision of the Doctrine of Disability of Mind." *Persona y Derecho*, vol. 33 (May 1995).

——. "Some Recent Work in Human Rights Theory," *American Philosophical Quarterly*, vol. 17 (April 1980).

———. "Some Reflections on Richard Rorty's Philosophy." *Metaphilosophy*, vol. 24 (January/April 1993).

———. "Two Senses of Human Freedom." *The Freeman*, vol. 39 (January 1989).

———. *The Virtue of Liberty*. Irvington-on-Hudson, N.Y.: Foundation for Economic Education, 1994.

———. "Wronging Rights." *Policy Review*, no. 17 (Summer 1981).

MacIntyre, Alasdair. *After Virtue*. Notre Dame, Ind.: University of Notre Dame Press, 1981.

———. "Nietzsche or Aristotle?" In Giovanna Borradori, ed., *The American Philosopher*. Chicago: University of Chicago Press, 1994.

McKibbon, Bill. *The End of Nature*. New York: Random House, 1989.

MacKinnon, Catherine A. *Feminism Unmodified*. Cambridge, Mass.: Harvard University Press, 1987.

MacLaughlin, Andrew C. *The Foundations of American Constitutionalism*. Greenwich, Conn.: Fawcet, 1961.

MacPherson, C. B. *Possessive Individualism*. London: Oxford University Press, 1962.

Marine, Brian John. *Individuals and Individuality*. Albany, N.Y.: SUNY Press, 1984.

Martin, Rex, and James W. Nickel. "Recent Work in the Concept of Rights." In Kenneth G. Lucey, ed., *Recent Work in Philosophy*.

Totowa, N. J.: Rowman & Allanheld, 1983.

Marx, Karl. "Critique of the Gotha Program." *The Marx–Engels Reader*. Edited by Robert C. Tucker. New York: W. W. Norton, 1978.

———. *Grundrisse*. Edited and translated by David McLellan. New York: Harper Torchbooks, 1971.

———. *Grundrisse*. Translated by Martin Nicolaus. New York: Vintage Books, 1973.

———. *Selected Writings*. Edited by David McLellan. Oxford: Oxford University Press, 1977.

Matthews, Lloyd J., and Dale E. Brown, eds. *The Parameters of Military Ethics*. New York: Pergamon-Brassey's, 1989.

Mendus, Susan. "Liberal Man." In G. M. K. Hunt, ed., *Philosophy and Politics*. London: Cambridge University Press, 1991.

Midgley, Mary. *The Ethical Primate*. London: Routledge, 1994.

Miller, Fred D., Jr. *Nature, Justice, and Rights in Aristotle's Politics*. Oxford: Clarendon Press, 1995.

Morris, Colin. *The Discovery of the Individual, 1050–1200*. New York: Harper & Row, 1972.

Nagel, Thomas. "The Limits of Objectivity." *The Tanner Lectures on Human Values, 1980*. Edited by Sterling M. McMurrin. Cambridge: Cambridge University Press, 1980.

Nederman, Cary J. "Property and Protest: Political Theory and Subjective Rights in Fourteenth-Century England." *Review of Politics*, vol. 58 (Spring 1996).

Nelson, John O. "Against Human Rights." *Philosophy*, vol. 65 (July 1990).

Norton, David L. "Individual Initiative." In Konstantin Kulenka, ed., *Organization and Ethical Individualism*. New York: Praeger, 1988.

———. *Personal Destinies: A Philosophy of Ethical Individualism*. Princeton, N.J.: Princeton University Press, 1976.

Novak, Michael. *The American Vision*. Washington, D.C.: American Enterprise Institute, 1978.

Nozick, Robert. *Anarchy, State, and Utopia*. New York: Basic Books, 1974.

———. *The Examined Life*. New York: Simon & Schuster, 1989.

Nussbaum, Martha. *The Therapy of Desire*. Princeton, N.J.: Princeton University Press, 1994.

Olson, Walter. *The Excuse Factory*. New York: The Free Press, 1997.

Pitkin, Hanna F. *Wittgenstein and Justice*. Berkeley: University of California Press, 1970.

Popper, Karl. *The Poverty of Historicism*. London: Routledge & Kegan Paul, 1961.

Popper, Karl, and John C. Eccles. *The Self and Its Brain*. New York: Springer International, 1977.

Posner, Richard. "Pragmatism and the Rule of Law." Lecture given at the American Enterprise Institute, Washington, D.C., 7 July 1991.

Rand, Ayn. *Anthem*. New York: Signet Books, 1946.

———. *Atlas Shrugged*. New York: Random House, 1957.

———. *Capitalism: The Unknown Ideal*. New York: New American Library, 1967.

———. *For the New Intellectual*. New York: New American Library, 1961.

———. *The Fountainhead*. New York: New American Library, 1968.

———. "The Goal of My Writing." *Objectivist Newsletter*, October 1963.

———. *The Moral Factor*. Palo Alto, Calif.: Palo Alto Book Service, 1976.

———. *The Virtue of Selfishness: A New Concept of Egoism*. New York: New American Library, 1964.

Rasmussen, Douglas B., and Douglas J. Den Uyl. *Liberalism Defended: The Challenge of Post-Modernity*. Cheltenham: Edward Elgar, 1998.

———. *Liberty and Nature: An Aristotelian Defense of Liberal Order*. La Salle, Ill.: Open Court, 1991.

Rawls, John. "The Independence of Moral Theory." In *Proceedings and Addresses of the American Philosophical Association*, vol. XLVII. Newark, Del.: American Philosophical Association, 1975.

———. *A Theory of Justice*. Cambridge, Mass.: Harvard University Press, 1971.

Reeck, Darrell. *Ethics for the Professions: A Christian Perspective*. Minneapolis: Augsburg, 1982.

Regan, Tom. *The Case for Animal Rights*. Berkeley: University of California Press, 1983.

Regan, Tom, and Peter Singer, eds. *Animal Rights and Human Obligations*. Englewood Cliffs, N.J.: Prentice Hall, 1976.

Reisman, George. "The Toxicity of Environmentalism." In Hans Sennholz, ed., *Man and Nature*. Irvington-on-Hudson, N. Y.: Foundation for Economic Education, 1993.

Rescher, Nicholas. *Distributive Justice*. New York: Bobbs-Merrill, 1966.

Rollin, Bernard E. *Animal Rights and Human Morality*. Buffalo, N.Y.: Prometheus Books, 1981.

Root, E. Merrill. "What about Ayn Rand?," *National Review*, 30 January 1960.

Rorty, Richard. *Objectivity, Relativism, and Truth*. Cambridge: Cambridge University Press, 1991.

———. "The Seer of Prague." *The New Republic*, 1 July 1991.

Rosenthal, Harry F. "Teacher's Firing May Symbolize a Cultural Trend." *USA Today*, 3 April 1996.

Ross, David. *Aristotle*. The Hague: Methuen, 1964.

Sadowsky, James. "Private Property and Collective Ownership." In T. R. Machan, ed., *The Libertarian Alternative*. Chicago: Nelson-Hall, 1974.

Salt, Henry S. *Animals' Rights*. London: George Bell & Sons, 1892; Clark Summit, Pa.: Society for Animal Rights, 1980.

Sandel, Michael J. "America's Search for a New Public Philosophy." *Atlantic Monthly*, March 1996.

Sen, Amartya. "Human Rights and Asian Values." *The New Republic*, 14–21 July 1997.

Shevoroshkin, Vitaly. "The Mother Tongue."The *Sciences*, May/June 1990.

Skinner, B. F. *Beyond Freedom and Dignity*. New York: Bantam Books, 1971.

——. *Science and Human Behavior*. New York: Macmillan, 1953.

Slote, Michael. "Ethics Without Free Will." *Social Theory and Practice*, vol. 16 (1990).

——. *From Morality to Virtue*. London: Oxford University Press, 1992.

Smith, Adam. *The Wealth of Nations*. New York: Random House, 1937.

Solzhenitsyn, Aleksandr. "A World Slit Apart." *Imprimis*, vol. 7 (1978).

Soros, George. "The Capitalist Threat." *Atlantic Monthly*, February 1997.

Spencer, Herbert. "State Tampering with Money Banks." In *Essays*. 1891.

Sperry, Roger W. "Changing Concepts of Consciousness and Free Will." *Perspectives in Biology and Medicine*, vol. 9 (Autumn 1976).

——. *Science and Moral Priority*. New York: Columbia University Press, 1983.

Stigler, George. "The Adam Smith Lecture: The Effects of Government on Economic Efficiency." *Business Economics*, vol. 23 (January 1988).

——. *Tanner Lectures on Human Values, 1980*. "Economics or Ethics?" Edited by Sterling M. McMurrin. Cambridge: Cambridge University Press, 1980.

Stone, Christopher. *Should Trees Have Standing? Toward Legal Rights for Natural Objects*. Los Altos, Calif.: William Kaufmann, 1974.

Strauss, Leo. *Natural Right and History*. 2nd ed. Chicago: University of Chicago Press, 1970.

Stroud, Barry. "Wittgenstein and Logical Necessity." In G. Pitcher, ed., *Wittgenstein*. Garden City, N.Y.: Anchor Books, 1969.

Taylor, Charles. *Philosophy and the Human Sciences*. Cambridge: Cambridge University Press, 1985.

Thomas, Lewis. *Lives of a Cell*. New York: Viking, 1971.

Tierney, Brian. "Conciliarism, Corporatism, and Individualism: The Doctrine of Individual Rights in Gerson." *Christianesimo hella Storia*, 9 (1988): 88–111.

——. "Origins of Natural Rights Language: Text and Contexts, 1150–1250." *History of Political Thought*, vol. 10 (Winter 1989).

Tolstaya, Tatyana. "The Grand Inquisitor." *The New Republic*, 29 June 1992.

Trigg, Roger. "Wittgenstein and Social Science." *Wittgenstein Centenary Essays*. Edited by Phillips Griffiths. Cambridge: Cambridge University Press, 1991.

Tuck, Richard. *Hobbes*. London: Oxford University Press, 1989.

Tucker, Robert C., ed. *The Marx–Engels Reader*. New York: W. W. Norton, 1978.

van den Haag, Ernest. "Against Natural Rights." *Policy Review*, no. 23 (Winter 1983).

van Dun, Frank. "The Philosophy of Argument and the Logic of Common Morality." In E. M. Barth and J. L. Martens, eds., *Argumentation: Approaches to Theory Formation*. Amsterdam: John Benjamins, 1982.

Veatch, Henry B. "Ethical Egoism, New Style: Is Its Proper Trade Mark Libertarian or Aristotelian?" In *Swimming Against the Current in Contemporary Philosophy*. Washington, D.C.: Catholic University of America Press, 1990.

Versenyi, Laszlo. "Virtue as a Self-Directed Art." *Personalist*, vol. 53 (Summer 1972).

von Mises, Ludwig. *Human Action*. New Haven, Conn.: Yale University Press, 1949.

———. *Socialism: An Economic and Sociological Analysis*. Translated by J. Kahane. New Haven, Conn.: Yale University Press, 1951. Originally published in German in 1922.

Walker, Michael A., ed. *Freedom, Democracy, and Economic Welfare*. Vancouver: Fraser Institute, 1988.

Walzer, Michael. "Are There Limits to Liberalism? Review of *Isaiah Berlin*, by John Gray." *New York Review of Books*, 19 October 1995.

Weingartner, Rudolph H. *The Unity of the Platonic Dialogue*. Indianapolis: Bobbs-Merrill, 1973.

Wittgenstein, Ludwig. *Philosophical Investigations*. Oxford: Basil Blackwell & Mott, 1953.

Zeller, Eduard. *Aristotle and the Earlier Peripatetics*. Translated by B. F. C. Costelloe and J. H. Muirhead. London: Oxford University Press, 1897.

Zweig, Paul. *The Heresy of Self-Love*. Princeton, N.J.: Princeton University Press, 1968.

INDEX

abortion, pro-life *vs* pro-choice approach
89–96
absurdism 185
Ackerman, Bruce 156
Adler, Mortimer 112
aesthetics 60
African Americans, collective identity 83
Aganbegyan, Abel 134
altruism 188, 190, 195, 199, 225n9
America 89, 194; capitalism 73, 186;
Constitution 77; Declaration of
Independence 75, 77, 186, 187
American political tradition 65, 68, 136,
170; founding principles and
multiculturalism 75–88
Americans with Disabilities Act 19
Amish people 85
Amnesty International 79, 82
amoralism: challenge to capitalism 187–8;
of radical individualism 2, 8, 12–13, 14,
15
animal liberation 105–7, 109
animal rights 85, 105–17
animals, classical individualism's case for
use of 109–11
anti-individualism 165–8, 170–4;
American 77–8; replies to 174–8
applied ethics: and free will 28–30;
inconsistencies 17–19 (consequences
of 19–20)
Aquinas, Thomas xi, 175
Aristotle 8, 10, 60, 111, 140, 165, 178,
183, 211n17; anti-individualism/
individualism of xiii–xiv, 98–9, 171,
174–5; Ayn Rand's debt to xi, 189,
190, 198; free will 99, 102; individual
rights and public welfare 144, 145, 148,
221n11; rationality, right reason xv, 46,

48, 68, 120; universality of human
rights 102–3; virtues 28, 102–3, 118;
see also neo-Aristotelian approach to
natural rights
Atlantic Monthly 77
atomistic individualism xii, 3, 161, 179,
182, 192
Augustine, Saint xii, xiii, 172, 175, 182
Austin, J.L. 33
Austrian school of economics 38, 52,
212n13
authoritarianism: metaethical subjectivism
as way of repelling 52; *see also* statism

Bad Seed, The (film) 31
Baden, John 146
Barry, Brian 20
Becker, Gary 4, 37–8, 39, 41, 212n4
belief, and action 37–8, 39, 40
Bell, Daniel 5, 182–3
Bellah, Robert 1, 2, 77, 171
Bellante, Don 52
Bennett, William 194
Bentham, Jeremy 97, 105, 107
Berlin, Sir Isaiah 52, 84
Block, Walter 71
Bondy, Francois 181
Bosnia-Herzegovina 83
Branden, Nathaniel 197, 207n22
Buchanan, Emerson 224n18
Buchanan, James 212n4
Burke, Edmund 157
Burundi 83
business ethics 12, 29

Calhoun, Laurie 31, 42
capitalism: and American political